$\mathscr{A}$ $\mathcal{N}$ourishing $\mathcal{L}$ife

A Nourishing Life

Katharine Parker Riddle

Pentland Press, Inc.
England • USA • Scotland

The front cover photograph of Katharine P. Riddle at the YMCA grounds in Estes Park, CO was taken by Zaida D. Chidester, a classmate in Woodstock School. Used with permission.

The back cover photograph of Katharine P. Riddle on Trail Ridge Road in Rocky Mountain National Park was taken by Cassandra M. Smith, a friend from San Antonio. Used with permission.

The back cover photograph of Woodstock School in the Himalayan Mountains of India was taken by Patricia K. Riddle, daughter of the author. Used with permission.

The World Food Day logo appearing on the back cover is also used with permission.

PUBLISHED BY PENTLAND PRESS, INC.
5122 Bur Oak Circle, Raleigh, North Carolina 27612
United States of America
919-782-0281

ISBN 1-57197-183-1
Library of Congress Catalog Card Number 99-074223

Printed in the United States of America

This book is dedicated to the many, many individuals who have nourished me and the world with love, especially to Margot, who not only has expedited its production but is the joy of my life.

Contents

Foreword

It seems like a long time ago—that year a handful of women gathered in Kittu and Margot's living room Sunday mornings, to talk about Nell Morton's *The Journey Is Home*, later to move on to Barbara Walker's *The Crone*.

Margot and Kittu always knew how to create peaceful, restful, engaging surroundings and on those Sunday mornings we soon discovered that they knew how to make community.

Now that I have read Kittu's powerful life story, I understand that making community comes as naturally to her, and to her partner of twenty-one years, Margot, as breathing does to the rest of us. Nurturing is what she does, wherever she lives and in whatever circumstances.

Before we came to know one another, I had heard of this amazing woman and was thrilled to see her in the back row of one of my Values Realization classes, to cross paths as she left and I arrived for our weekly massage appointments. Then she called and asked if I'd be interested in joining a small group of women on Sunday mornings to talk about women's writings and, as it turned out, come to know and enjoy one another.

Not an early morning person, I still managed the shocking 7:30 A.M. rising, picking up Robin at her house, and getting to Kittu and Margot's house on time, for a variety of rolls and coffees and teas as we gathered. Kittu and Margot's friends chosen for this experience included ranges of religious and non-religious believers, a Buddhist woman from Bhutan, a Hindu from India, ages from young to old, and, even though we all lived what could be called a middle-class lifestyle in the U.S., a range, too, of economic conditions and educations.

I did not know then, but came to understand, that this was typical behavior for Kittu, even as I gradually realized she was a prominent professor at the University of Nebraska, and an international citizen by virtue of her birth in India and her life there and in the U.S. and

China. Yet Kittu did not just have little gatherings, she made a difference in the lives of the women she touched. Now that she and Margot live in San Antonio and, in the summer months in Estes Park, Colorado, she continues to work steadily and without fail at projects that support and encourage women around the world.

I cannot begin to count the ways *I know* that Kittu has forged ahead, quietly and with enormous intelligence and care, putting women around the world in touch with each other, writing newsletters, beginning groups, networking, coming up with brilliant new, even small, ideas for nurturing women. While in Lincoln, she began an international center, funding it mainly herself, the year after she retired from the University. That is only one of the many things she did; I remember most that she made soup for the Soup Kitchen at the Gathering Place, reminding us to boil left-over soup at least three minutes.

A founding partner of Old Lesbians Organizing for Change, Kittu also writes and collects stories for a newsletter, "Storyletters," funded by the Doté Foundation and emphasizing women from all countries.

This is not meant to be a collection of Kittu's good works; I need to say that whenever I have been around her over the years, I end up feeling better about myself, more encouraged with my own possibilities. Kittu told me once, me the non-believer, that there is a stream of goodness in the world and that all we have to do is step into it. Those words, that power has resonated with me ever since. I think she's right and I wish I could believe it. Every once in a while, I mentally step into that stream of goodness, an act of supreme trust for me.

For this woman whose journey has taken her from devout Christianity to a wider belief in the oneness of all the world, her Christmas letters are gems of true, earthy, believable wisdom. I read and re-read them aloud to classes as an example of a woman who is a role model for me, a role model of aging, of nurturing, of creating, of finding the good, of supporting women, of not being afraid of the truth, of lifelong friendships, of remarkable courage.

In a letter which included words about fog, the setting sun, a family wedding, a class reunion, the second surgery for melanoma on Kittu's left thigh, experiences with Tibetan Lamas and Jean Houston, Margot's work, the summer retreat in Colorado, Kittu hopes that the vindication of Alger Hiss is "a manifestation of the dispersal of bigotry in our society." The letter concludes: "May the season which calls forth re-membering for us all, be over/ever flowing with the assurance that this world and universe has a possible future more grand than we can recall or imagine. And may each of us take our place of responsibility joyfully to assure the possible."

Another year, their letter asks: "How can we heal our planet and provide environments that are adequate, appropriate and healthy for all life?" In a recent year, Kittu and Margot tell about watching scientists on PBS discuss strings or strands of space/time and chaos mathematics . . . "As we watched *The Colours of the Universe*, we learned that it is with remarkable fractal geometry that the essence and nature of the creative universe are now being defined . . . It seems to us that perhaps *the* important 'job' we have as individuals is to live lives of gratefulness, *grace-filled-ness*." On another occasion, they spoke of "the expectation that we are all of us on the verge of breakthrough, of achieving a transcendence in our understanding." These remarkable women urged their readers "to consider ways in which [these principles agreed upon at the Beijing Women's Conference] can be implemented in your lives and your communities." Expressing their daily theology in words that speak to my heart, they "celebrate the elegance, complexity and mystery of the Life Force of the universe" realizing that "what is visible comes forth out of the invisible, the void." The void "is the great birthing place . . . Creation in evolution is the work of us all . . . There is no way to learn this other than from our own experience of living. As we learn we become part of the deep dimensions of Life, maintaining that which is sacred!"

I could go on quoting from these splendid missives. In them is just one place where the principles that have sustained and energized Kittu Riddle may be found. In her extraordinary story, one may find other threads that make up the rich garment of her life. And yet, if we could look everywhere, in every university department, and church education office, and government and non-government nutrition agency, everywhere Kittu has lived and thought, "What can I do here to help women help themselves?" and then studied and worked, made a telephone call and walked out the door to the unknown, we would find the results of her life, in the countless programs, big and little ideas put into practice in the lives of women and children made easier, richer, more productive and better.

A Nourishing Life is so full of energy and love, an emerging spiral of inner nurture and reaching out to others—without a single "How can I do this?" doubt, without a hesitation about what its author is called to do in this world, that its publication becomes a gift not only to everyone and every group Kittu has touched in her strong sweet life, but to anyone whose journey needs cheering and supporting.

I am deeply grateful for the presence of this humble, gifted, loving woman in my life, for her nourishing life, and for this amazing story sent out among us.

Ruth Raymond Thone
May 1999
Lincoln, Nebraska

Acknowledgments

I've always wondered why authors thanked so many people. Now I know. Literally hundreds of friends have contributed to the richness of the nourishing life I write about. I couldn't begin to name them all on this page or even in the context of my story. But, those among you who read between the lines will recognize yourselves.

To friends who grew up with me, were my companions; to those who taught me in Woodstock School, in Park College and the University of Chicago; to Chuck and our wonderful years together; to those who knew us and our children during our early years, in China and India, who followed us with love through our dwelling choices in the U.S.A., I am eternally grateful.

To peers in my professional life who participated with me in countless projects and seminars; to friends in many countries, especially those who still correspond and inspire me with their world view; to the women who nourished me and themselves in the women's communities of Tucson, Lincoln and San Antonio, I am deeply indebted. To members of my family, all of whom have been encouraging and supportive, my abiding love. To my children and grandson, I bequeath my vision and hope for the future.

Those who contributed directly to the writing of this book I want to thank specifically. Don Holloway taught me to use a computer. Sally Stoddard (from Woodstock) urged me to write my stories. Carol Barrett (from Union Graduate School) introduced me to Rachel's Journal Writing Group at the Doté Foundation's Resource Center in San Antonio. There I met Louita, Pat, Susan, Katharine, Maggie, Helen, Norma, Rachelle, Loretta, and, after Maggie became leader, Melanie, Debbie, Sandy, Martha, Leslie, Jenda and Vickie joined. They all listened to my stories and made suggestions from which I've benefitted.

Maggie Reasor encouraged me to keep writing and to publish. Sarah Nawrocki showed me how to put chapters together. Melanie Stafford introduced me to Jody Berman and Deborah Korte who edited, trimmed, rearranged, and guided me through the launching.

My gratitude to each of you and to Ruth Thone for her generous foreword.

The Doté Foundation Board played a part in this book by encouraging my periodic publication of women's stories as *Storyletters*. They and Melanie S., Lesley S., Margot K., Anita F., and the many writers who contributed deserve my sincere thanks. With their help, I gathered the courage to make a biography out of what, up until then, had been just my stories.

I hope that readers of *A Nourishing Life* will find nourishment not only from my stories but also from their own.

Katharine Parker Riddle

Abstract

A Nourishing Life is an intimate account of my venture to better the world through the empowerment of women. Inspired as a child in India by a missionary/mother's interest in nutrition, I followed her example in China and India, becoming a home economist to the world through the Agricultural Missions program and developing special programs to meet the needs of mothers and their infants and children in Asia and Africa. Through this I experienced deep spiritual growth, completed a Ph.D. on nourishment, and set up a "Nourishing Space for Women." With my three children grown and independent, I stepped out of my marriage of thirty-five years and entered into a long-term relationship with a woman. Opportunities for university teaching opened up that included promoting women's roles in international development. Since retiring, I have published women's stories and, in my ongoing role as a world watcher, followed such events as the U.N. Conference on Women at Beijing. I continue to be amazed at the myriad opportunities for women today, particularly in the vision of nonsexist, nonracist South Africa.

Chapter One
A Passage from India

They say the cobra foretold an auspicious future for me. Our Indian servants, who came running when they heard my mother's shrieks, stood in awe. Its head was reared above my playthings, where I had been only moments before. A six-month-old infant, I had been carried outside to go for a ride with my parents in their horse-drawn carriage when my mother realized my bonnet was missing. When she went to retrieve it, she found the snake. Though Mother didn't understand the servants' reverence, she was impressed by their assurance that the cobra meant I had a special destiny.

Their prediction proved to be true; I have been very fortunate. Providence has shaped my interests and talents for use in situations where fresh vision and new ways of doing things were needed. I have dedicated my life to promoting nourishment—a word whose definition is far broader than we typically realize—among women and families. This journey has taken me both inward to the depths of my own soul and to the far-flung corners of the earth.

From missionary work in China and India to the nutritional support programs I developed in Appalachia to the Arizona desert retreat I brought into being, where women learned to honor their true selves and experience their inner strength, I have labored to amplify the status and potential of women. This work enabled me to reach out and explore new ways of thinking. I found myself moving away from the religious fundamentals that had guided the earlier part of my life and instead embracing a more freethinking spiritual outlook. To my surprise, I discovered it was even possible for me to leave my husband, a wonderful man who had fathered my three children, and fall in love with a woman.

Looking back on my life, I am filled with wonder. Now I know that love and compassion are commonalities that spread far beyond the missionary community I was raised in. I know that, despite tragedy, life has a way of working out, providing surprising and beneficent discoveries along the way. Even the hardships I have faced—meningitis, breast cancer, melanoma, numerous surgeries, and rape—brought their own form of healing. On this journey, challenge, grace, and fulfillment have been my constant companions.

I have seen the world awaken to the needs of its impoverished peoples and respond by creating new ways to help. Out of economic depression and devastating wars has come a growing sense that we are all responsible for each other. Renewed hope for the future has led parents to strive toward a better heritage for their children—a chance at self-improvement. I could never have predicted the eye-opening opportunities that have evolved, nor the chances I've had to create nourishing circumstances and offer nourishment—in the forms of food, caring, and information—to women and families. It is literally a different world from the one I grew up in.

I was born to missionary parents in Landour, India, a British cantonment, or military post, adjoining the beautiful mountain resort of Mussoorie. At 7,500 feet, this vacation spot popular among missionaries, stands majestically atop the first rise of the Himalayas. At night, its lights could be seen from Dehra Dun, the end of the railway line 5,000 feet below. To the north were breathtaking views of the eternal snows that stretch 1,500 miles across the roof of India, rising range upon range to the mysterious country of Tibet, where none could enter. My parents were here temporarily, studying Hindi high above the heat of the plains, when I arrived on May 21, 1919.

Before I was even a month old, the monsoon swept north from the Indian Ocean and showered the subcontinent, lashing

Katharine, 6 months, with her Ayah, Shanti, who gave her the nickname "Kittu." Allahabad, U.P. India, 1919.

against our steep mountain slopes and dropping heavy rain, leaving coolness in its wake. It was time for us to go home to Allahabad. Our family of three took the winding road down to the train station and spread our bedding on the benches of an express train that took a day and a half to reach home. Allahabad, a large and bustling city, stood at the meeting place of two sacred rivers, the Ganges and the Jumna. According to Hindu mythology, a third river descending from Heaven makes it a triple confluence, a very holy place to bathe.

My *ayah*, Shanti, cared for me while Mother and Daddy continued their language studies. She found it hard to say "Katharine," my given name, so she gave me a pet Indian name, "Kittu." My parents picked it up from her, and the name stuck. This name, unusual in western circles has followed me throughout my life, identifying me immediately to friends I haven't seen in years. Friends of mine who had never met before even been brought together simply by hearing it spoken.

Mother and Daddy arrived in India in 1918, just before the November 11 armistice that ended World War I. They had met in seminary in Hartford, Connecticut. My father, Allen Parker, a tall, long-legged farm boy with an agricultural degree from Ohio State University, planned to put his training to use doing mission work overseas. A pacifist, he was opposed to the war raging in Europe; seminary proved to be an alternate form of service. My mother, Irene Glasgow, a short, vivacious Quaker from Whittier, California, felt called to pursue mission work overseas as a Christian educator. They were both quite poor during their courtship and had to pool their resources to manage financially. They were married in a simple ceremony on May 29, 1918, the day after graduation. They had volunteered to go to India as missionaries, and the Presbyterian Board of Foreign Missions assigned them to work at the Agriculture Institute in Allahabad.

In those days, missionary service was the primary overseas employment opportunity for Americans. The British and other Europeans could find jobs in their respective colonies, but apart from a few posts in embassies, consulates, and businesses, the Protestant mission stations were where Americans clustered. The mission boards of many denominations employed thousands of workers in Asia, Africa, and South America, until World War II. Then travel was interrupted and living abroad became less safe. In the wake of the war, the relationship between American churches and newly formed indigenous churches changed. Even in countries where they had long been posted, missionaries were now to be sent only at the invitation of these churches that were exerting their leadership for the first time, and fewer American workers were being invited.

Mission boards in the United States were dependent on the support of member churches, both large and small, to meet their financial obligations. Local churches, with many calls on their funds, often needed encouragement to make good on their pledges. Typically, a missionary or missionary family would be assigned to a particular church and would establish a personal connection with its congregation. Visits from that special person or family on furlough, or leave, made their financial support more meaningful. Daddy and Mother had close ties with churches in Auburn, New York, and Portland, Oregon, where we visited each time we returned to the States. Our friends there kept in touch with us throughout their lives.

When my parents originally set out for India, they knew the salary would be low compared to wages in the U.S. and there was no prospect of financial improvement. Each missionary received the same sum of money regardless of the job performed or the number of years served. There were, however, other forms of compensation. Housing and medical care were provided free of charge, an allowance was added with the birth of each child and continued through their college or vocational training. In addition, every five or six years, missionaries and their families were granted a twelve-month furlough that included travel costs to and from the United States.

In America my parents would have been considered poor. In India, however, they were looked upon as incredibly wealthy. But because all missionaries' salaries were equal, my American friends were neither richer nor poorer than I. I knew only that we had more money than most Indians. It wasn't until I arrived in the U.S. that I realized the value of the American dollar.

Embarking from Vancouver in the fall of 1918, Mother and Daddy crossed the Pacific by ship, stopping in Japan, China, and other ports en route to India. Bouts of morning sickness made the two-month trip a queasy one for Mother. Upon arriving in Allahabad, they settled into a small second-floor apartment at the Agricultural Institute and began the work they had been commissioned to do. Daddy began learning about Indian agriculture, and Mother worked in a home for uninfected children of lepers. In those days, it was common practice to take disease-free newborns from their leprous mothers and raise them in special orphanages.

The climate in Allahabad was enjoyable in winter, but by April it had become quite warm. Temperatures soared into the nineties. Overhead fans provided the only respite from the heat. Mother and Daddy were encouraged by the Mission to continue their language studies in the cool of the hills, so they relocated to a boarding house in Landour for those attending the language school. Their lessons in Hindi would continue for several years until they passed certain proficiency exams. It was in this boarding house, named 'ZigZag,' that I was born.

My character was molded and nurtured not only by childhood friends of different nationalities, but also by listening to the earnest conversations around our dinner table. From the time I was small, I heard talk about the political struggles in China, India, and other countries. Daddy's ideals as a pacifist resonated with those of Mahatma Gandhi's nonresistance movement then taking shape in India. There was much discussion about how this movement might help India obtain independence from England. Though I wasn't encouraged to comment or to ask questions, I would stay awake as long as I could, knowing that what I was hearing was important. And as I listened, I imagined that if only my father could run the world, it would be a better place and there would be no more war.

The tenor of these conversations was unfailingly kind and generous. There was no negative criticism, no cynical wisecracking or ridiculing of the protagonists. To this day, it is difficult for me to criticize harshly or to hear such criticism myself. And I still seek out the bright side of any calamity or alarming situation.

As a child, having a stable home life made it possible for me to cope with the fact that my life in India wouldn't last forever. I knew that after graduating from high school, I'd have to go to college in the U.S. I was, after all, an American. There, I'd have to start life on my own—prepare for a career, or get married, or both. I knew the only way for me to return to India would be as a missionary because in those days no agencies other than churches employed Americans. And I didn't want to work for the U.S. Embassy.

This awareness that I didn't really belong in India instilled in me a lifelong sense of living between countries and cultures, though I developed the ability to make my home on whatever shores destiny carried me to. My anchor was my tie to Woodstock, the school I attended in Landour. Though we gravitated to opposite ends of the earth, chance meetings with fellow graduates always provided a sense of connectedness and the opportunity to reminisce about the cultural milieu in which we grew up.

My earliest recollections are of Landour, of climbing up and down steep hillsides and looking with awe at mountain views—the snows to the north and the plains to the south. My parents and I moved there before I was three. In 1922, Daddy had accepted the invitation to be principal of Woodstock School which had been established in

Landour in 1854 to educate the daughters of foreign missionaries and Indian Christians. Before this time, while sons of British and American families had been sent back to their home countries to attend school, girls remained with their parents and were usually educated at home. As a result, they were often isolated from other Americans and Europeans their age. The founding of the Woodstock School had meant that such girls could live in dormitories and study together for the nine-month school year from March through November. Not long after I was born, Woodstock's board of directors decided to open enrollment to boys and sought a married couple to spearhead its expansion into a coeducational institution.

At first, Daddy and Mother had hesitated over this invitation. Both had wanted to work with Indian families in the plains. After giving it some thought though, they realized that providing a good education for missionary sons and daughters would contribute to the overall mission effort. Parents would be less anxious if their children could be well-educated here in India, and Daddy could still contribute to the improvement of agriculture in the mountains.

Woodstock, already 66 years old, was already a major institution, one of eight or nine English-speaking schools in Mussoorie run privately for the children of special populations such as railway workers or members of a particular church. As Woodstock's principal, Daddy, somewhat shy and already bald at age thirty-one, stepped into a very influential position. He fostered cooperation among the various schools and worked with the Cantonment Board to provide running water and electricity to all establishments. Asked to oversee property and to erect buildings, he quickly learned how to lever grant monies for the school.

He and Mother, being both friendly and outgoing, established good working relations among Woodstock's faculty and staff and improved morale. They involved parents and teachers in developing the school curriculum as well as extracurricular programs for both girls and boys. The student body rapidly grew from fewer than 200 to more than 350 as families enrolled their sons and daughters. A welcome was extended to all children, regardless of religion or nationality. Soon children from Catholic, Parsee, Hindu, Jewish, and Muslim families were attending alongside those from Protestant denominations.

Mother concerned herself with many things—among them, the meals served at the boarding school. Food was hard to obtain in quantity or variety, and she knew that the boarders were homesick for familiar dishes. With no background in nutrition, she learned the nourishing properties of Indian foods from Charlotte Wiser, a nutritionist whose children attended Woodstock. Native foods were also much cheaper than those the foreigners ate. Drawing on her own knowledge, Mother taught the baker how to make healthy brown bread out of whole wheat flour instead of using white flour mixed with brown sugar. While she worked to make foods taste more like home for American boys and girls, she also encouraged the frequent serving of Indian dishes—lentils, vegetables, rice, and *chappati* (unleavened bread), which we ate every day for lunch.

She also helped Indian women nourish their newborns. If breast milk wasn't forthcoming, Mother demonstrated how to make a clean substitute using boiled, diluted cow's milk to feed to the infant through a small funnel. I didn't often have time to go with her into the homes of servant families or other Indian families on the hillside, but she talked about her work and how the babies were thriving. She encouraged those she had helped to share their experience with other mothers.

Mother's way of helping seemed, to me, quite sensible, especially since the Indians were so poor. Frequently, Indian women visited our home to ask for help. As I watched over their children playing on our Persian rugs, I listened to their distress and heard Mother's counseling.

She encouraged women missionaries who summered in Landour to donate food and clothing which she, in turn, distributed to needy homes. She also attended frequent meetings at Landour's community center. Among the groups she founded and participated in was the Reading Club, whose members discussed the latest offerings from American and European presses. With these books, she started a small lending library for the community.

An agriculturist and humanitarian, Daddy devoted efforts towards the well-being of farmers who brought in milk, vegetables, eggs, and fruit from their small hillside plots to sell to the school and the summer residents. He also earned the eternal gratitude of school staff and servants by finding ways to increase their benefits and by building them better living quarters.

I saw my parents strive each day to make a difference in the lives of those around them. They felt great empathy and love for these people and were very aware of the difficulties they had to surmount. They were a team who worked together even though each had a full and busy life. My parents knew that God had led them to this service and would provide guidance in coping with the criticism or problems that accompany newness. They relied on their own inner resources to deal with stressful circumstances in their personal lives and never let these issues spill over into family life.

The Parker Family. Allen, Clara Jo born in 1922, Kittu and Irene, Landour, Mussoorie, U.P. India.

I both admired and loved my mother and father. I knew that though their work was arduous, all of it was done for the school—its students, staff, and parents—and the community. I grew up feeling fortunate to have been well-parented. By their example, Mother and Daddy showed me how to live as a loving, caring person.

I was proud of my parents and knew that as the principal's daughter, I had to behave well. School servants constantly reminded me of my position by rising and greeting me formally or standing at attention when I passed. I was seldom out of sight of some school employee. Any mischief on my part would quickly find its way to Daddy's ears. I knew not to take advantage of my position by acting proud. When I walked along the Tehri Road and through the bazaar, the narrow shopping strip between Landour and Mussoorie, I'd frequently hear, "Parker Sahib's daughter is going by" and would call out a friendly greeting.

Some of the girls teased me mercilessly, calling me a goody-goody and stuck-up. This was my first taste of children's cruelty, and I didn't understand it. Why, with all my good intentions, would they try to make me feel miserable? It was extremely upsetting. To comfort me, Mother suggested that these girls had probably experienced similar badgering in their families or communities and took out their frustration on me because I seemed more fortunate. Mother's words aroused in me a sense of empathy that helped me refrain from yelling back. After that, not only did I simply ignore their insults, I was able to be friendly to my tormentors. This was made easier by the fact that I had close friends of my own.

My sister Clara Jo was born during our family's first year at Woodstock. She was a welcome addition, particularly because my parents had lost a second daughter, Dorothy, to dysentery in Allahabad the previous November. I don't remember Dorothy, but I was enchanted with my new sister and wanted to carry her around on my hip just like the little Indian girls did with their baby sisters.

Clara Jo was one-and-a-half and I was nearing five when we went back to the States on our first furlough, a year's leave. In Ohio, uncles, aunts, grandparents, and cousins we'd heard about only in letters magically came to life, eager to spoil us with ice cream and candy, dolls, and new dresses. Though I don't remember Mother's relatives in California, I do remember Yellowstone Park and being warned not to feed the bears. The uncertainty as to whether our Model T would make it up the steep inclines was also quite a thrill.

We spent the winter in Chicago where I attended kindergarten and Daddy started work on a master's degree in education. We lived in an apartment building right next to the University of Chicago with other missionaries. I remember jumping down the hall stairs with a boy who lived above us. I must have been something of a tomboy. We took turns jumping down two, three, four steps. Then he dared me to jump down five. I couldn't let him beat me, so, although I was scared, I gathered my courage and jumped. Everything would have been fine if I hadn't landed on a small rug that slid—with me on it—across the polished floor and crashed into the glass front door. A small nail holding the curtains gashed my left eyebrow and I had to get stitches. The scar, an odd memento from Chicago that is still with me, reminds me that I took that dare!

When the furlough was over, I was glad to get back to life in Landour. Helen Pittman, my best friend who was also my age, was living just above our house, Tehri View. We picked up right where we had left off, playing on the hillside, imagining elves and fairies among the lush undergrowth and building pebble-and-leaf houses for them.

The day before my sixth birthday, she and I were at her house swinging, when we heard shouting. Looking over the stone fence, we saw a bunch of *coolies*, workmen, down by the school, struggling up the hill with something. Suddenly Helen said, "Let's go play near the Smith's house." I gladly agreed. They had lemon verbena bush with leaves I loved to smell. Then she suggested we slide down the steep hill behind Tehri View. Though I knew this was dangerous, the excitement of the challenge overrode the fact that we weren't supposed to play there. By the time we returned home, it was nearly dark. But surprisingly, nothing was said about it.

The next morning Mother and Daddy sent me out into the front yard, and to my amazement, there stood a little wooden house with a corrugated tin roof and a front porch. It was the best birthday surprise I could have received. Helen came running down the hill saying she'd known all along that the grunting coolies had been delivering the playhouse, built for me down at the school. She'd been told to divert my attention and keep me away from the front yard.

The playhouse was tall enough for us to stand up in, and we could even push a small trap door and climb into the attic. I was delighted! Helen and I played out there every day after school, and friends on their way home from classes stopped to join us. Because all my schoolmates were welcome, even when I was not there myself, the playhouse boosted my standing, and I was teased less about being the principal's stuck-up daughter. That tiny house was quite special to me—not only was it a place of my own, it was a place where children could gather and be themselves.

Sadly, when I was ten years old, Helen's family resigned from mission work and went back to the States. I was heartbroken when she left, sure I'd never have a friend like her again. Though we wrote frequently, I didn't see her again until our next furlough when I was nearly twelve, and by then, we had grown apart.

For me, life in Landour was bicultural. I felt equally comfortable in the homes of Indian servants and those of American missionaries. School was conducted in English and we spoke English at home, yet we were also fluent in Hindustani, used in conversations with

Indians. I went in and out of the one-room homes of school servants on the hillside, squatting near the cooking fires of Christian households, enjoying a piece of freshly baked *chappati* or playing with the babies. But in Hindu households, I knew I had to be careful not to go near their food, lest I defile it. All foreigners and those not Hindu were considered outcast—a cultural belief I simply accepted.

I was taller than most girls my age and resembled my mother. Because I thought she was pretty, I decided I must be, too. When I looked in the mirror, I saw brown eyes, straight brown hair parted on one side and held by a bobby pin on the other, and pink cheeks glowing from exercise. Though an avid reader, I was also an active and adventurous child. My clothes were often awry and my knee socks drooped. I wore out the backs of my dresses riding landslides and climbed huge old oak trees with long moss-covered branches. There were places I knew not to go—the burning ghat at the bottom of the hill where Hindus burned their dead, and the hidden gullies where garbage was emptied out—but I must have gone there anyway because I recall the ashes on the pyres, the whiteness of human bones, and the stink of refuse.

I also remember the beauty of Landour. Starting in June, when monsoon rains transformed the dry brown hillsides into carpets of fresh green moss and ferns, flowers began to bloom. Pink and yellow dahlias grew wild, orange ginger-root blossoms sprayed over steep hillsides, and small lavender orchids shot up from the ground. Yet the roots of this abundant, colorful foliage were not enough to hold the hillsides together. Heavy monsoon rains often washed out the familiar paths and tore down *pushtas*, or retaining walls, creating unexpected dangers. The rainy season was three months long and caused quite a change in summer activity.

The school year started in early March when it was still quite cold. Schoolchildren from the plains came uphill to live in the dormitories while their parents remained below. It seemed like all of the fun happened in the dorms, and I felt left out because I had to live at home. By mid-April though, parents started coming uphill and moving into the small houses on the hillside and taking their children out of boarding. With the days now sunny and cool, the social season, with its parties and picnics, plays, concerts, and contests, began in earnest. In mid-June, with the advent of the monsoon, many parents went downhill again and put their children back in boarding. For three months, there were very few hours of sunshine, and the smell of mildew pervaded our houses. It was hard to keep anything dry, much less dry it out. We resorted to using racks pulled up to the ceiling or large baskets fitted over charcoal braziers to dry our laundry.

At the end of the monsoon, the sun returned in a blaze of autumn. The days were exhilarating and the nights began to get cold. This was the season for sports. Hockey contests and track and field events all led up to the Mussoorie Olympics in which Woodstock students competed against children from other English-speaking schools. There were few level places big enough to hold such events, so we often had to hike a few miles before competing. The school year ended with a Christmas celebration on November 25, after which pupils departed for their homes on the plains.

During the summer months, wandering salesmen, or *wallahs*, carrying baskets of fruit or tin trunks filled with baked goods on their heads, or with bolts of cloth strapped to their backs, climbed up and down the hillside going from house to house each day. The cake wallah was the girls' favorite. Whenever we met him, we would beg him to put his trunk down and open it so we could smell the goodies. We would look longingly at the petit fours, curry puffs, macaroons, fudge balls, and peppermint canes. Then, pooling the few *annas* we had between us, we'd have a long consultation on what to buy. Usually the peppermint won. No mint I've eaten since has had such a crunchy consistency and delicate flavor as these.

Daddy's first big building project was a hostel for boys with a winterized residence for our family at one end (Tehri View was not insulated and best used as a summer residence). He also retrofitted cottages and dormitories with electricity and indoor plumbing. I'd accompany him on his daily inspection tours, skipping along to keep up with his long strides. He walked rapidly, swinging a cane. I'd ask questions about how buildings went up—information that would one day be useful in my life's work—and he was more than willing to answer. Frequently though, the contractor, plumber, or someone else connected with the building would join us and assume that he had priority in the conversation. The time I spent with my father was important to me because it was rare. Although I knew I had his support and approval, his duties as principal kept him busy. As a result, I did not feel particularly close to him.

The hostel featured a covered swimming pool fed by local springs. The water was ice-cold. Rajah Bandy, a young teacher who lived in the hostel and supervised sports activities, offered to teach me to swim. I understood we'd start at 5:30 A.M. The only way I knew to get to the pool was through the boys' bathroom but figured it'd be empty that early in the morning. When I opened the door to the pool, however, Rajah was indeed holding a swimming class—but it was for boys, and they were all naked. I ran back to my room, confused. Their nudity didn't embarrass me, but I was pretty sure they wouldn't welcome me in their class. Later, I found out he had meant 5:30 P.M. I never admitted my mistake to him, but I did learn to swim.

My sister Patty was born just before the hostel was completed. Her crib joined the little white beds in the room that Clara Jo and I shared. Outside, Mother planted a lovely garden with many different flowers, including large double dahlias, shasta daises, huge red begonias, and blue forget-me-nots. As a toddler, blue-eyed Patty would run out and bury her face in their lacy branches.

I was now eight, old enough to take some responsibility for my new baby sister. One day I found Patty licking juice off the skins of some litchis nuts left on a plate, and I immediately informed my Mother. Litchis, a sweet, pulpy fruit, were kept fresh at the bazaar by soaking them in water, but everyone knew that this water was unsafe to drink. At home we had ways of disinfecting the fruit, but even so, Patty contracted dysentery and got quite sick. In 1927, there were no sulfa drugs or antibiotics so her illness was life-threatening. Dr. T. B. Butcher, the school doctor, cared for her around the clock in a nursing home in Mussoorie.

When Clara Jo also became ill with dysentery, Mother went to stay with them in the nursing home. I was very lonely without my sisters, so at night Daddy let me sleep in Mother's bed next to his. In the evening, he would call her for the latest news. It was never encouraging.

One morning I awoke to hear Daddy and Mother talking softly in the bed beside me. I jumped up, happily assuming Patty was well since Mother had returned home. They took me in their arms and told me that my baby sister was as well as she'd ever be—she had died and gone to Heaven. Mother had brought her body home during the night, carrying her in her lap as she rode in a *dandy*, a sedan chair carried by four men. I ran into our room, where Patty was lying in her crib peacefully, as if she were asleep. Only a few weeks ago, she had been jumping up and down in it, full of life. Mother and Daddy came in, too, and wept with me.

As we stood there hugging each other, mourning the loss of Patty and worrying over Clara Jo who was still gravely ill, my parents shared a secret with me: five months from now, in November, we would have another baby. They encouraged me not to say anything about it. Right now it was our private news to comfort us alone. It felt so good that I tucked the secret away in my mind and forgot about it, never even noticing Mother's growing tummy. When it became the gossip of the school though, I proudly said that I had known all along.

But that day we busied ourselves with preparations for Patty's burial, which, according to law, had to take place the same day. First,

Daddy instructed the carpenters to make a simple pine box. Mother, our friends, and I padded it inside with cotton covered in soft white voile. Next, Daddy sent word to the caretaker of the terraced cemetery on the north side of the hill to prepare a grave under a tall fir tree, where Patty could lie facing the eternal snows.

Making plans for Patty's funeral was comforting because it made her death real, made it more concrete. I told Mother of my guilt at not having prevented her from licking the litchis and received assurances that it wasn't my fault. When it came time to put Patty in the coffin, I couldn't bring myself to lean over and kiss her even though I badly wanted to do so. I later expressed my grief in poetry and by burying my face and tears in the blue forget-me-nots as Patty once did.

By afternoon, all was ready. Coolies carried the casket, followed by Mother in a *dandy*, with Daddy and me walking behind. We went up to the top of our ridge and into the cemetery, where Patty would lie among the graves of military personnel and missionaries. While still at the gravesite, the service not yet over, a messenger brought urgent word that Clara Jo had taken a turn for the worse. Daddy and Mother left as soon as the casket had been lowered. Friends gathered around me and walked me down the hill, but I felt deserted.

It was a joyous day when, after being ill for two weeks, Clara Jo finally came home. I was so relieved she had survived. Her recovery took a long time, and our bedroom still seemed strangely empty without Patty's crib. Then one night in mid-November, our beds were moved out to the glassed-in porch, and we knew Mother was having the baby. Dr. Butcher arrived, and sometime after midnight, we were thrilled to hear the first cries of our new sister, Barbara Irene. Her arrival filled our hearts, and her bassinet made our room feel complete again. Still, I missed Patty.

Before I turned eight, I had started violin lessons with Miss Edith Isles, head of Woodstock's music department. The discipline of the lessons and the soothing sounds of the notes helped assuage my grief in the wake of Patty's death. But it wasn't until high school that I began to truly appreciate music, eventually becoming confident enough to play solos in concerts and participate in orchestra. Later, I realized just how important music was to our small community. Phonographs were few, and radios played little music. Live performance was all we had, and musicians who sang or played at teas or social occasions were greatly appreciated.

When I was nine, all the girls my age were invited to Mrs. Mhow's house to discuss becoming ladies. I expected a lecture on manners. Instead, we were presented with a discourse on what would happen to our bodies as we mature. She used charts of the male and female anatomy to illustrate the physical changes and explained in detail how a baby was conceived. As she talked, we were silent—we were all too embarrassed to look at each other. Though our mothers had told us about getting our periods, we weren't aware that this subject was discussed outside the family.

Some months later, I was appalled to find brownish stains in my pongee bloomers. I rushed down the hill to the boys' hostel where Mother was in the kitchen giving orders to the cook. She could see I was distraught. Once she learned why, she explained that I'd started my period just as she'd told me I would. I had forgotten. She showed me the cloths (napkins) I'd have to fill with cotton and pin to an elastic

Allen, Barbara (born in 1927), Clara Jo, Irene, and Kittu Parker, in front of the "Playhouse." Landour, Mussoorie, U.P. India.

belt and explained that I'd have to wash them out so that most of the stain was gone before they could be sent to the *dhobi* or washerman. Then she calmly told me which of my friends had already gotten their periods. I was horrified that our mothers discussed this subject and that every mother would soon know that I too had reached puberty. But even more upsetting was the fact that she told me to slow down and not run so much during my periods. She wouldn't even let me walk the half-mile uphill back to school and instead called coolies to carry me in a *dandy*. I was so embarrassed that I insisted they put me down before we reached the school, hoping no one would see me.

For a while I felt overwhelmed with what I had to put up with as a girl. But a few years later, I realized that Mrs. Mhow and Mother had left out the most amazing part about bodily changes—the wonderful, throbbing feeling between my legs when I was around boys.

However, also around this time, I became increasingly concerned by the poverty that surrounded me. I asked Mother why so many Indian women sat by the side of the road, nursing their new babies and holding out bowls for alms. She didn't know the answer, but it bothered her too. After some discussion, we worked out a plan: I would adopt one of the mothers and give her a banana about once a week when I walked by. The first time I did this, the woman seemed grateful for the gift but looked furtively over her shoulder as if fearful someone might suddenly grab it. The second time, she seemed distraught. The third time, she wasn't there.

It was then that I learned how dependent the destitute were on protectors and how vicious the repercussions of that protection could be. It was as difficult for the beggar woman to be singled out for charity, attracting the jealously of her peers, as it was for me to see her suffering.

In April 1931, before I turned twelve, our family of five headed for the States on our second furlough. We set sail from Karachi, which is now part of Pakistan, and headed up the Persian Gulf. At Basra we boarded the train to Baghdad, stopping overnight in Ur of the Chaldees to view excavations of artifacts from the time of Abraham. There at the diggings, Mother pointed out a thick layer of dirt ten feet tall containing no artifacts and explained that it was evidence of the great flood described in the Old Testament. I was impressed with her knowledge—until then I hadn't realized how much of a biblical scholar she was. I felt thrilled that she had chosen to share with me something so important to her.

From Baghdad, we crossed another large desert en route to Damascus. It took forty-eight hours by bus including stops at oases.

The sand dunes all looked alike to me, and I couldn't figure out how the driver knew which way to go.

Next, we took a train north through Aleppo into Turkey and got off at a tiny town early the following morning. The car that was supposed to meet us never arrived, so we bargained for a truck to take us 150 miles farther north to Kaiseria-Phillipi where some missionary friends lived.

From there we went on through Turkey into Europe, stopping in France and taking an ocean liner to the U.S. Again we went to Chicago where I spent my first year of high school. Mother had proudly bought French fashions for us, but they were so different from America's teenage styles that I only felt unattractive and awkward, particularly around boys. I wanted them to like me, but I couldn't seem to figure out what to do—or not to do—around them. One evening, a boy walked me home from a church party, and I invited him into my bedroom to talk because my parents were busy with guests in the living room. It never occurred to me that this was inappropriate, that is, until I saw the look of consternation on Mother's face when she opened the bedroom door.

Soon furlough was over. On our trip back to India, I developed a painful crush on a young man aboard the ship. I was so lovestruck and so miserable at being tongue-tied around this fellow that I wondered if I'd ever feel comfortable around boys. I looked forward to getting back to Woodstock and my friends. Still, because I was the principal's daughter, even these relationships were sometimes fraught with problems.

One of the greatest things about life in Landour was that we had to entertain ourselves. Radio brought us the BBC news but little other programming and movies were only an occasional treat. So we put on plays, went on hikes, and spent lots of time planning parties, paying particular attention to the games we'd play and the foods we'd eat there. I enjoyed many games, but when they involved kissing, I became uncomfortable. Kissing, I felt, was not something to be taken lightly.

At a class picnic when one particular kissing game was announced, I left the group and went around the hill to where our teacher was putting out lunch. I offered to help her. She told me not to be a poor sport and encouraged me to go back and participate, even after I explained what was going on. I didn't mention the game to my parents though, so I was shocked when my father, a frown on his face, came into our classroom on Monday morning and rebuked us. Everyone was sure I had tattled. From then on, I felt left out. I was not included in parties where there might be kissing, hugging, or dancing. I still had fun with the girls in my class, and boys still walked me home from class parties, but I knew they would not ask me out for dates. Mother and Daddy were aware of what was going on and ached for me, but there was nothing they could do.

Though my social life was not busy, life at home was very full. Our guest room was often bursting with visitors to the school and our dining table was usually stretched to its limit. Mother included me and my sisters in her planning and counted on us to help keep the house neat and help entertain guests. She was not a robust person, and in the afternoons, I'd pitch in and do whatever she felt had been left undone.

Friendly, warm, and open, Mother gave exquisite tea parties for summer vacationers, complete with cheese puffs and date bars. She made sure that everyone on the hillside who had anything to do with the school was invited at least once during the season. Clara Jo and I helped with the baking over the weekend and on tea days we would hurry home from classes to help set up the parties. Curly-haired little Barbara, a favorite among the guests, would help Prema, our Indian sister, pass the sandwiches.

Prema, the daughter of the prime minister of the state of Gwalior, came to live with us when she was twelve. Her father felt it important that she receive a good education. Her brothers were already enrolled in Woodstock as boarders, but Prema had lived such a sheltered life in the women's quarters of Gwalior Palace that she couldn't be put directly into boarding. Daddy suggested that she come live with us, and we agreed to invite her to be our sister. So she was part of our family during the school year.

We now lived in the principal's bungalow that Daddy had built before we went to the States on furlough. It was a comfortable home. Downstairs, two large rooms the width of the house opened into each other and provided ample room for entertaining. Behind the dining room was Daddy's office. It had an outside door where local people, school servants, and anyone else who wanted to speak with him would line up and wait their turn. The house had two kitchens—one indoors where kerosene was used, and one outdoors where meals were prepared using charcoal.

Upstairs were four bedrooms. Mine was a corner room with beautiful views. Sitting at my desk, I could look through pine trees down to the *doon*—the plains—5,000 feet below. I loved the privacy but that changed when Prema joined the family. Clara Jo moved in with me so that Prema could share Barbara's room. My single bed became bunk beds. I quickly claimed the bottom bunk and loved to tease Clara Jo by pushing up on her mattress with my feet. On summer nights when the windows were open, an occasional unwelcome bat would fly in. We detested these creatures and soon developed a routine to deal with them. As I closed the windows and turned on the light, Clara Jo reached for the two badminton rackets she kept nearby, and we'd play "bat-minton" until we could throw its dead body out the window and down the hillside.

The only time we were alone as a family was during the winter when school closed down and the hillside emptied out. It was during this time we'd begin planning for Christmas and working on projects that had been put aside. In the evening, we'd sit around the fire, and while someone read out loud, others would work on stamp collections, knit, or play cards.

One winter we hiked 120 miles along the Tehri Road, the main thoroughfare that stretches from Landour bazaar, past our house, and on into Tibet, though the latter was closed to outsiders. Coolies carried our bedding and supplies, and we stayed overnight at rest houses installed by the British for civil servants inspecting the area. Along the way we met mule trains carrying produce to town, herds of goats going to slaughter, and passed Hindu pilgrims walking barefoot toward the source of the holy river Ganges. Travelers, usually men, sang plaintive songs that echoed through the mountains. It took us over a week to get to where we could look out at the forbidden land of Tibet. Then we visited friends in Pauri before returning to Landour by bus and train.

Sometimes during the winter, we'd visit Isabella Thoburn College, in Lucknow, where Mother served on the board of directors. But often, the faculty members would spend Christmas with us instead. These "aunties," as we called them, always brought new games, books, or goodies to eat. Several days before Christmas, we'd take an all-day picnic to "Witches' Hill," where we'd pick out our tree, cut it down, and carry it home, singing carols on the way. Later, we'd decorate it with ornaments, garlands, and candles.

We had many callers on Christmas Day, and to each we gave a packet of peanuts and *ghur* (chunks of hard brown sugar) wrapped in red and green tissue paper tied with tinsel ribbon. Between visitors, we opened stockings containing funny little surprises, packages from the States full of new clothes and toys, and presents we'd wrapped for each other. Of all the delicious food we ate on Christmas Day, I remember most the stew made from specially ordered tinned oysters.

After Christmas, we usually went downhill to visit friends in various parts of India. Riding a bicycle was one of my activities on the plains. Sometimes we would cycle long distances with friends and meet for picnics. Road traffic consisted of horse carriages, ox carts, men pulling lumber or carts of produce, women carrying loads on their heads and babies on their hips, and an occasional motorized vehicle. Visiting the plains gave me an entirely different perspective on life in India.

Upon realizing how sheltered and narrowly focused my view of India truly was, my parents arranged for me to spend a month with Clara Mariner, a woman engaged in evangelistic work among village women. Typically, these villages were little more than clusters of houses, usually on a slight elevation, between fields of lentils, wheat, and other cereal grains. Clara had a regular staff of servants who set up camp for her in groves of mango trees near the villages she planned to visit. It was fun sleeping in one tent, eating in another, then venturing out along the narrow irrigation ditches to watch the farmers working their fields. Clara and I would walk or cycle to the surrounding villages and find the outcast section, where the Christians were, to meet with the women. We would inquire about their health, discuss family news, conduct literacy classes, give simple Bible lessons, sing Indian songs called *bhajans*, and pray together.

We planned our activities around the women's schedules because they were extremely busy with their regular daily tasks—gathering manure to use for fuel, forming it into cakes and drying it in the sun, winnowing wheat, preparing food for the men in the fields, caring for children, washing clothes, and other chores. In addition, some of them cleaned the houses of upper-class women to help make ends meet. Though there was a clear separation of caste, I noticed a distinct loyalty even among the women of different castes. They all had burdensome lives.

During this time I also learned more about the work of Charlotte Wiser, the nutritionist who had taught Mother about Indian foods. I watched as Charlotte squatted with Indian women to discuss their diets and what they fed their infants and toddlers. She studied the food they cooked, noting how they fixed it, how much they prepared, and which members of the family got how much. The ideas she developed over the course of several decades as a Presbyterian Missionary resulted in better-fed infants and children and healthier families.

While at Woodstock I had many inspiring teachers. My father taught American History my junior year and my mother taught Old Testament my senior year. Miss Isles, my violin teacher, not only conducted the school orchestra but led oratorios including singers from the whole hillside. I treasure the watercolors she gave me. Miss Frances, also a painter, took me through the rigors of algebra, introduced me to drama and poetry, and was my spiritual inspiration.

Kittu and her Daddy ride in a rickshaw pulled by two coolies and pushed by three. Her sister Barbara rides in a Kundy, *on the back of a coolie. They are on their way to the bus depot from which Kittu will leave Landour, Mussoorie, U.P. India, for college in the USA. May, 1936.*

Miss Marley, eternally renowned by her ability to remember each alumnus, taught Latin and was head of the library.

In December 1935, I graduated from Woodstock. The experience was bittersweet—my classmates and I were very proud of ourselves and glad to be finished with high school, but each of us was terribly uncertain about the future. We wondered which college to apply to, how we'd get back to the United States, and whether we'd ever see Woodstock or each other again.

I applied to Park College, a Presbyterian college near Kansas City, Missouri, because it offered a work-study program which made the tuition more affordable than other colleges. I also liked the idea that every student worked. When I was accepted, my parents arranged for me to travel to America with two of my India "aunties," Sarah Chakko and Florence Salazar, from Isabella Thoburn College.

In early May 1936, before I turned seventeen, life with my loving, nurturing family in India came to an end. After helping me pack my trunk, Mother and my sisters went down to the bus station where I said a tearful goodbye. Daddy and I took the rattling bus down the hill, then a train to the city of Lucknow, where he left me in the care of Sarah and Florence and returned home. It is not surprising that these kind women taking me away from my family and escorting me to the other side of the world became temporary scapegoats for my unhappiness, unwanted chaperones against whom I could rebel.

For three days and nights we traversed the sweltering Indian subcontinent, our train doggedly pushing south into strange territory. As I watched the tilled terrain fly by, I wept inside. Outwardly, I maintained a sullen silence to mask my homesickness. This part of India seemed barren. The station stops were unfamiliar and the calls of food vendors unintelligible. The sense of alienation, setting in even before I had left the land of my birth, was almost more than I could bear.

Still, as each day went by, I gained more emotional distance, separating myself from where I'd been and what I'd known.

Sarah and Florence ordered *dal bhat* (lentils and rice) at station stops, and food trays were passed through the windows into our compartment. Though it smelled delicious, I was unable to eat. Even the special date bars Mother had packed went untouched.

It was oppressively hot. An Indian woman chewing betel nut was seated cross-legged on one of the wooden benches of our ladies' compartment. Seeing my discomfort, she offered a hand fan to supplement the overhead fans. Her genuine concern softened my notions of rebellion. She was curious about me—a tall, skinny girl with straight, short brown hair, wearing a skimpy cotton dress that probably, in her opinion, didn't cover enough of my arms or legs to be modest. Another woman, bangles jangling on her arm as she adjusted the *chadoor* over her head, bluntly asked me, "Why hasn't your father gotten you married off yet?"

"I'm going to America to go to college first," I replied.

She shook her head and looked at her companions. The women exchanged skeptical glances.

Her next observation was right on target, "You are sad to be leaving India."

I agreed. But in leaving India, I knew I was doing what had to be done. I was leaving the country in which I'd grown up, the land I loved. It was my home, but it wasn't my home country. I had an American passport even though I didn't yet feel I belonged there. I trembled inside, knowing that soon I would arrive in a land that, despite my visits there on furlough, was still alien to me, a land of people who knew hardly anything about India. I was the one who would have to change, to make adjustments, and I dreaded it.

Americans would say I was stuck-up, that my accent was British, that my homemade clothes looked strange. No wonder I was rude to my escorts who were leading me into this uncharted territory.

As I rested on a wooden upper berth, I remembered the cobra and wondered whether the special destiny that the servants had predicted awaited me in America. All the same, something new was coming into being within me—a gladness for the chance to be independent, to be free of the stigma of being the obedient principal's daughter, an eagerness to make a fresh start in a new place.

Chapter Two
Finding My Way

Near the southern tip of India, our train was loaded onto a ferry and carried to northern Ceylon where it proceeded south to Colombo. Our ship, the *SS Yasakuni Maru*, awaited us, ready to sail east to Japan. From there, we would board another ship for the trans-Pacific journey. Ocean travel, relaxed and luxurious, gave us weeks in which to transpose body and mind from Orient to Occident. I hoped there would be congenial companions and plenty of activities.

Looking the passengers over, I spotted a youngish man, thin, quiet, and observant, whom I recognized as Al Kearns-Preston, a teacher in Allahabad. He, in turn, recognized me as Allen Parker's daughter. I liked him, and we found we had plenty to talk about. I told him I was glad to be away from Woodstock and the pressures of being a principal's daughter. He was looking forward to visiting his girlfriend after a two-year separation.

Over the next two weeks, we walked the decks, played games, danced at night, and watched the porpoises from the stern. In the lounge, we wrote letters back to India and mailed them from Singapore and Hong Kong. There were no romantic implications between us, but my chaperones kept a close eye on us just in case. Nevertheless, his companionship during this interlude at sea felt very reassuring.

Upon arriving in Shanghai, Sarah, Florence, and I disembarked to visit China. We left our trunks on board the *Yasakuni Maru* as it headed to Japan where they would be transferred to our next ship, the *SS Chichibu Maru*, in Yokohama. Al, too, stayed on board. He had planned to cross the Pacific earlier than we were. We thanked each other, said goodbye, and promised to write. However, the next Sunday, Al appeared unexpectedly at an evening church service we were attending in Nanking. He had decided to visit China after all and was even booked on the same train we were taking to Peiping.

In Peiping, Sarah, Florence, and I stayed at the Methodist compound and never saw the Presbyterian compound where Al was staying, the place where I would one day live and give birth to my daughter Patty. I kept watch for Al as we visited the special delights of this famous city—the Temple of Heaven with its blue-tiled circular roof, the courtyards of the Forbidden City with its gold roof, and Coal Hill, the elevated garden in its center. Outside the city walls, we toured the Summer Palace of the Dowager Empress. She had built a stone boat in the large lake where she kept cool while her subjects fanned themselves in the heat.

From Peiping, we headed north by train across Manchuria and Korea. Chinese trains were much like those in America, with double seats on both sides of the aisle. At night, these seats could be turned into berths just like in Pullman cars. There was also a dining car that served European as well as Chinese and Korean food. Despite these comforts, it was a most uneasy journey.

We knew Japan had taken control of Korea, but we hadn't realized they were also infiltrating Manchuria. Armed Japanese soldiers boarded our train, patrolling the aisles in silence. When the train stopped and we got out to walk around, our movements were closely watched. After Mukden, the train halted many times with no explanation. None of us knew what was happening though rumors flew back and forth among the passengers. We were not at all sure that being on the train was safe or that being American citizens would protect us if fighting broke out.

At one stop, we heard shots. When the train pulled out of the station, three people lay by the tracks, bleeding. This upset us so much that we canceled our plans to stop in Seoul. We stayed on the train, even though we had to pay a supplement and no sleeping berths were available. We didn't even get off to stretch our legs.

The next day, at the docks of Pusan in South Korea, we boarded an overnight ferry, rented cabins, and slept our way across the Korean Strait to Japan. Another train met us at Shiminoseki and took us along the south coast of the island of Honshu to Kobe. Upon arrival, we went directly to the American Express office where tourists collected mail and exchanged money. Much to our surprise, we found Al there. Unfortunately, he was soon headed for Tokyo and his Seattle-bound ship in Yokohama, so we hadn't much time to talk. Another farewell.

As my chaperones and I settled into our small but comfortable YWCA rooms in Kyoto, the first stop on our two-week tour of Japan, I remembered I was supposed to deliver a gift from an American physicist in Lahore, India, to a Japanese physicist somewhere in the city. Unfortunately, both the gift and instructions were in the trunk I'd left on the *Yasakuni Maru*, and I couldn't remember the physicist's name. I did recall that he lived in a tall house with a flat roof, did research on cosmic rays, that his name began with an "N," and that his daughter had studied piano in Europe. But these details were so sketchy, I wasn't sure I'd ever be able to find him.

Each day was an adventure. In the morning, a staff person at the YWCA would write out in script the names of the places we wanted to visit and explain how to get there by public transportation. In each instance, the ticket collector would read the instructions, sell us tickets, make correct change, bow to us respectfully as we got on and off his vehicle, and indicate the direction of our destination. There were very few English-speaking people, but we managed fairly well even without a guide. Everyone we met was cordial and helpful.

We walked through beautiful gardens and visited ornate temples and fascinating museums. In tiny shops along the street, we bought wonderful finger foods such as sushi, small sandwiches, fruit, and pickled vegetables artistically arranged on decorative platters. Our experience in Kyoto was so different from our exposure to the Japanese military in Manchuria and Korea that we didn't know what to think.

I'd almost forgotten the gift I was supposed to deliver when, walking back to the YWCA one evening, I heard piano music coming from the second floor of a building. A two-storied-building was uncommon in Japan—was it tall enough, I wondered, for cosmic ray research? Could it be Dr. N's daughter playing the piano? Was it possible I had stumbled onto the physicist's residence?

The YWCA staff answered all my questions in the affirmative. I immediately went back and rang the doorbell, introduced myself, and was warmly welcomed. In a city of more than a million people, I had found the man whose name I couldn't remember. Like my chance meetings with Al, this encounter was typical of the serendipity I would experience throughout my life.

As we traveled north up the west coast of Honshu to the island of Hokkaido, the terrain changed to steep mountain gorges and hillsides terraced with rice paddies. Countless small islands dotted the ocean beside us. Though there was hardly any open space, each view was enhanced by sculptured temples, graceful trees, lakes, and gardens. The residents had cultivated almost every available space with trees, shrubs, and crops. In their day-to-day lives, they demonstrated grace in all activities no matter how mundane. Even the lunch boxes we purchased on the train were not only filled with delectable food but were also attractively decorated. People went out of their way to be kind, assist us, and make our visit comfortable. Their solicitous courtesy was impressive and most appreciated. Again, we couldn't help noting the marked contrast to what we had observed in Manchuria and Korea.

Uncle Paul Parker and cousin Verlene, Audubon, IA July, 1936.

By the time we reached Tokyo, it had been more than a month since I'd left India, and I had yet to cross the Pacific. The *Chichibu Maru* lay waiting in Yokohama Harbor, our trunks in one of her cabins, and we boarded shortly before final announcements blared from the megaphones. I wondered what lay ahead. Too excited to go below, Sarah, Florence, and I stood on deck, fascinated by the thick wall of fluttering streamers reaching out from every deck and porthole and held tight by those on the dock. The band played "Auld Lang Syne," and to the calls of "Bon voyage!" the ship pulled away, tearing the streamers and literally breaking our links with the land.

Over the next two weeks, I made friends with five recent high school graduates—three boys and two girls—of different nationalities and religious traditions. This experience was priceless. We became inseparable. We celebrated leaving behind our childhoods in Asia and our readiness for the future, wherever it might lead us. Our easy camaraderie reinforced the growing sense of myself as a likable person. To my newfound friends, I was simply Kittu, a fun companion. I realize only now how much my horizons were broadened by meeting those young people from various cultures. My shipboard experience proved to me that I was attractive and pleasant to be around.

We sailed beneath the Golden Gate Bridge, then under construction, and spent several days in San Francisco before heading south to Los Angeles, where we disembarked and reluctantly parted.

Our tight clique was dispersing, our friendships about to unravel across continents. We were each whisked away by happy and excited relatives—in my case, my Uncle Paul and Aunt Vema who were waiting to take me back to Iowa. Their house would serve as my home base while I attended Park College.

On the long drive to Iowa, I was more homesick than I'd been since the train trip in India. And yet I was looking forward to college, to being in a new environment where no one knew me. Uncle Paul recognized how immature and inexperienced I was and spent a lot of time with me in the evenings answering my many questions. Aunt Vema, in turn, acquainted me with housekeeping, helped me get clothes for college, and introduced me to some girls my age from their church.

Letters from home arrived, establishing a lifeline of contact. Though it took a month for mail to get to me, halfway around the world, I answered the letters as soon as I could, knowing it would be a couple of months before I'd hear back. When my trunk arrived, I basked in memories of the day Mother and I had packed it. As I sifted through the scrapbooks and mementos, I told my six-year-old cousin, Verlene, about each item. The trunk remained in Iowa when I went off to college, but each vacation I'd spend hours savoring my treasured remembrances of home—looking at pictures, taking out my sari, opening and closing fans or jewelry boxes, smelling the sandalwood.

To my horror, when I reached Park College in September 1936, I discovered that others from Woodstock had enrolled there too. Two of us had even been assigned as roommates. I desperately wanted to be an ordinary college student and asked my friends from Woodstock to respect this. There were also missionary children from other countries there, many of whom were homesick and longing to get back to the mission field. I worked hard not to be lumped together with them to avoid being stereotyped a "mish kid." There were too many other social groups and friendships I hoped to explore. I was forging a new identity—this time it would be an American identity.

As I sought to redefine myself, I confronted many issues that simply hadn't come up during my childhood in India. Park College, for example, had rules banning smoking, drinking, and dancing. Though I didn't care to smoke or drink, I did want to dance. I obeyed the rules but worked to change the college's position on dancing. It astonished me that many students had no intention of living by the rules. In fact, I learned that a young woman we had elected as dorm president often sneaked out on the roof to smoke. Things like this were hard for me to understand.

Despite my desire to venture out in new directions, I took my Christian upbringing seriously. I'd grown up in the church, been baptized, taken Communion, and was sincere in my belief that God meant universal love. Jesus modeled an all-inclusive, caring, forgiving and loving way of life that prevents people from harming each other and challenges them to serve in ways that contribute to a better world. I prayed daily, both in support of the ones I loved and for people in special need. I asked for, and received, the guidance of the Holy Spirit in how to live my life.

Having grown up in an interdenominational atmosphere, I had seen many ways people expressed their Christianity. Some groups, however, believed that they, and only they, possessed the full truth. To me, such thinking was unfortunate. I believed we are all seekers of truth. It had taken a great deal of generous understanding to get along, even in the Christian community of Landour, but this experience taught me how important a loving and accepting community is to the freedom to pursue new ideas. I certainly had much to pursue here!

At Park College, I had to work to supplement my allowance from the Presbyterian Board. Each student spent twelve hours a week doing "family work." These duties varied, and we could change them each semester if we so desired. For the first two years, I waited tables at the dining hall. During my last two years, I served as a dormitory assistant for the senior girls' dorm, answering the phone and taking care of permissions and routine requests. These and other extracurricular activities helped me to discover that I enjoyed taking leadership roles and being involved in strategic planning.

Family work was a good leveler—it brought me into contact with individuals whom I otherwise might not have met. It made me increasingly aware that my view of the world was much broader than that of the average American student. Many had no concept of what the rest of the world was like—the poverty, the long history, the cultural customs—and thought "the American way" was the only way. Still, as an American, I wanted to understand the values of those who had grown up in small towns and learn how the severity of the Great Depression had limited opportunities to learn and change, and contributed to narrow-mindedness.

Despite—or maybe because of—the challenges I experienced, I truly enjoyed college. I became active in my sorority and took part in the student YWCA, eventually becoming its president. Academically, I wrestled with the choice of a major. Though I was very interested in religion, philosophy, and music, I really wanted to be a nutritionist like Mrs. Wiser, who educated and empowered Indian women. To do

Kittu and Clara Jo in front of Mackay Hall, Park College, Parkville, MO, 1939.

this, I could either major in chemistry and spend hours in laboratory research, or I could study home economics. I chose the latter because it included course work in behavioral sciences, family management, textiles, and interior design, as well as nutrition and meal planning. It proved to be a good choice. I also earned my high school teaching certification and later did graduate work in nutrition education.

In 1939, I took a summer job as a waitress at the YMCA camp in Estes Park, Colorado. When I arrived at the Administration Building to check in, I noticed quite a few good-looking men, among them a tall, rather lanky young man drying glasses at the soda fountain. I soon learned his name—Charles Riddle—and that the straight black hair and high cheekbones that had first attracted my attention were part of his Cherokee heritage. He had grown up in Enid, Oklahoma as a Christian Scientist, and was deeply concerned about the welfare of the world. As an undergraduate at the University of Oklahoma, he had become active in the Presbyterian Church.

Chuck, as he preferred to be called, wooed me with frozen malts, which I thought was very special. I was captivated by his ancestry and his interest in becoming a social worker. He was fun to be with and after work, we'd often stroll down by Glacier Creek. He loved to whistle during these outings, and sometimes we'd sing songs together. We both took part in the Gilbert and Sullivan productions the staff staged that summer. One night following a performance, he borrowed a car and took me up to Bear Lake to see the full moon. We sat on a rock and kissed, and it was there he told me he loved me. I was ecstatic and felt sure we would spend the rest of our lives together.

That summer, Chuck and I attended leadership training and other YMCA-sponsored seminars. We were both committed to promoting social change, and we gained invaluable tools in learning how to work with people. Also during this time, the excitement of my romance spilled over in letters home. Airmail had been introduced and was more expensive but took only two weeks! My folks were

The Parker Family in Parkville, MO just before Kittu's graduation from college in 1940. Kittu, Irene, Barbara, Allen and Clara Jo; friend Helen Wentz in background. Taken the next to last time the family was together.

excited about Chuck but concerned about my letter saying I was so in love that I was considering transferring to the University of Oklahoma where Chuck would be a junior. They sent a cabled reply urging me to hold steady for their forthcoming letter. Their advice was actually a relief—it put things in perspective and helped me realize how much I'd regret giving up my investment in the Park College community during my senior year.

At the end of the season, Uncle Paul, Aunt Vema, and Verlene drove up to Estes Park to get me. I was devastated by having to leave Chuck. We hadn't made firm plans for the future, and I didn't know when we'd see each other again. Soon after we reached Iowa, Clara Jo arrived from India ready to begin her freshman year at Park College. I was glad to see her but so caught up in my romance with Chuck that I did little to ease her loneliness.

In early 1940, Mother, Daddy, and Barbara returned to the States on furlough, my father having resigned as principal of Woodstock School. Clara Jo and I eagerly looked forward to their visit. Delighted as I was to see them after three years' separation, we were, in some ways, strangers. No matter how frequently we'd written, letters couldn't adequately describe the changes in how I felt about myself. I wanted their approval of my newfound independence yet was afraid they would still try to guide me, not recognizing that I was now a grown woman. I'd met the man I wanted to marry and, of course, wondered how my parents would react when they met him. My worries were soon dispelled, however—they liked him. In fact, they liked him so much that Daddy clapped him on the back and said, "Young man, you'd make a good missionary!"

Good missionary? I was appalled. There was no way I could envision being a missionary's wife. I'd come to the United States to attend college, firmly planning to adjust to life in America, to feel at home in my own land. During the three years before I met Chuck, I had dated many young men, carefully avoiding those who planned to enter the Christian ministry because I found them naive, arrogant, and narrow-minded. Their main focus seemed to be on finding wives. Some of them actually told me that because I was a kind and generous person, I'd make a good hostess and that my unusual background would be an asset as a minister's wife. This prospect was not even remotely appealing. The wives of ministers, as far as I could see, were placed on pedestals and expected to set a good example for their congregation. I had recently managed to climb down from one pedestal and was not interested in gracing another. Daddy was putting what I considered to be treasonous ideas into Chuck's head, and I hoped Chuck would forget all about them.

The following June, I graduated from Park College. My parents, sisters and Chuck attended the ceremony, proudly sharing the honors I was awarded. And they were as excited as I was over the diamond engagement ring Chuck gave me. Though I had a scholarship for graduate study the following fall, I deferred it and waited for Chuck to graduate from the University of Oklahoma. In the interim, I worked for the student volunteer movement going from campus to campus discussing overseas missionary opportunities. Despite my personal aversion to returning to the mission field, I believed strongly in the value of overseas service knowing how greatly it could enhance and enlarge a person's world view. There were still few organizations that provided opportunities to work in underdeveloped countries. But the foreign mission enterprise offered postings in Christian colleges and schools, teacher training institutes, agricultural centers, hospitals, medical and nursing schools, and many other opportunities.

That year I traveled to more than eighty campuses in the central and western U.S. making contacts, cementing new friendships, and rekindling connections with classmates from Woodstock. In Oregon, I ran across a classmate who told me that he was truly seeing me for the first time. He apologized for the way he and the rest of the class had ostracized me. Needless to say, I was very touched by his kindness and understanding. Unfortunately, he was killed in World War II.

Mother, Daddy, and Barbara spent the last few months of furlough in a missionary apartment in Pasadena, California. Clara Jo was now attending Whittier College nearby. They invited Chuck and me to come out for Christmas, and we spent a memorable week together, joined by relatives from Iowa and Ohio. On New Year's Day 1941, we watched the Rose Parade before sitting down to a wonderful holiday meal and later taking family pictures. Little did we know it was the last time we would all be together.

It was very hard to say goodbye knowing that my parents and Barbara would leave for India in February, crossing the South Pacific by boat. With the growing threat of war, the seas were already considered unsafe. They were headed for Allahabad. The cable I received in March announcing that they had safely reached Bombay was a welcome relief.

A month later, while attending a conference in Colorado, I received an unexpected phone call from my Uncle Paul. Somehow I knew that one of my parents had died. "Which one is it?" I asked. He told me that Mother had died suddenly of an intestinal obstruction. Her death was completely unforeseen. I was stunned. Leaving the conference, I took the train to California to be with Clara Jo. There was no funeral service in the States that we could be a part of, but at least we could console each other.

The two-day rail journey gave me time to weep and remember. I chuckled over a conversation in Pasadena, California in which Mother complained that Daddy was concerned mainly with seeing his relatives and put very little effort into helping her see hers. Then, regretting the outburst, she asked me to forget her words and forgive her. Though brief, it was probably the most meaningful conversation we ever had. Through it, she became much more human to me— suddenly I saw her as a real person, someone who actually harbored resentful thoughts. Until then, she had always seemed so good and kind, nearly perfect. I thought I'd never measure up.

I also remembered the day we had packed my trunk back in India and she had said to me, "Kittu, remember you are beautiful." Gangly as I was at the time, I thought she had said this only because she was my mother. But I was glad she felt that way. I treasured her words and felt certain that by remembering and believing them, I would feel more sure of myself.

During our last conversation, she told me she would send a white silk sari to make into a wedding dress. As the train hurtled westward, I wept anew for my mother and for this cherished gift that would never be. Much to my surprise, a package arrived a few weeks later containing a beautiful ivory silk sari patterned in silver and gold thread. As soon as she'd reached Bombay, Mother had enlisted Prema's help in choosing the sari and had shipped it to me via the stewardess, who gave it to my aunt in Boston. I spent what seemed an enormous sum of money, twenty-seven dollars, to have it fashioned into a wedding dress. I felt this was the best way I could honor Mother, to do justice to her gift, her last message, a memento of her love.

I wished we'd had the chance to discuss my feelings about marriage, although at the time, I'm not sure I could have articulated them. I loved Chuck and we'd made many plans together. Furthermore, I couldn't see my life proceeding without marriage. In those days it was particularly important for a woman to marry. In the wake of the Depression, the job market was open mainly to men, who were considered to be the primary breadwinners, and women had few other options. Though they could teach or nurse, women were expected to marry early and keep house for a male wage-earner. Life for a single woman was difficult.

I realized that when Chuck and I married, I would be giving up my hard-won autonomy. By the time I graduated from Park, I had become strong and capable. My only doubts revolved around

Kittu and Chuck were married on September 2, 1941, in Chicago, IL. Kittu is wearing the dress made from the sari her mother sent from India a month before her death.

whether I would be able to earn a living if I didn't marry. After working for a year, I saw that I could indeed support myself, but where would I live? If I married, I would always have a home with Chuck. Still, I knew that I could easily become trapped by societal expectations of how a wife should act. Pursuing personal and professional ambitions in this context could be difficult at best.

With Mother gone, I had no one with whom to share these uncertainties. After all, in the eyes of my friends and family, I had found a wonderful man—intelligent, kind, tolerant, creative, and fun. How could I question this relationship? Attributing my doubts to premarital jitters, I set them aside.

After Chuck graduated from the University of Oklahoma, we moved to Chicago, where he enrolled in George Williams College to study social work, and I started a master's degree in nutrition at the University of Chicago. We married on September 2, 1941 in a small ceremony conducted by Uncle Paul in the presence of friends. I wished Daddy could have returned to the States to marry us, but the oceans weren't safe and no passenger planes were available.

Chuck's mother made the trip from Enid, Oklahoma, to be with us. Mom, as I called her, very kindly took me aside and told me about contraception. It wasn't easy for her, but she found the courage to do so out of concern for me, knowing that I had recently lost my mother. She explained that she tied a string around a ball of cotton soaked in vinegar and inserted it before intercourse. Afterwards, she would get out of bed and douche. I thanked her but didn't tell her that I had already been to the doctor and been fitted for a diaphragm. I knew I was fortunate to live in Illinois where the dissemination of contraceptive information was legal. As she shared her knowledge, I realized just how many women had no access to legal contraception. It was then that I began to comprehend why women had so many children. Like Chuck's mother, they had only makeshift methods at hand.

After our honeymoon, we moved into the House of Happiness, the privately run settlement house where Chuck worked. It provided social services such as child care for working mothers, classes and clubs for mothers, and afterschool activities for girls and boys. It was here that we heard the shocking news of Pearl Harbor—a day that would change our lives in ways we could not anticipate. For one thing, Chuck, a conscientious objector, was forced to find an acceptable alternative service. After considerable negotiation with his draft board, he transferred to the ministerial studies program at Chicago Theological Seminary. Suddenly, I was the wife of a ministerial student—exactly what I had worked so hard to avoid!

Even worse, if Chuck heeded Daddy's suggestion, I would find myself the wife of an overseas missionary.

I had several objections to returning to mission work. On a practical level, I didn't see how we could be assigned overseas in the first place, since we had no home-based church to sponsor us. On a personal level, I feared the lack of anonymity, the visibility of life in a fishbowl. The actions of missionaries were scrutinized closely. Those who served were expected to conform and live up to high standards, to be almost holy. Moreover, I was beginning to feel at home in the United States and didn't want to leave its plethora of interesting activities and useful contacts. But more importantly, on a fundamental level, I did not want to do evangelistic work— persuading people to change religions. The process of conversion is extremely difficult, both spiritually and emotionally. It was daunting to think of asking people to forsake the security of the faith and community that had nurtured and supported them. I lived with these objections for several years. But as my life unfolded, they were gradually resolved, and Chuck and I came to a mutually agreeable understanding.

During this period, I missed my mother, her letters, and her responses to my letters. But Daddy rose to the occasion. His letters throughout the first years of my marriage were a continuous source of surprisingly good advice and comfort. His ability to empathize, to share his own grief and loneliness, yet to understand and counsel me, led to a deeper appreciation of him as a person. Hoping he would eventually remarry, we were pleased to receive word in early 1943 that he had proposed to Dorothy Dragon, a missionary in India, and that she had accepted. They were married in April.

Despite the inner turmoil I felt at the time, I dove enthusiastically into my master's studies in nutrition. As a scholarship student at the University of Chicago, I was required to work part-time for my mentor, Dr. Lydia Roberts, a nutritionist and head of the College of Home Economics. She was on the cutting edge of the emerging field of nutritional health planning and served on several national committees. My task was to keep her filing system—twenty-four-cabinet drawers full—current. Having never been near a research program, I could hardly comprehend the scope or importance of the information those cabinets contained. But the more familiar I became with their contents as I searched for just the right place to insert an article or report, the surer I was that I had chosen the right field. There were many new and exciting discoveries being made about nutrition, and I wanted to be part of the process.

By 1941, studies had been undertaken to identify most of the major vitamins, to determine the quantities of vitamins and minerals present in various foods, to calculate the amount of each nutrient required by the human body at various stages of life, and to evaluate which foods were actually being eaten and in what quantities. Based on the results of these studies, national committees were able to develop recommendations on how to improve the national diet.

A major concern among nutritionists was low consumption of B vitamins and iron, which are found in basic staple foods—the seeds of cereal crops such as wheat, rice, and corn. In their complete, natural form, these seeds and grains contain B vitamins, iron, fiber, complex carbohydrates, and (incomplete) protein. When eaten unrefined, along with vegetables or fruit to provide vitamins A and C, and milk or eggs to complete the protein, they provide an excellent mix of nutrients. Most people in the U.S., however, rarely eat these cereals in whole form. Rather, they consume wheat, corn, and rice products that have been refined in a process that removes B vitamins and iron—the very nutrients so lacking in the American diet.

Several possible courses of action were considered. In England, where the war drastically cut into the food supply, a rationing program was in effect and people had to eat what they could get. All bread was made with a mixture of whole flours of various grains for maximum nutrient value. It was called "Victory bread." However, in the United States, cereal was plentiful and could not be rationed. The remedy to this deficiency was to enrich the wheat and corn flours by replacing the nutrients that had been lost during refinement.

To implement an enrichment program, legislation was needed and Dr. Roberts was instrumental in shaping it. Passage of this legislation, which required the addition of three B vitamins, thiamin, niacin, and riboflavin, and the mineral, iron to all refined (white) flour, did more to improve the nutritional value of the American diet than any other single action, paving the way for many other food enrichment and fortification programs. Careful analysis and extensive debate went into setting these enrichment standards. As a result of this and related efforts, the U.S. has an excellent, varied, and well-monitored food supply.

As I began my graduate studies, development of a national school lunch program was in progress. It was the second major step toward improving national nutrition levels. Studies of American eating patterns had shown that in poverty-stricken neighborhoods, children seldom got anything approaching adequate nutrition at breakfast or lunch, and their learning ability was consequently in peril. The goal of the National School Lunch Program development committee, on which Dr. Roberts served, was to provide children with a good midday meal that would satisfy at least one-third of their daily nutritional requirements. Dr. Roberts suggested that for my master's thesis, I research and propose standards for school lunches that would fulfill this goal. I gladly accepted the challenge.

After surveying the available literature, I created a tentative list of policies regarding desirable lunchroom practices. These I circulated to more than one hundred people who had experience or a vital interest in this area and asked them to indicate agreement or disagreement. From their responses, I drew up proposal guidelines on administration, education, food arrangement, atmosphere, and sanitation for school lunches. To my amazement, these guidelines were used in framing the original "Type A" school lunch, the first standardized lunch adopted into the program. These guidelines also served as the basis for other beneficial nutritional programs around the country such as the National School Breakfast Program.

In pursuing my goal of helping people improve their diet, I was not keen on laboratory research, consumption studies, or statistical tabulations. Rather, I preferred the practical approach, always asking myself, *How can I actively encourage people to eat better*? An amusing example of the benefits of such pragmatic methodology occurred in the summer of 1942. At this time, I was running the kitchen at a settlement house summer camp in Michigan. The camp had a victory garden that provided fresh vegetables. The main crop was turnips— not a favorite among the children, who came from underprivileged families with poor nutritional backgrounds. Turnip greens, a good source of vitamin A and minerals, could be used in soups and stews, but the turnip root itself is best served raw to preserve its vitamin C value. However, raw turnip is not to everyone's liking. Hoping for the best, we prepared turnip sticks, put a bowl of them on each table, and stood back to watch the children's reaction. One of the counselors, sensing there might be difficulty in "selling" these snacks, reached for a stick and held it in her mouth like a cigarette. Each child at her table immediately grabbed for a turnip stick. Other tables followed suit. That summer, the children "smoked" their way through the entire turnip crop.

In December 1942, I received my master's degree in nutrition education and quickly found a job as a nutritionist at the Elizabeth McCormick Memorial Fund, a private welfare agency. In the days before public welfare, social services were dispensed by such organizations as this one and the settlement houses where Chuck and I had worked.

One of our tasks was to distribute surplus foods to low-income families. Unfortunately, staples such as flour and lard constituted the bulk of the distribution, although there were some canned vegetables and dried fruits, including prunes. I remember the day a woman asked me how to use prunes. I showed her several recipes, and was prepared to copy down any that interested her. However, her mind was on other matters.

"You married?" she asked.

"Yes," I replied.

"How long?"

"Two years."

"Any children?" she inquired.

"No, not yet," I replied.

She took the card from me and turned it over, saying, "Please write the recipe for that on the card."

Clearly, prunes were not going to satisfy this particular need. I referred her to Planned Parenthood at the YWCA, glad I was able to do so.

One of the nutritionists at the McCormick Fund came up with the idea of developing nutritional profiles for a wide variety of foods. She involved us all in the arithmetic to determine what percentage of the known daily requirement for particular vitamins and minerals was found in each item of food. We then drew up bar charts showing these nutrient levels in the different foods. None of us foresaw the widespread ramifications her work would have in the field of nutrition. The National Dairy Council used these nutritional profiles to produce comparison charts that, with considerable updating, are still utilized today in nutrition education. But more importantly, the information provided by nutrition profiling was so valuable that it would ultimately spawn a national nutrition labeling program. As an outgrowth of our work, RDA (Recommended Daily Allowance) percentages are now available on every item of packaged food in the U.S.

The next few years continued to be filled with change. Despite contraceptive protection, I became pregnant. I hated to leave the Elizabeth McCormick Memorial Fund after having been there just over a year. I had also been employed on a part-time basis by the National Dairy Council to produce two nutrition brochures for national distribution—"Mealtime Melodies" discussed menu planning and "War Fare" dealt with wartime rationing. I continued to work as long as I could and finally went home a month before the baby was due.

Dorothy Irene Riddle was born the morning of January 12, 1944, at Chicago Lying-In Hospital. I was thoroughly convinced there had never been such a wonderful baby. When Chuck and I took her home, I felt confident that we would have no difficulties, particularly in light of my training in infant care and feeding. With Clara Jo there to help, the early days went smoothly and Dorothy took easily to breast-feeding. After Clara Jo's departure, however, I was overcome with a heavy sense of responsibility for this new little life. Thoughts about all the things that could go wrong brought me to tears. I was especially worried when Dorothy did not conform to the regular feeding schedule I had been trained to expect and instead preferred to feed frequently and at odd intervals. Several midnight phone calls to her pediatrician finally convinced me that she would eventually settle into a rhythm, and within six weeks, Dorothy had proved him right. Once I was able to get something done between feedings, I began to relax.

It was evident that the war would not last forever, and we had to make plans for the future. Chuck would graduate from seminary in June 1944 and was very interested in going to China to do rehabilitation work. He didn't want to go to India—the British were still in power and we both supported Indian independence. We talked to the Presbyterian Board of Foreign Missions about our interest, and they agreed to take us on, offering us a posting in Peiping.

I paced the floor trying to sort out what my role would be if we decided to go. I couldn't simply be a wife. I needed to continue growing, to have my own identity, to make my own contributions. We would have servants to help with housework, and though that sounded luxurious, it would be a mixed blessing—servants have their own ways of doing things. It would make running a household a challenge I didn't welcome. I thought of ways I could participate in any community in which we might live. I could teach, develop nutrition projects, and work with other mothers as we raised our children.

I also struggled with my objections to returning to the mission field. Fortunately, as my internal debate continued, we were informed that the role of American Christian missionaries was changing. Before the war, U.S. missionary boards had funded their own programs and decided autonomously which countries to send their recruits to, what projects they would undertake, and how long their service would last. During the war, however, Asia had been cut off from the West. Without support from Western countries, they had developed their own indigenous churches, raised their own funds, and carried out their own missionary projects. In many instances, these local churches—even those of different denominations—had joined together to form a united church.

The U.S. Presbyterian Board of Foreign Missions had begun discussions with these indigenous churches, inquiring as to whether foreign help was still needed in countries where Presbyterian missionaries had previously been posted. If so, it was agreed that foreign personnel would be sent only at the request of a local church, serving as "fraternal workers" under its direction. All evangelistic work, or efforts to convert others to Christianity, would be carried out by the indigenous church, not by foreign missionaries. In light of these new circumstances, most of my fears and objections were allayed. I told Chuck that if he still wanted to go and the Chinese Church truly wanted us, I'd accompany him.

Even though I was hesitant and doubts still lingered, I made the right decision. Our lives were immeasurably enriched by the nineteen years we would serve overseas, first in China and then in India.

Chapter Three
Grab That Kite

Though commissioned to go to China, we could not leave immediately, because wartime restrictions prohibited civilians from traveling overseas. In the interim, we moved to California, where we studied Chinese at U.C. Berkeley and waited to ship out as soon as the war ended.

I felt the need for regular spiritual practice and joined a Bible study class led by Mary Chaffee. We examined every detail of the text, placed ourselves in the situations described, and examined the insights that emerged. Reading the first chapter in Mark, where Jesus says that the Kingdom of God is here and now, affirmed that everyday life is immensely valuable and that we are surrounded by goodness. Daily Bible study became my spiritual nourishment for many years.

Our contented existence in Berkeley came to an abrupt halt when the Presbyterian Board transferred us to Yale University because its Chinese language and culture program was supposed to make us fluent more quickly. Housing in New Haven, Connecticut was in short supply, and we ended up in a duplex over a gas station far from our friends. We couldn't afford a car and public transportation was problematic. Getting groceries was also challenging and time-consuming because many foods were rationed. In addition, there were no laundromats—quite an obstacle for a young mother. A church member kindly allowed us to use a machine in her apartment. So I'd load the wood-framed baby buggy with baby and laundry, push it three blocks, carry the essentials downstairs, and when the washing was done, lug wet clothes home to hang in our kitchen. To supplement this, Chuck and I scrubbed diapers on a washboard while reciting vocabulary for the next day's lesson. Child care was hard to find and we often took turns going to class. These difficulties hindered our studies, but our living situation improved in early 1945 when we found a more suitable apartment.

Though my time for leisure reading was limited, I couldn't resist the popular book *Anna and the King of Siam*. One day, as I sat engrossed in descriptions of the women of the Siamese court who lived behind the veil, I was reminded of Prema and her stories about women in *purdah* in her native state of Gwalior. It dawned on me that I hadn't heard from her in years. As I continued reading, I felt her presence. Just then the doorbell rang and the postman handed me an envelope addressed in her handwriting! Prema wrote that she had chosen a husband from among the suitors her father had selected. I smiled as I read, remembering how she once said she felt sorry for me because I had to go out into the world and find a husband for myself. She was happy with her choice and her marriage. Her only sorrow was that Barbara, Clara Jo, and I had not been present on her wedding day. My delight at this surprise communication, that brought both India and Prema closer to home, was tinged with sadness. I wondered whether I'd ever see her again.

In late summer, news of the atomic bomb that had been dropped over Japan was tragic beyond belief. Thinking about the wonderful Japanese people I'd met suffering such terrible devastation and hardship was awful. Although we didn't agree with it, the bombing did end the war and we joined the jubilation on the streets. Chuck wanted to go to China immediately to help with reconstruction there. We had to face reality and decide where the children and I would live until we could join him. Dorothy was not yet two and another baby was on the way.

Chuck and I completed our course and graduated on February 22, 1946. Feeling as if I could go into labor at any time, I elected not to walk up on stage during the ceremony. Though Chuck collected my diploma, I can still say I was among the first women to earn a graduate degree in Chinese Language and Culture from the then all-male Yale University. After lunch, Dorothy and I napped until about 3:30 that afternoon. I awoke in labor. Chuck got one of the few taxis to take us to Yale University Hospital, where things were pretty relaxed because of the observation of George Washington's birthday, a holiday. The nurse barely got me prepped before William Parker Riddle made his appearance around 5:30 that evening. There was a great deal of joking about naming him George Washington Riddle instead.

When Billy was six weeks old, we headed west, visiting supporting churches in Chicago and Lincoln, Nebraska. Dr. Ruth Leverton, whom I had known in graduate school, was department chair of Home Economics at the University of Nebraska. Our paths would cross many times though I didn't know it then. We traveled south to Enid, Oklahoma to visit Chuck's mother and finally reached Berkeley at the end of May. In early June, Chuck boarded a freighter bound for Shanghai. The rest of us stayed behind. Women and children weren't yet allowed to enter China, which had been so badly disrupted by the Japanese withdrawal. I was alarmed to learn that his freighter carried high-octane gasoline since its course led through mine-filled waters. "If you don't hear from me, you'll know why," he called out cheerily as the boat pulled away from the San Francisco dock. I had desperately wanted to stay with Chuck and was terribly upset by our parting. I began pestering the shipping companies and called San Francisco daily trying to secure reservations. By mid-July, I was told that if I received permission from China, I could leave on the *SS General Meigs* scheduled to sail October 1. I was determined to go. Permission finally came, and with great eagerness, I delivered my luggage to the pier on Saturday, September 29—two days before our departure. But a sudden maritime strike changed everything. I was told to retrieve my luggage and wait. Our ship would sail four days after the strike ended.

After an agonizing two-month wait, during which I could make no plans, the strike was finally settled, and I got word that we would sail December 2. By then all West Coast seaports were crowded with people wanting to get to Asia, and all available ships were hastily retrofitted for civilian use. Passengers were crammed into spaces too small for comfort. My first-class cabin, for example, held eighteen women in six sets of three-tiered bunks. It had only two wash basins and no bunk lights, only overhead lighting that turned on and off at the door.

I was issued a lower and a middle bunk plus a crib for the baby. The woman assigned to the top bunk in our tier had physical limitations and begged me to give her the bottom berth. By doing so, I gained a friend with whom I could discuss my lingering misgivings about becoming a missionary. She brought to my attention something I hadn't yet seen—that missionaries are truly lucky because, through service, they meet a genuine need and feel valued and become engrossed in their work. She felt certain that this would be true for me as well.

Despite my apprehension, I was excited about moving to China, knowing I would be contributing to efforts to improve education and alleviate suffering in the wake of the Japanese occupation. I had valuable skills I was eager to offer—I could teach English, provide advice on nutrition, and share what I had learned about child rearing. On a more personal note, I was looking forward to becoming part of a new and different community and building friendships among my neighbors and professional peers.

I knew no one on board and had no help in caring for the children. The cabin stewardess was willing to take Billy's bottles and sterilize them, but that was it. We spent most of the day outside on the deck— Billy strapped in the old wooden pram and Dorothy and I in a deck chair reading books and playing games when not walking around. We went to the cabin only when I washed diapers and hung them to dry over our bunks. Getting the children settled in at night was difficult because the overhead lights were on. Both children woke early—they didn't know that our time zones changed as the ship proceeded west. The highlight of our seventeen day crossing was a stop in Honolulu where Clara Jo, head nurse at Queens Hospital, rescued us, took us to the beach and replenished our toy supply.

We finally entered the estuary of the Yangtze River. As I watched the color of the water change, I remembered sailing up this river after my high school graduation. Now I had come to live in China to join my waiting husband. I didn't know that within two years I would sail up this river again as a refugee, escaping great political changes in Peiping.

All formalities of debarkation were held aboard ship and passengers had to queue up for each inspection. Dorothy and Billy were too young to wait patiently in line, and I wondered how I would manage. Then I realized that no line would be closed until everyone had gone through so we could simply be last in every line. The children and I spent the day wandering back and forth, keeping track of the lines, making sure we got to each before it closed. Finally, after a customs inspector checked my suitcases, we were ready to disembark.

We could feel the ship being tied up alongside the riverbank and went out on deck to watch. It was only then that I realized that Shanghai had no piers—they'd been destroyed by the Japanese. We pushed our way over to the rail and there, far, far below, amid the crowd of people who had come to meet the ship, we saw Chuck. We waved and shouted, and I wondered how long it would be before we could disembark, before I would feel his arms around me. Just then came the announcement that those who had completed luggage examination could leave the ship. With papers and kids in hand, I raced down the stairs, which turned into ladders the farther down we went. Somehow we got through. Chuck was quite surprised when we were the first to emerge from the ship. After a joyous reunion, I went back to claim our luggage and we were on our way.

Our excitement was soon overshadowed by the dreariness of Shanghai. Occupying most of China during World War II, the Japanese had stripped the city of metal to send to Japan to make armaments. When they surrendered, they left a barely functional city behind. Public services had been disrupted, electric supply was low, and in the evening, lights were dim. This misery was compounded by fog and rain, deterrents to any outdoor activities.

Though Chuck had been living in Nanking, we were headed for what was then called Peiping (now called Beijing) and planned to fly north as soon as possible. Unfortunately one night, three airplanes crashed while trying to land at Shanghai's airport and all flights were subsequently grounded. As our wait stretched from days into weeks, we stayed in an old bungalow—a guest house run by the indigenous Church of Christ in China as a courtesy to fraternal workers passing through Shanghai. In an effort to dispel the gloom of the war-torn building, I fastened some paper to the wall of our room, and on it Dorothy and I drew a Christmas tree about four feet high. We decorated it with anything glittery we could find and put a few little gifts under it. I'd brought along a fold-up cardboard crèche which we set up under the tree, telling the Christmas story as we did so. Little did we know how many times this crèche would be folded and unfolded in the years to come as we moved around the world.

After New Year's we learned that flights had resumed, though we felt somewhat uneasy about leaving. It was scary knowing that we'd be on the first scheduled flight out of Shanghai following the accidents. Worse, we would be heading into territory currently being fought over by the Communists and the Kuomintang (Nationalist) government of Chiang Kai-shek. We boarded our plane from the rear and sat in the canvas bucket seats that lined both sides of the aisle. Luggage was piled in the middle and tied down with ropes. The flight proceeded without incident and we were met at Peiping's airport by Jessie Mae Henke, a nurse and the wife of one of our missionary doctors. She shepherded us into the Presbyterian mission compound at Erh Tiao Hutung and took us into the large, two-story house that would be ours while we were in the city.

The compound was a large, walled space containing a group of missionary homes intermingled with gardens, patios, and a tennis court. Like the other dwellings along the walled alley, the entrance was through a gatehouse. Cars and other modern vehicles couldn't get through, so they parked outside, but rickshaws, palanquins, and stretchers could enter. A gatekeeper monitored the comings and goings, keeping beggars out.

The house was full of well-worn furniture belonging to the Hayes family, who had lived there before fleeing the Japanese occupation. I walked through the rooms admiring the tall windows and the way the front room adjoined the dining room. There was also a large study plus a separate first-floor apartment. Upstairs were two good-sized bedrooms connected by a bath—perfect for our family—and a large guest room with its own bath. To my surprise, I discovered the first-floor apartment could be entered unobtrusively from our front hall as well as from outside. It was a most intriguing mansion.

Once we had looked over the house, Chuck thrust a large packet of paper money into my hands, saying, "Use this to buy something tomorrow. Maybe curtains for the house. It may seem like a lot of money, but soon it will be worthless." I knew China suffered from inflation, but I did not yet comprehend the extent to which the yuan had been devalued—a result of the continued fighting between the Communists and Nationalists. Money lost value daily and the only recourse was to buy goods.

I was aghast at the thought of shopping so soon in an unfamiliar country, but Chuck's suggestion of cloth for curtains made sense. Jessie Mae walked in to invite us to dinner and, seeing the amount of money I was holding, agreed that it should be spent right away. Curtains were a good place to start. The following morning, she and I set off by rickshaw for the Clock Tower cloth shop. There was no adequate way to camouflage the twelve-inch-square packet of money in my lap, but I noticed that other shoppers carried equally large bundles without embarrassment—a true sign of inflation.

Since I didn't know the currency or the exchange, I decided the best thing would be to choose what I really liked without trying to keep track of the price. It seemed almost too easy. I gave the window measurements to the clerk. He cut the pieces of cloth and presented me the bill for $550,000 in Chinese currency! I nearly choked. Of course, in American currency, the price was reasonable. Curtains for four rooms for only $85 was a good deal.

Still, I had no idea how much money I had in the packet. Was there enough? It took twenty minutes for the clerks to count it out and inform me that I had $530,000. I was $20,000 short. My heart sank again. Still thinking in terms of American dollars, I wondered where I would get such an astronomical sum. But Jessie Mae stepped right in, generously offering to loan me the money. "You'll get used to the inflation," she said comfortingly.

Chuck and I couldn't manage a household and fulfill our work duties without help in shopping, cooking, cleaning, and child care. When word circulated that we were looking for servants, a cook and his wife appeared at our door. Jang Shih Fu (*shih fu* meaning "cook") helped me purchase supplies and equipment for the kitchen, and his wife, whom we called Amah, took over the cleaning and the care of Billy, who was just learning to stand and walk.

Jang Shih Fu fed us skillfully, preparing Chinese food at least once a day. I remember writing a letter back to the States saying we'd had a delicious lunch of spinach stems and turnips. When I re-read what I'd written, it didn't sound all that appetizing. I amended it to say that the cook had cleverly used crisp stems along with a little beef to make one dish and a little pork with the turnips for another. Both were delicious with rice. He saved the precious spinach leaves for another meal.

During my years there, I learned much from my Chinese friends about the exquisite nutritional economy and balance in Chinese cooking. A few ounces of meat or an egg, scrambled and cut up, were used to flavor the vegetable dishes. Fresh soy beans, ground into milk and made into bean curd, took the place of cow's milk or cheese, and cooked soy beans complemented the protein of flour noodles.

During the winter of 1947, food was limited in supply and variety. The only vegetables on the market were onions, potatoes, spinach, cabbage, turnips, and several varieties of radish. There were dried winter fruits, small hard pears, and, surprisingly, persimmons. Picked in the fall and stored frozen in caves in the western hills, they were brought to market as demand dictated. Soon, nothing looked or tasted more appealing at breakfast than an icy, juicy, orange persimmon.

Chuck and I began teaching English at Truth Hall, the boys' Christian high school across the alley behind our house. Because the buildings were unheated, I dressed as warmly as I could in an overcoat, scarf, hat, and mittens. The students, though eager to learn, had only thin cotton shirts, cotton pants, and cloth tennis shoes to wear. I don't know how they stood the cold. I encouraged them to move around as we did word drills.

An American dietitian brought in by the United Nations Relief Agency visited the school to suggest improvements in child nutrition. She decided that the best dietary supplement would be eggs, and she planned to give each boy an egg per week to take home. Nutritionally speaking, this was not a bad idea. Eggs—an excellent sources of protein, iron, and other nutrients—were easy to dispense and easy to use. But I wondered whether she had inquired about how the Chinese used eggs or how many eggs were available on the market. And neither of us took into account the fun-loving spirit of Chinese schoolchildren. The eggs had no sooner been handed out than an egg fight erupted and the school yard became a scramble of eggs and boys. It was a hilarious sight, but such a mess and such a waste. Undeterred by this incident, the dietitian ordered that the following weeks' eggs be hard-boiled so that the boys would eat them. This strategy worked better, but most of the eggs were still used as missiles so the project ended.

The experience reinforced for me how essential it is to take people's customs and preferences into account for good nutrition planning. The Chinese, at least in those days, seldom ate eggs whole. They used them sparingly as part of a main dish. Consequently, there was not a large market for eggs. In just two weeks, the project had consumed the city's entire supply. It was several weeks before they became available again to egg-loving foreigners.

The value of eggs came home to me when I went to see Mrs. Yin, the wife of our pastor. Graciously offering me hot water to drink—tea leaves were far too expensive—she explained that she was cooking for the Christian refugees streaming into the city to escape the fighting between Kuomintang and Communist soldiers. The skirmishes taking place each night outside the city walls were destroying their homes and crops. When I asked what she was cooking, she apologized for the meagerness of what she had to offer them explaining that it was only sorghum. But then she took two eggs out of a basket and insisted they be given to my children. Aghast at this munificent gift yet knowing it would be impolite to refuse, I reverently took the eggs home, marveling at her generous spirit and vowing to find her some help in feeding the refugees.

Meanwhile, the schoolboys at Truth Hall continued eating wah-wah-tou—heavy, soggy dumplings made of ground sorghum. Grainy and tasteless, they were hard to choke down, even when accompanied by pickled turnips. But they were familiar and the only food besides peanuts that the school could afford to purchase in quantity.

In seeking to improve the schoolchildren's diet, Dr. William Adolf, a nutritionist training dietitians at Yen Ching University, proved to be an invaluable and experienced ally. Nutrition was a budding science, but there were a few places in China where it was taught.

Easter came early that year. It was still cold, so we put on our padded garments before boarding a bus to the sunrise service. It was held south of the city at the Temple of Heaven, which had a beautiful blue-tiled circular roof. Potholes in the street made the bus ride very rough. On the return trip, I started to bleed. I was then two months pregnant.

I hadn't intended to become pregnant again so soon when everything about China was still so new. I explained to my doctor, Gene Henke, that the New Haven gynecologist who had given me my postpartum exam had said nothing about my diaphragm, so I had assumed it still fit. Gene told me that laws in Massachusetts and

Connecticut prevented doctors from discussing birth control with their patients, even with those who specifically asked about contraception. Seeing how depressed I was about the pregnancy, he told me that it would be easy to lose the baby and that if I walked around a lot, I would probably miscarry. If I wanted to keep the baby, I would have to commit to five months of bed rest. "Even then," he said, "you might lose the baby. Early bleeding is sometimes nature's way of indicating an imperfect child."

I walked home from the appointment feeling more depressed than ever—and with a crucial choice to make. Considering the war-torn situation we were in I had ample reason to take deliberate measures to end the pregnancy, but I simply couldn't. Instead, I immediately arranged for my classes and household duties to be covered and took to bed. I did what I could to nurture the child, feeling that if the fetus aborted itself, I'd be able to accept the loss of the pregnancy. Wrestling with this showed me that as difficult as some choices may be, having that choice is vitally important. No one can say for another what that choice should be.

Chuck and I moved into the downstairs apartment. From my bed, I could look out the windows and appreciate the emergence of spring at the compound. The bushes and trees that had once stood with bleak precision now sprang into bloom with forsythias, lilacs, and flowering quince. Crocuses, daffodils, and hyacinths bloomed in the flowerbeds. Fruit trees burst forth. The show was spectacular but brief—within two weeks summer arrived and the beautiful spring flowers were gone. But then, to my surprise, another pageant unfolded. Gardeners from nearby nurseries brought flowering plants on long carts to sell in the compound. And better still, planting was included in the price.

We were glad the harsh winter was over, but the sudden arrival of summer brought with it a new unpleasantness. Alleys and streets, once iced over, became sweltering thoroughfares that reeked with the stench of humanity. I hadn't realized that the so-called "honey carts" that went up and down the alley carried human refuse away from dwellings lacking modern sanitation.

In the past, foreigners had refused to live in Peiping during the hot months, preferring to summer at Beitaho on the seashore instead. But now, with Nationalist and Communist armies fighting in the countryside we were restricted to the city. We had to devise alternate ways of keeping cool. Sleeping downstairs helped. We got fans and an icebox and improvised a pool for the children to play in. Activities slowed down, and we rested in the heat of midday.

I was no longer teaching, but students and friends visited me at my bedside while the children played nearby. A Chinese tutor came to the house to continue my formal language lessons. It was in many ways a wonderful time of enforced rest.

As I lay quietly, I reflected on the beginnings of the mother's group formed several months earlier to help me speak Chinese. I had been dissatisfied with my inability to speak this new language easily, and I'd read that an immersion experience was the quickest route to fluency. Wondering how to arrange this, I had invited all the Chinese women I'd met to come for tea—those who lived up and down the alley, those who were teachers and nurses, and those I had met in church, including the pastor's wife. About fifteen women showed up. It soon became obvious that my language difficulties severely limited our conversation. My guests were polite but puzzled about how to communicate with me.

Hesitantly, I asked them to continue conversing without me, explaining in halting Chinese, "You can see that I am unable to speak your language fluently. Please help me by carrying on conversation amongst yourselves and allow me to listen and participate when I can." My request was greeted with polite silence and discreet questioning glances. "What would you like us to talk about?" one older woman ventured. "Your homes, your families, your lives—anything you want to talk about," I offered.

Again they looked at each other, and then they started talking. At first they discussed my request. As the conversation moved on to family matters, I was able to answer a few questions and to let them know I was following the gist of the conversation. Then, they really took off, telling lively stories about their children, questioning each other, and sharing ideas about what to do in a particular situation.

Suddenly, one woman stopped the conversation by saying loudly, "Do you realize what time it is? It is 5:30. We must all go home to fix the evening meal." I laughingly explained that I understood. "You are saying the same thing as homemakers say in the U.S.A." They laughed with me. "But we've been having such a good time, we hate to break this up. Could we come and do this again?" They all spoke at once.

"Of course!" I replied eagerly. "You are providing exactly the kind of immersion I need. Would you want to come back two weeks from now?" They agreed. Evidently, they'd never taken time to talk like this as a group. Each was busy in her own realm, working outside the home and caring for family.

Now, as I lay on my bed fondly remembering that afternoon, I wondered what might be next for our group. Perhaps we could expand, inviting women who lived in extended, multi-generational families to join us. I'd have to discuss it with them. I also thought about extending my own contacts. I had heard there was a Beijing chapter of the American Association of University Women, an organization I belonged to back in the States. Its membership consisted of female graduates of American colleges and universities including Chinese women who had studied abroad. Later, I learned that this chapter was encouraging its Chinese members to establish their own association—a Chinese Association of University Women. Fortunately, it came into being in 1948. Never before had there been a group like it in China.

In August 1947, a new American friend, Adeline, died in childbirth. The baby died, too. Though full of grief, I, somehow, wasn't fearful about my own condition. Three-year-old Dorothy was curious about Adeline's death, and I explained that Adeline could no longer move and talk because the part of her that cared and thought and loved had left her body. Wanting to see Adeline, Dorothy went with me to the room where her body was lying. She ran in and crawled up on the bed looking earnestly at Adeline's face. When I reached the bed, Dorothy was satisfied. Turning to me, she said, "Adeline's not here. This isn't the Adeline I know!" I was happy that Dorothy got to experience the reality of death, as well as the gladness Adeline's friends felt at her spirit being free. We could still experience her love even without her physical presence.

By the end of October, I was weary from being pregnant and eager to see the baby and know all was well. Ironically, the doctor was now urging me to walk around frequently. It was certainly no hardship—cool weather and all its beauty had set in. Leaves were falling, the skies were deep blue, and there was a nice nip in the air.

Patricia Karen Riddle was born at 11:30 P.M. on October 28, 1947. The Chinese nurses were delighted with her. When one nurse brought Patty in for nursing, she said, "We think your baby, with her dark hair and eyes, looks healthy. Other foreign babies with light hair and pale, watery eyes don't look healthy to us." I told them that Patty's father was part Cherokee, one of the Native American tribes in America. Visitors peeking into the nursery saw only bundled-up, black-haired infants, so when the nurses invited them to guess which baby was foreign, they shook their heads and said, "There are no foreign babies here." By the time our eight-day hospital stay was over, Patty was thriving. Her Chinese name became "Ping Sheng" meaning "born in Peiping."

Christmas of 1947 was a miserable time. I was worried about Daddy, then in the United States on furlough with his wife, Dorothy, and their two children, Harriet and Donald. His heart had acted up in early December and he had been hospitalized in Berkeley. There had been no further word, so I was truly shocked to receive a letter just before Christmas informing me that he had died on December 11. I was bewildered that Dorothy had not cabled me when his condition deteriorated, though I later learned she had hoped to spare me a shock. Still, I had not had the chance to see my father before he died and it was hard to believe he was gone. I was grief stricken, and my heart ached for my stepmother and her children, who would now grow up without a father.

As Christmas approached, I developed a bad cold and terrible headaches. But I wanted Christmas to be fun for Dorothy, Billy, and Chuck, so I kept wrapping presents and baking goodies. I thought that keeping busy would help me forget the pain I was in, both physically and emotionally. Despite how badly I felt on Christmas Day, I didn't want to bother the doctors. Finally on December 26, I let Chuck seek medical help. When Gene Henke arrived, he took one look at me and called for a stretcher to carry me to the hospital.

The next few days were hazy—I slept a great deal. Gene suspected that I was suffering from spinal meningitis. He ordered a spinal tap to relieve the pressure and to test for meningococci. The results confirmed his suspicions. As I drifted in and out of consciousness, I had a sense of being cocooned within love, knowing I was being cared for and trusting in the healing process. Amazingly, I wasn't anxious and truly didn't think I was in danger of dying. I didn't realize how serious my condition was until one evening when I awoke to find a nurse kneeling by my bed, praying. "We're very concerned about you," she told me, "and I'm asking God to heal you. Also, I was very lucky today. I was given six tangerines and I'm giving you three of them to make you well." Citrus fruit was practically unavailable in north China because of shipping difficulties. Her generous and sacrificial gift touched me deeply.

Consultations took place in hushed tones outside my room. Dr. Weiss, an Austrian refugee who had fled to China, suggested treating my meningitis with a newly discovered drug called penicillin. At his recommendation, the next time a spinal tap was performed penicillin was injected directly into my spinal fluid. The effect was miraculous. I believe I have him to thank for saving my life.

My reflexes came back and eventually I was well enough to walk across the alley to our home and resume everyday life. I was extremely lucky to have had no lasting damage from such a serious disease. Dorothy came back from her long stay at a friend's home where she had been while I was sick. She returned just in time for her fourth birthday party. I had asked Jang Shih Fu to make cupcakes so that each child could have one with a special, animal-shaped candle on it. When I set the plate of blazing cupcakes down in front of her, Dorothy looked at me earnestly and said with disappointment, "But, I've been practicing how to cut a cake!" During our few weeks of separation, she had grown up a great deal, and we had grown apart. Though this situation seemed temporary, the seeds of an emotional distance that would later plague us were planted at this time.

Once our women's group began meeting again, we were eager to pursue topics concerning the improvement of home and family life. We invited a woman who lived in an extended family to share some of the difficulties of dealing with her mother-in-law, and we asked a stepmother to join our group and explain how it felt to be in her position. After getting together for about a year, we decided to hold a picnic so that we could meet each other's children. After all, they had figured quite prominently in our discussions. Thirteen mothers and thirty-nine children, including Dorothy and Billy, participated. After we had eaten, one mother led games until the children felt comfortable on their own. Then we had great fun watching them, talking about them, and comparing notes.

These women had become a significant support group, for me and for each other. We were, in essence, a consciousness-raising group long before the term was coined. We learned from each other and we learned about ourselves. Most importantly, we trusted each other with our private thoughts and worries. Of all of us, Mrs. Yin, the pastor's wife, was the most reticent. Eventually, we learned why. Her son was a juvenile delinquent and she and her husband were stricken with shame. But she had no one besides us to turn to, and though she hated to burden us, she needed our understanding and support. She finally felt able to trust us with her confidences. I was pleased with my role in bringing the group together, and through our meetings and all that we achieved, I gradually became aware that I wanted to dedicate my life to women's service.

As my health improved, I began doing the household accounts and planning menus with Jang Shih Fu again. I fed Patty, made sure Billy and Dorothy were happily situated, taught school, practiced violin, checked on the garden, answered the mail, prepared for guests, and responded to whatever else turned up each day. I was hopeful about the future of China, feeling sure that somehow a coalition between the warring Communist and Nationalist factions would be formed and the Chinese could return to the business of living and pursuing their dreams. Though I didn't see exactly how my work fit in, I had a tremendous sense of being involved in causes much larger than myself, causes to which I was making a significant contribution. I had found my mission. I was where I was supposed to be. It seemed that before I opened my eyes each morning, a kite hovered over my bed and I was expected to reach upward and grab hold of its tail. As soon as I grabbed that kite, it would lift me up and yank me here and there all day long and gently deliver me back to bed late in the evening. I felt I was being shown what I could do to help in the world—my main task was to be present and grab every opportunity. I realized that the prediction of my bunkmate on the *General Meigs* had come true: I was indeed engrossed. I loved what I was doing.

Chuck had joined the Rotary Club of Peiping, which met every Thursday for lunch. We found it pleasant to take Thursday afternoons off and cycle the four miles through the city to the hotel where the Rotarians met. From there, I would go on to the American Consulate compound, have lunch with Ruth Forman, the wife of a consular official, and visit friends until Chuck came to collect me. Then we would become tourists, visiting museums or historic sites such as the Forbidden City, sometimes taking in a show and dinner. We enjoyed trying out the cuisines of many countries.

Roberta Lewis, a cellist who was keen on getting musical ensembles together, encouraged me to play my violin in string trios and quartets. A gifted musician, she organized weekly practices of Handel's *Messiah* in Chinese during the summer of 1948. It was an awesome task and we worked very hard. Unfortunately, only a few weeks before we were scheduled to perform, foreigners had to leave Peiping. Though our Chinese *Messiah* was never performed there, it was produced some years later in Manila and has been produced in other Asian languages since then. I've been glad to tell this story to young Chinese musicians who were raised during the Cultural Revolution and were not aware that European classical music was part of their musical heritage.

During the time I was working on the *Messiah*, other ventures were also in full swing. Dorothy had started kindergarten in the consular compound. Chuck preached a forty-five minute sermon in Chinese—a heroic feat considering he'd had great difficulty learning the language. During this service Patty was baptized. In addition, our mothers' group was writing its story and planning to publish it through the Methodist Press as encouragement to other mothers' groups.

But national events were taking a somber turn. Cities to the north were falling to the Communists one by one. No one knew what was going to happen. We didn't feel we were in physical danger, but all around us, the stable elements of Chinese society were crumbling.

Our Chinese friends were getting poorer by the day. Inflation was soaring—prices of food and other goods rose weekly. We rarely kept cash on hand. Salaries of teachers were figured not in Chinese yuan, but in sacks of flour, the staple food of the north Chinese diet. The economic situation deteriorated so badly that the Chinese began selling their family treasures to stay afloat. Almost every day I was implored to buy a set of plates or an ornate vase. The polite thing to do was to offer a ridiculously low price knowing it could be honorably refused. But the day I offered $2 for a large Peiping blue porcelain vase and my offer was accepted, I knew that people were getting desperate.

We sent a trunk with our irreplaceable possessions back to the States. Years later, when we retrieved and unpacked it having forgotten what it contained, we found the Indian rugs and tables from my parents, albums, pictures, and the $2 vase—an odd collection, but those items and the suitcases that accompanied us out of the country are all that remain of our two years in China.

It was said that General Chiang Kai-shek did not believe inflation existed. In fact, when he came to Peiping and visited the street where he bought his hats, the storekeepers lowered their prices to what they had been the last time he shopped there and he was able to say, "See, the prices are the same. There is no inflation." No one knows why the people colluded to keep him in the dark when they were the ones who suffered.

Meanwhile, corruption and bribery were widespread and the black market flourished. We felt that we should not support the black market because it aggravated economic catastrophe, but sometimes, out of necessity, we did. When one of the checks I cashed on the black market came back endorsed with the mayor's signature, I decided my scruples had been misplaced.

In August 1948, the Generalissimo, as Chiang Kai-shek was known, acknowledged that inflation did indeed exist and decided that something needed to be done about it. The exchange rate at that point was 65 million yuan to one dollar. The country suddenly underwent a great monetary exchange. The old paper money, printed in denominations of 100,000 yuan or more, was recalled. New currency was then issued at the rate of four yuan to one dollar. This announcement came as both a relief and a shock. Under the old system, the ridiculously large numbers had been quite difficult to work with. If I bargained with a rickshaw puller to take me to the market for 100,000 yuan, I could easily miscount the zeroes on the paper currency and pay him ten times as much. And I knew that the

Chinese were having similar problems. But now, instead of carrying around bundles of money, I could use a wallet again.

Our servants were greatly pleased with this evidence of economic overhaul and decided it was time to convert their savings into the new currency. Each pay period, I had allowed them to leave some money on the books as savings. Though it was illegal to do so, I had kept track of the amount in American dollars and told them that when they needed it, they could withdraw it at the going exchange rate. Now was the time, they said, taking it all to purchase the new money.

For about a month, the country flourished under a stable currency. Then it began to weaken. Prices began to rise. The Communists, watching the situation closely, precipitated the end of the Nationalist regime by starting a huge buying spree. Toward the end of September, stores were completely sold out of medicines, cloth, shoes, canned goods, books, and other supplies. Money was worthless again. The monetary reform had been in effect only six weeks.

At this point, we saw the heart go out of the Chinese people. Those who had supported the Generalissimo through war and peace now saw that his show of power was meaningless. They knew that he could not defeat the Communists, who had been waiting in the countryside for the economy to fail. The people's hopes were dashed. They had lost everything and now faced even greater uncertainty than they had during the war with Japan. Our servants, having lost their savings and fearing that we would be leaving with the other foreigners, were crushed.

In October, several major northern cities sold out to the Communists. There were no battles, only payment by Nationalists for the safe retreat of their armies. Foreign embassies and consulates monitored these events closely, ready to advise their citizens about their safety. Chinese church leaders suggested that we prepare to move to western China to wait out the present difficulties, hoping that a coalition government between Chiang Kai-shek and Mao Tse-tung would ultimately be created and we could return to Peiping.

But the Kuomintang Army was no longer effective—as the sale of several cities proved—it was riddled with corruption and no longer even pretended to defend a city against Communist takeover. Chiang Kai-shek fled to Canton before heading to Taiwan. Diplomatic relations between the United States government and China were now up in the air.

We were lunching with American friends on November 2, 1948, when a messenger from the consulate appeared with a letter addressed to every American. Those who did not wish to forgo the protection of their country were to leave the city by train on the morning of Tuesday, November 6, at 8 A.M. Arrangements for the evacuation had been made by the American government. There were no guarantees of safety for anyone who did not take advantage of this opportunity to leave the city, and our intentions had to reach the consulate within twenty-four hours. Each of us then signed our names in a large black book indicating that we had received the notice. But when the messenger left we all laughed, feeling sure we'd never have to leave.

We found Mr. Lo, one of the teachers at Truth Hall and the brother of the principal, waiting at our house. He had heard about the message and wanted to know our plans. "We don't have to leave," we said generously. "We're willing to stay and continue teaching."

Mr. Lo looked at us pityingly, choosing his words carefully. "Aren't you aware of the situation we Christians are in? By being your friends, our status with the Communists is already compromised. Their rallying cry is 'Get rid of the foreign imperialists.' We don't know how we will be treated when the new regime takes over." He was being blunt—very un-Chinese—but his words were those of a true friend, and they changed the picture entirely. We realized that our presence was a liability. We thanked him for his courage in speaking directly and said we would tell the consulate that we would take part in Tuesday's evacuation.

My first thoughts were for our mothers' group. At our next gathering, held in a teahouse, our meeting was despondent. "What will you do? Where will you go?" they queried. "I don't know," I replied and asked, "How will it be for you under the Communists?" They answered, "We don't know either. It was awful being cut off from the rest of the world when the Japanese occupied our land. Christians and those with foreign friends were not treated well and that will probably happen again." I then thanked the women for their individual and collective support. Not only had I learned their language, I had became familiar with their country and culture. They, in turn, each expressed gratitude for what the group had meant to them. Then we exchanged gifts. They gave me an angora scarf knitted with wool from the rabbits one woman raised. It was dyed a beautiful orange, my favorite color. I told them that when we left, I would not embarrass or endanger them with letters that would further identify them with foreigners but that I would never forget them. Though we probably would never meet again in this life, I was sure we would meet in the hereafter.

Reluctantly, Chuck and I started sorting through our belongings. Our bicycles and mechanical equipment were given to the school in the hope that they could be sold for cash. We packed a trunk of pans, dishes, and housekeeping equipment to take with us—we didn't yet know where—and sorted out the children's clothes and toys. We sent a truckload of furniture to the American consulate storeroom. Yet what we really wanted to do was spend time with friends who came to call. We asked them to take whatever they wanted, but they didn't dare take anything because doing so would only further identify them with foreigners.

On Tuesday, we rose early, planning to do some last-minute packing, but friends began arriving at 6 A.M. We thought they'd say goodbye and quickly leave, but they stayed. The living room filled up and overflowed into the hall. No longer able to pack, I put essentials in a bag and instructed Jang Shih Fu to wrap whatever he thought we could eat in dish towels. We never ate breakfast. The gatekeeper came to tell us that the truck taking all of the Americans to the train was leaving. Grabbing a dish towel, I shoveled Patty's tins of baby food into it and walked out the door, thanking our servants and saying to all assembled, "Help yourselves to anything that is left," knowing as I spoke that it was an empty invitation.

Instead of taking interest in our household goods, they followed us to the gate and joined the huge crowd gathered around the truck. As we joined others from the compound and scrambled up onto the flatbed, the crowd began to sing, "God be with you till we meet again." We rolled down the alley with the refrain in our ears. The tears I'd been holding back now flowed freely down my cheeks. I felt like I had been cut in half with a sword and half of me would remain in Peiping.

I truly loved China and loved living there. I'd made friends who had patiently helped me in many ways. I'd been an inexperienced foreigner, and these newfound friends had shared their routines, their traditions, their hopes and worries, and in the process had deepened my comprehension of life. In China, I'd been able to be myself, express myself. Without any previous connections, there had been no set expectations about how I should act. I valued the artistry that defined not only the structure of buildings and landscapes, but also the structure of life itself. I had thrown myself wholeheartedly into my work there and had been richly rewarded. Considering all that China had given me, I hated to leave.

At the station, a reporter snapped a picture of me. "You look like a refugee, with a babe in arms and two children tugging at your coat," she said. And I realized that's what I was: a refugee, homeless and without my usual resources. For example, I'd had household help for two wonderful years. Now I would have to do household chores myself. And for the first time, the care of three children rested fully on my shoulders.

The train was crowded. We sat knee to knee with other refugees. For the moment, our future was in the hands of the U.S. government—we had no idea where we were going. In Tientsin Harbor, two flat landing transports were tied up along the dock. I was assigned a tier of three bunks in the officers' quarters upstairs, but Chuck had only a cot on the flat bottom of the ship. He helped me set up Patty's crib, leaving Dorothy, Bill, and me each a berth. At the last minute, our captain took pity on the horde clamoring on the docks. These refugees from the Russian Revolution had escaped to Manchuria and north China and were now fleeing the Communists yet again, desperate to head south. We took one hundred on board. They were assigned all the top berths in our section. Therefore I had to get Dorothy and Bill to sleep at opposite ends of one bunk, or else have one of them sleep with me. As it turned out, I sat up most of each night.

One morning as I trudged into the bathroom to wash diapers, I said to the woman who had been allotted our top berth, "You're lucky. You can go upstairs into the sunlight. I'm stuck here washing diapers." She shot back with, "Don't you call me lucky! You have a country." That set the issue straight, reminding me how lucky we were indeed. The night before, U.S. citizens had been served ham, sweet potatoes, oranges, pineapple, and soft white bread, none of which (save the sweet potatoes) I'd tasted in over two years. These refugees had no one to care for them—no one to care about them—and nowhere to go. I was glad that our government was taking them at least as far as Shanghai.

Although Shanghai appeared greatly improved since our time there, it was bulging with refugees who had escaped the Communist takeover of the western and northern provinces. Housing was at a premium. Fortunately, a church committee was responsible for finding shelter for the fraternal workers flooding into the port. At first we were billeted in the attic of a missionary family, but when their own children were evacuated from west China, we had to find other accommodations. We were assigned to a brand new three-story townhouse where several families could live. It was a temporary arrangement. Each of us was deliberating where we would go next.

Our family of five had the top floor—one main room and a bedroom connected by a bathroom. Another family had identical accommodations on the second floor. The first floor, occupied by single missionaries who came and went, had a kitchen, a small dining room, and a main room. The first-floor occupants had to let us traipse through their living space in order to get upstairs.

Interiors were stark; furniture, meager. We were allotted one large table, four folding chairs, and cornhusk floor mattresses. There were no closets, shelves, cupboards, or bureau drawers. It was forbidden to pound nails into the walls or woodwork. A rope strung across each room from door hinge to window hinge sufficed for hanging clothes and drying laundry. A two-burner kerosene stove we had brought with us made it possible to cook in our rooms, boil drinking water and heat bath water. Food supplies stayed in boxes on the floor. The table was always in use for cooking, eating, washing dishes or clothes, writing, and playing games.

Because the weather was cold and wintry, our children stayed inside. The mattresses became their daytime playgrounds, and unless we locked our suitcases, our clothes and other belongings were frequently ransacked. We'd been offering meals to the transient missionary population, and as Thanksgiving Day approached, we decided to hold a big dinner in the first-floor rooms. Amazingly, even though World War II had ended three years earlier, there were still U.S. army surplus rations on the black market. It was not difficult to get canned turkey, sweet potatoes, cranberries, peas, and even mincemeat for pies.

The pies had to be baked downstairs, but the other cooking was divided among the upper floors, resulting in much consultation up and down the stairwell. It was a happy, busy, noisy occasion. On the third floor, we worked on the turkey. Just as it was beginning to smell good, we heard friends arrive downstairs and excitedly dashed out the door and down the steps to greet them. Alas, we heard our door close behind us with a decisive click and knew we had locked ourselves out—and the turkey in.

After hugs all around, we broke the news to our guests that our dinner was in jeopardy. Silently, we gazed up at the third floor wondering how we could scale the walls. Eventually, we asked the occupants of the townhouse next door to allow one of us to go up to their third floor and climb out a window onto the rooftop that connected our apartments. They agreed, and one of our members eventually edged across, reached a window on our floor, and smashed his way in to save our dinner.

We had a wonderful meal and shared lots of laughs. When the mailman arrived with a letter from my stepmother Dorothy inquiring as to whether we would consider serving under the United Church of Northern India, it was a welcome invitation—one that paved the way for the next chapter of our lives. We were truly thankful that Thursday.

Chapter Four
A New India

When our invitation from the United Church of Northern India was approved by the Presbyterian Board, Chuck spent many days processing the innumerable papers that would allow us to leave China. We hoped that the Communist armies, marching south after having swallowed Peiping, would not reach Shanghai before we slipped out. Finally, on December 20, 1948, our visa was granted. If we could book a flight, we could be in India for Christmas.

The airlines claimed they were completely full until after New Year's, but we didn't want to wait that long and risk getting trapped in Shanghai. Chuck called the airlines several times a day, inquiring about cancellations and using every argument he could muster. Finally he managed to secure tickets for December 23.

On our last full day in China, it rained heavily. Clothes I'd handwashed the day before and expected to be dry for packing were still hanging limply from lines across the room. Jessie Mae Henke and Signe Merwin, who had fled with us from Peiping, arrived to care for the children so that Chuck and I could head downtown for a last shopping spree and a nostalgic meal of Shanghai's specialty, sweet-and-sour pork. Seeing the damp clothes, our caregivers proceeded to iron them dry, a real labor of love.

On the morning of our departure, our downstairs neighbors gave us a waffle breakfast and sent us off in the mission's car—more reliable than taxis, or so we thought. To our dismay, it broke down five miles from the airport and we had to hitchhike. An Air France van rescued us—up until that moment we'd never heard of Air France—and delivered us to Pan Am in time for our flight. Our plane took off right over our apartment house, and as we looked down, we said a tearful farewell to China.

After a stop in Hong Kong, our flight headed to Bangkok. There we would change planes in the middle of the night. Exhausted, we waited on a hot, steamy, mosquito-plagued tarmac for our connection to Calcutta. To our great relief, we found the plane had marvelous "sleeperette" seats that allowed us to stretch out our legs and recline.

With all the tension of leaving China, we surely needed that space and a good sound sleep before we confronted the unknowns of India.

All too soon it was 3 A.M. and we were descending into Calcutta. Tears welled up in my eyes as I realized we had made it—safely. But a shiver of uncertainty ran through me as I thought of all we still faced in this new India. When the tires hit the runway, the children awoke in querulous outbursts, eager to get off the plane but unaware of what lay ahead.

On the bus ride into the city, I became alarmed because we seemed to be hurtling straight into oncoming traffic. Sure that our end was near, I shrank back, closed my eyes, and braced myself for the crash. But nothing happened. I opened my eyes and then realized that, this being India, traffic was passing on the left, just as it always had.

At the Grand Hotel, a phalanx of waiters in formal red uniforms complete with gold braid served us an early breakfast in the center of an enormous dining room. They stood at attention around us, ready to respond to our every wish. The children gladly thought up new requests—toast with jam, scrambled eggs, bacon, cocoa, bananas. I asked the waiters to fill our thermoses with boiled drinking water for the train trip that awaited us.

Chuck had eaten hastily before going to the railway station to make the necessary arrangements. He returned in high spirits announcing that he had finessed tickets to Allahabad on the morning train. Insisting we leave immediately to claim our seats, he packed all of us and our luggage into taxis. When we arrived at the station, it was swarming with holiday crowds. Even in India, where most people are Hindu, Christmas Eve is a popular day for travel.

The bustling railway station felt very familiar. I felt I was in my element. However, when I spoke, everyone looked at me strangely—the words tumbling out of my mouth were neither English nor Hindustani, but Chinese. Tired as I was, I couldn't recover the Hindustani that had been pushed to the back of my mind during our years in China. Later that day, as the train traveled northwest toward Allahabad, I pointed to a woman's bracelets and heard her say *bangles*. It was the first Hindustani word to come back to me.

We settled into our second-class compartment, and my excitement began to mount as we pulled out of Calcutta, crossing the Hoogly River on the huge, new Howrah Bridge, and headed out into open country. We had exactly two seats on a bench running beneath the windows—a great accomplishment in a compartment where twenty-eight people occupied seating for twenty. Our children sat on our laps or on a blanket spread on the floor between us and the passengers opposite us. Every inch of space on the seats, under the seats, or in the berths above was crammed with people or luggage. There was no connecting corridor running the length of the railway car. Each compartment opened on both sides but was separate from the rest of the train. Tight quarters soon led to camaraderie. Singing and laughter went hand in hand with sleepy nods and quiet reflection. Our children were agog, watching and listening. They found the bathroom daunting because they had to squat over a hole in the floor while the ground rushed by underneath. But its two faucets were appealing. The lower one released water for flushing, the higher one for washing hands. As the day grew hotter, passengers had to choose between the cool breeze of open windows, which also brought in cinders, or the cinderless benefits of closed windows, which trapped the heat. In both cases, ceiling fans worked overtime.

Soothed by the rhythmic cadence of the speeding train, I watched the scenery flow by and reflected anew on what my return to India would be like. This was the land of my birth. I had traveled these railways, built by the British to unite the subcontinent, for much of my life. But the British no longer ruled here. In 1947, India had reached the milestone my parents and I had longed for—independence. And in many ways, after thirteen years, I was coming home to a different country. This was clearly brought home to me as I gazed at the faces around me. They were all Indian. We were the only foreigners in sight.

Other things had changed as well. My parents were both dead, and my only family in India was my stepmother, Dorothy Dragon Parker, whom I barely knew, and her children, my half-sister and half-brother, Harriet and Donald, who were the ages of my own children. I admired Dorothy for her courage in returning to India with Harriet and Donald, and her letters were warm and welcoming, yet I wondered how our two families would mix and mingle.

It was to Dorothy's home in Allahabad that we were now traveling. She knew only that we'd obtained our Indian visas and were trying to get out of China but didn't yet know we'd actually left. In the tumult of our sudden departure, we hadn't sent word to her. We'd been in such a hurry to board the train in Calcutta that even then there was no time to call or telegraph.

However, feeding the children was my immediate concern. Vendors passing our window called out their wares that included *narangi* (large, loose-skinned tangerines), bananas, hot tea, Indian sweets, hot fried *purl* (bread), and other fare. I ordered fruit that could be washed and peeled and would assuage thirst as well as hunger. We were brought trays of tea with boiled milk. Later, Chuck and I enjoyed

Indian meals. I wasn't sure how to get boiled water, so at every major stop I asked Chuck to run up to the engine to fill our thermoses.

The children were entranced with the colorfully dressed people who were talking, arguing, singing, and asking us questions. Dorothy and Billy squeezed up to the windows to watch fields and villages pass by. When fellow passengers offered them candy, I had to say tactfully, "We are new to your country. Perhaps their digestive systems are not ready for new foods." When Chuck and I read the children's books out loud, an interested audience leaned across the bench to listen to our English.

The sky grew dark and night descended. We dozed, lulled by the chugging of the train as it steadily pushed its way north along the banks of the Ganges, the engine bravely tugging its overloaded passenger cars to distant destinations. At last, before dawn, I heard the familiar words *Allahabad agaiya*, Allahabad has come.

Collecting and then loading our baggage onto coolies' heads, we emerged from the station to find *tongas*, or horse carriages, to take us to the girls' school where my stepmother Dorothy taught. Our procession clopped through dark, unfamiliar streets, then turned into a compound where we were challenged by the night watchman. I asked for Parker Memsahib and he directed us to one of the houses, running ahead to wake her and warn her of our arrival.

Dorothy quickly appeared, wrapping her robe around her and asking, sleepy and puzzled, why we hadn't let her know we were coming. There was a moment's awkwardness. We had no excuse except our preoccupation with escaping China and could only say that we hoped our arrival was as welcome a Christmas present for her as it was for us. A smile broke over her face as she hugged us and our discomfort vanished. She guided us to several beds and apologized that the servants would be off until later that Christmas Day. We snuggled gratefully under the covers knowing that after some sleep and a refreshing bath, we'd be ready for anything. Our children were delighted to discover their new playmates, "Aunt" Harriet and "Uncle" Don, when they woke up later that day.

Word of our arrival spread quickly. Over the next few days, friends from childhood came to call and missionaries in other Allahabad institutions who had known Daddy and Mother invited us over. Most exciting of all, we received invitations to an important wedding reception that provided an intimate and revealing portrait of the new India.

In a private ceremony, as is customary in India, Nayantara Pandit, niece of Indian prime minister Jawaharlal Nehru, married Gautam Seghal. Later on, at the reception, when photographers signaled that they were through taking pictures of the famous politician with his beautiful sari-clad niece and her groom, Prime Minister Nehru absentmindedly picked up a knife and began to cut the wedding cake. He was intercepted by his daughter, Indira Gandhi, who tapped him on the shoulder and asked teasingly, "Who do you think you are, Papa? The bride?"

Those of us gathered there with her chuckled over her watchfulness and audacity. Her aunt, Vidhya Lakshmi Pandit, mother of the bride, joined the merriment and chided the prime minister, saying, "You don't have to do everything, *bhai* (brother). Today is Tara's day!" He was ruefully apologetic as he turned the knife over to the bride and started joking with her sisters by asking which would be the next to marry.

I had only been in India a few days and was at the reception because Mrs. Pandit insisted that Dorothy Parker bring Chuck and me along. Mrs. Pandit and her husband, Ranjit, had been friends of my parents and had stayed in our home when they visited their daughters at Woodstock School. I hadn't seen her since 1936, and in the interim, both of our worlds had changed. She had lost her husband, and I, my parents. When I left India for college, she and her brother had been prisoners of the British. Now he was prime minister and she was India's first ambassador to Russia.

It was at this joyous celebration that I met Mr. Nehru. Daddy's descriptions had not adequately prepared me for this vigorous, delightful man. Never had I encountered anyone who radiated such charisma. I told him I was glad to return to an India under his leadership and asked about his book *Glimpses of World History*. He affirmed that it was the first history of the world written from an Asian point of view. I couldn't believe that he, an author and maker of history, was standing there chatting with me, with his customary red rosebud tucked into a buttonhole of his *atchkan*—the famous Nehru jacket.

He told me how much he missed my father, a loyal supporter of Indian independence. But all too soon, others interrupted, and this poignant moment ended. The day was, after all, a significant occasion. It was the first state wedding in newly independent India and many notables were in attendance. Precedents were being set and the entire country was watching.

Indian friends later asked me about the event—how much pomp was displayed, how much money had been spent on the reception. When I mentioned that a wedding cake had been served, some shook their heads, worrying over the "infiltration of foreign influence." But it seemed to me that such fears could be allayed. It was a simple, gracious affair carried out in a home setting. All of the food except for the wedding cake was Indian, and though delicious, it wasn't fancy.

As I wandered among the crowd, I remembered the large garden parties held in Allahabad when I was a teen. They were official, formal-dress British occasions attended by Europeans and Americans with only a sprinkling of Indian guests. Now, in the garden of *Anand Bhawan*, the Nehrus' home, I was one of about ten foreigners. To me, this change truly symbolized the new India.

I was delighted to be embraced by such a dedicated and selfless family. I knew that each of them had valiantly and voluntarily sacrificed for India. Beginning with Prime Minister Nehru's father, Motilal Nehru, each had turned over his fortune to the independence movement. As followers of Mahatma Gandhi, they had lived simply and endured imprisonment. Mrs. Pandit's husband Ranjit had died as a result of prison conditions. And Mr. Nehru's wife had passed away in a sanatorium in Switzerland during the early years of his incarceration. These losses made the family's struggle for independence even more difficult.

Then another realization swept over me—this wedding not only pioneered a fresh mix of Indian and European simplicity, but it also challenged the old system of arranged marriages. Tara, and Indira before her, had each selected her own husband.

Back then, none of us knew that both Indira and her five-year-old son, Rajiv, would eventually become prime ministers of India. But we were aware of the adjustments and responsibilities required of Indira, who served as both wife and mother in Lucknow and as international hostess for her father at the prime minister's residence in New Delhi. Eventually, Indira and her husband, Feroze Gandhi, would move to Delhi and live in a wing of the prime minister's mansion, making it easier for her to conduct occasions of state.

Feroze, a Parsee lawyer from Bombay whose background was quite different from the Kashmiri Nehrus, disagreed with his father-in-law's politics. He is probably given insufficient credit for quietly carrying out his profession and minimizing the embarrassment his political views might have caused the Nehrus. When he died in 1960, many thought that Indira would be glad to be rid of him. Her hand-written reply to my letter of condolence indicated otherwise.

During the years she was prime minister, I often wondered how she managed. After having supported her father and husband, she now had to carry the affairs of state without the help of either.

Our days in Allahabad were leisurely and enjoyable. I was delighted to renew acquaintances with childhood friends and introduce them to my family. Chuck, the children, and I visited spots that evoked potent memories for me, and together we found the cemetery where Mother was buried. Looking down at her grave brought tears of regret for all I had missed, but also a sense of closure. Her grave was near that of my baby sister, Dorothy, who had died of bacillary dysentery at seven months when I'd been just two-and-a-half. Having these family connections made our adjustment to life in India that much easier.

Chuck and I still had to decide where we would live and work. Several invitations were extended—one of them from Jumna High School, where Daddy had served as both teacher and administrator. Regretfully, we declined. There, Chuck would have been expected to live up to Daddy's reputation, a formidable, if not impossible, task and one of the reasons we hadn't come to India earlier. We chose instead to move to Moga, a small town in the Punjab, where the Moga Teacher Training School was located. It had been founded by Irene and Arthur Harper, friends of my parents who were well known in educational circles. I had visited the school many years ago. Now the Harpers were ready to retire. The principal, Mr. Sudhir Roy, a gifted, caring person, was grateful we had come. Chuck felt sure he could make a real and immediate contribution, even though he had yet to learn Hindustani and we weren't entirely sure what our duties there would be.

When we arrived in Moga in February 1949, we hired a *tonga* to carry us from the train station to the school. As we passed through the main gate, I looked around at the familiar brick buildings neatly arranged and enclosed by low walls. Students were sweeping the pathways, trimming hedges, and planting flowers. Mrs. Harper welcomed us into the old missionary residence, which would soon be our new home, with a delicious chocolate cake set out on a tea table and a cheery fire in the fireplace.

English was widely used in training teachers, and Mrs. Harper explained that when educators and students from other colleges came to visit, Chuck and I would help orient them. Such groups often arrived unannounced wanting to observe classes in session and engage in dynamic discussions about how education should be delivered in Indian villages. Chuck and I would show the visitors around and answer questions which allowed Moga's teachers and administrators to continue their own work.

Interest in Moga was keen because the national government was considering implementing Mahatma Gandhi's basic education model and the Moga school came close to fulfilling his ideals. The Moga model included eight school years of integrated curriculum that would prepare boys and girls to be self-sufficient in rural India.

Reading, writing, and arithmetic were learned in conjunction with planting vegetables, cooking school meals, planning farm crops, raising cotton and spinning and weaving cloth from it, sewing clothing, tanning leather, making shoes, and undertaking countless other practical projects. The students even learned to build and use smokeless stoves, or *chulas*.

The fact that we were refugees endeared us to many in Moga's Christian community who understood what that meant. They had harbored refugees at the time of India's partition in 1947, putting themselves in danger for doing so.

As a condition of independence from Britain, political groups within India had to agree on the form the new state would take. The majority party under Jawaharlal Nehru and Mahatma Gandhi planned to launch a secular India. This upset Muslim political leaders and they threatened to derail the independence process at the last hour. As a concession, Gandhi agreed that India would cede a third of its land to create the new Islamic state of Pakistan. Relations between Hindus and Muslims in India had been relatively peaceful for years, but the partition of India created a nightmare. The newly drawn border split extended families apart—a very unpopular effect—and though there was no policy forcing Muslims to leave India, or Hindus, Pakistan, members of the minority religion in each country felt threatened. People unwillingly abandoned their land holdings to flee across the border—Hindus to India and Muslims to Pakistan—and their anger fostered unspeakable acts of carnage.

Moga was on the rail line to the nearby Pakistani border where Hindus streamed into India and Muslims fled in the other direction. During this upheaval, many trains were stopped and every passenger slaughtered. The perpetrators were fanatics—Hindus against Muslims and vice versa. The Sikhs in the Punjab aided refugees from both religious groups, but there were also Sikh fanatics who took the opportunity for revenge. In the short four hundred years of their religious history, the Sikhs had been brutally persecuted by both Hindus and Muslims.

We heard many stories about what people in the Punjab had undergone. It had been a lawless, dangerous time and a time of hourly uncertainty and great suffering. Someone had to clean up the remains of the death trains, so the Christians of Moga and the surrounding villages volunteered to do so as a service to their country and out of gratitude to God that they, a small, neutral, and relatively powerless minority, had been spared.

Now, two years later, in 1949, a new country was coming into being before our eyes. Everyone, Indian and foreigner alike, felt a tremendous sense of hope for the future. I wanted to fit into this spirit by living simply, like the Indian families around us. We hired one full-time servant, a cook named Charanji Lal, and a part-time *ayah*. I did much of the housework and supervised the children indoors. The *ayah* sat outside and played with the children, seeing to it that they didn't run into the road or get into difficulties. This way, I could be in close touch with them as they came in and out and observe their adjustment to this new country.

They did amazingly well. They were even willing to drink the milk of water buffaloes, which tasted different from cow's milk. They watched me boil it and set it aside for the cream to rise overnight. We used some of the cream with brown sugar syrup on hot *chappatis* for breakfast and the rest was churned into butter.

Moga, a small rural town, was quite a contrast to Peiping, a large sophisticated city. In each place, however, I tackled the same challenge—to improve the diets of children in boarding schools where there was not much money to do so. Suggested changes had to be realistic in terms of available foods. In Moga, school meals consisted mainly of *chappatis* baked fresh for each meal by the schoolchildren on the smokeless *chula*. The whole wheat flour for making them came from the school's own wheat crop. The children also ate *dal*, or lentils, and a curry made from vegetables raised on the school farm. They also boiled milk from the school buffaloes and served it in tea.

Depending on the season, the farm produced carrots, cabbage, cauliflower, mustard greens, onions, turnips, eggplants, gourds, and potatoes. I analyzed the nutritional benefits of these various crops and listed them in order of their comparative nutritional value. Then I presented my compilations to the school farm director who used them to time and rotate the planting of crops so that the most vitamin-packed vegetables would be available on a regular basis, thereby keeping nutrient levels in student diets as high as possible. The children not only ate good nourishing food, they also learned the nutritional values of what they consumed. They were not picky eaters. They knew that at school a good meal was assured and that they were eating better than they did at home in the village.

The weather turned warm in March but was already hot by mid-April, signaling that it was time to go uphill to Mussoorie. Chuck was allowed only a month's vacation and decided to take it at the end of summer. The children and I would spend the entire summer at the hill house we'd been assigned. It seemed more than a little strange that my children would now be attending Woodstock, the school where I had learned to read and write and where Daddy had been principal.

We were better prepared for an overnight train trip than when we had arrived in India several months ago. Charanji Lal, our cook, went with us and helped me stretch bedrolls out on the compartment benches. I didn't sleep much. I was concerned that the children might fall during the night. More importantly, I was terribly excited knowing that in the morning I'd have my first glimpse of the Himalayas in thirteen years. At dawn, there they were, stretching across the northern horizon, filling my eyes and my heart.

From Dehra Dun—the station where I'd boarded the train to leave India so long ago—we retraced my steps to Landour, traveling first by bus to an altitude of 7,000 feet. The journey felt very familiar. Not much had changed. We walked the last three miles, and when the children got tired, they rode in a *dandy*. I'd forgotten how steep the hillsides were. Coolies carried our luggage on their backs.

My eyes took in all the sights, most of them dearly familiar. At the top of Mullingar Hill, the road leveled out and headed east past the school and on to Tehri. On Landour Hill, one new building, the community hospital, had been built since I'd left. Dotting the hillside were familiar cottages, school buildings, and dormitories. The slopes contoured the school campus, and in the background stood the familiar landscape of Witch's Hill, so named because lightning always struck there. Memories came flooding back and exclamations of joy escaped my lips.

To my surprise, I'd been recognized by shopkeepers in the bazaar, those who had been Daddy's friends. Some burst into tears and *salaamed* deeply (formal greeting), asking where they could come call. I conveyed that we would share a duplex, Woodside, with my stepmother Parker Memsahib and her children Harriet and Donald, who would join us from Allahabad.

Though Woodside was fully furnished, settling in was complicated by the fact that there were many callers. Every day for weeks, I sat out on the porch while shopkeepers, watchmen, *wallahs*, school servants, and other friends sat with me and wept, remembering Daddy's goodness to them and relating the afflictions they had suffered at the time of partition. If only Parker Sahib had been there, they lamented, none of this would have happened. If only he hadn't died! I would reply, "Even Mahatma Gandhi and Pandit Jawaharlal Nehru couldn't stop the killings, and I fear that my father couldn't have stopped them either. But I am convinced that the news of the terrible slaughter and rioting broke his heart and contributed to his death."

I was deeply suffering the loss of my father. Seeing Woodstock School without my father, once so integral to it, brought his death into the present and revived my sorrow. Still, even as I yearned for him, I knew I was carrying out an important duty. As his eldest daughter, I was listening to his other mourners, hearing their suffering and sense of loss. It was a powerful healing experience.

When I was invited to tea by Rhea and Margaret Ewing, Woodstock's principal and his wife, I was excited to get a glimpse of my former home. I felt Mother's presence and fondly recalled the parties she'd thrown and the waffles with creamed chicken she'd served each Sunday because it was an easy recipe to stretch, and we never knew how many guests she'd invite home after church. The carved black desk she'd used, a beautiful piece belonging to the school, still stood by the stairs in the dining room.

I was comforted to learn that just as I missed Mother, many others did too. All summer long, people I scarcely knew would stop me at church or some social function to tell me a story about how much she had helped them. Remembering her warmth and goodness helped me complete my grieving process and showed me my place as an adult in the daily activities on the hillside.

On Sunday evenings when our servants went to the Hindustani church, we made Chinese *jyaudz*, small steamed dumplings filled with ground pork and cabbage. Dorothy and Bill remembered them fondly from China. Making enough for our large crowd was a task that involved every member of the family including Harriet, Donald and their mother. We formed an assembly line, rolling out small rounds of dough, filling them, pinching them together and boiling them. Once they were cooked, we would dip them in a mixture of vinegar and soy sauce and devour them using chopsticks. This became a weekly family custom that lasted for many years.

It took some time to get used to the monsoon rains again. From the second half of June to September, the paths were muddy and water streamed down the hillsides. We wore rain gear everywhere and had to be careful to keep our shoes and suitcases from becoming mildewed. Leeches lurked everywhere. But I hadn't forgotten the payoff—with the heavy rains came gorgeous flowers—every shade of dahlia and orchids, which when inverted looked like miniature peacocks, ginger-colored lilies, and others. The hillsides were a riot of color. Mossy ferns grew in the huge oak trees, beetles flew around in droves at night, and evenings brought breathtaking sunsets.

I slipped easily into the familiar framework of life in this hill station. There were no phones so we sent all our messages in the form of notes via a coolie. The daily mail delivery was an important event. Vegetables, milk, fruit, meat and bread were delivered to the door by *wallahs*. The *dhobi*, or washerman, collected soiled clothes and brought them back laundered and ironed. I knew something of the hard conditions under which he worked, standing knee-deep in icy mountain streams, soaping each piece, and slapping it against stones. I marveled that the clothes came out so clean.

At the end of the summer, Chuck joined us for his vacation. He desperately needed rest, and to our alarm, he suddenly fell ill. He ran a high fever, couldn't keep food in his stomach, and complained of aching joints. Suspecting malaria, our doctor began quinine treatment but changed her opinion when his urine turned dark, his stools turned light, and his skin became jaundiced. She shipped him off to the hospital where Dr. Bethel Fleming confirmed the diagnosis of hepatitis and advised me to visit infrequently because of its highly infectious nature.

Here we were safe in India, having survived the uncertainties of evacuation from China and the adjustment to a new country, and now my husband was bedridden and maybe dying. I was terribly discouraged. The mile-long walk to the hospital was rocky, dusty, and exhausting, and I had three children aged five and under to care for.

It was late September, the days were getting shorter, the season was over and cottages were emptying. Many of the hospital's summer staff had returned to winter jobs on the plains and the institution was shorthanded. To make matters worse, the young female nurses on Chuck's floor were afraid to be alone with a man so he received only minimum care. He needed far more attention than he was getting. He itched all over and scratched until his skin bled and patches of body hair fell out. Topical applications didn't soothe for long and medication was hard on his liver.

As his condition daily deteriorated, my fear of losing him grew. Dr. Fleming told me she'd cabled her medical school in the States for suggestions because she had never seen such a bad case. Chuck himself grew frightened. The day came when he took my hand and begged me not to leave, saying, "I don't think I can make it through the night."

In desperation, I sent a note to several friends, begging them to care for the children so I could remain at Chuck's side. When Dr. Fleming agreed with my decision and said, "Kittu, I've done everything I know how to do. I think you *should* be here tonight in case he doesn't pull through," the shock of her words galvanized me to further action. My despair was replaced with a fierce sense that it was up to me to save my husband. I sat by his bed all night forcing fluids, reading to him, and praying. He pulled through the night, sleeping soundly, and seemed stronger in the morning.

Soon after he woke, I trudged wearily home and explained to the children that because we needed to get Daddy well, I would be away each day. Dorothy offered to stay with a friend after school and a neighbor recommended a very capable *ayah* to care for Billy and Patty. I then enlisted help for Chuck. I composed a letter with a sign-up sheet asking anyone who could spare the time to come to the hospital and sit with him to prevent his scratching and give him liquids. A coolie took it to every occupied cottage on the hillside, going from house to house for the next three days. The response was overwhelming—the sign-up sheet was full. People I didn't even know had volunteered.

Thanks to this loving care, Chuck began to heal. Gradually, his skin became less sallow and his hair started growing back. He gained enough strength to sit, then stand, and finally, to walk. Even when he was well enough to come home, he was still pitifully thin. I did all I could to tempt his appetite, but everything I cooked had to be low-fat. We celebrated his homecoming on October 28, Patty's birthday, with an angel food cake. The mission hospital in Ambala generously sent a nurse to stay with us and help me with his home care. She taught me how to give him his liver shots.

The nights were now growing cold and the days, though sunny, were chilly. We needed to move down to the plains to warmer weather. But Dorothy told me she didn't want to leave school and begged to stay in the boarding department until Woodstock closed for the winter. I could hardly bear to pack up her things and leave her there. She was so young, not quite six. With a heavy heart, I took Billy, Patty, and a still-weak Chuck down to Dr. Peterson's home in Saharanpur, where we broke journey long enough for Chuck to recoup before continuing on to Moga. When Dorothy came home some weeks later, traveling by train with other schoolchildren, it was a joyous reunion for me. I had worried about her and wondered if I had done the right thing.

Years later when Dorothy was an adult, she admitted that during Chuck's illness, she thought he had gotten sick due to my incompetence. Her decision to go into boarding was made not out of a love for school, but because she believed I had my hands full with Chuck and the younger children and thought that taking care of herself would help me. She sensed my worry upon her return to Moga and interpreted it as confirmation that she was simply an additional burden. She decided then that she would get used to taking care of herself. This drove a painful wedge between us and it was many years before we understood each other again.

Dorothy entered the Moga kindergarten. It was a joy to see her and children from Hindu, Sikh, and Christian families, some wealthy and some poor, all playing and learning together. Her teacher, Mrs. Joseph, organized meetings for the mothers to discuss child development and share our experiences.

I enjoyed the meetings and wished I had more time to get to know the other mothers better, but we were getting ready to go on furlough in May 1950. As that time approached, Mrs. Joseph suggested that they organize a farewell tea for me. The first I knew about it was when rugs were being spread out on the lawn at our house so guests could sit around the low kindergarten tables and my tea set and cups were commandeered. When all was ready, I was invited to attend. Nearly forty women had come.

I was touched by the thoughtfulness of the occasion, but my heart quailed when I saw the two women seated at my table, both from very exclusive Hindu families. "They'll never drink tea with me," I thought to myself knowing that those of high caste never ate with those they considered "outcast foreigners."

My fears were confirmed. As tea was offered, they declined, saying, "We've already had our tea. We just came to bid farewell to Mrs. Riddle." But the wife of a well-known and highly distinguished local doctor had evidently anticipated this interchange. She rose quickly, called the group to order, and gave a little speech about what had brought us together as mothers. She spoke of the preciousness of our children, praised Mrs. Joseph as a gifted teacher, and referred to India's first Republic Day, reminding us that caste was now illegal and urging us as mothers to rid ourselves of the inner prejudices that divided us. She concluded with, "As we say farewell to Mrs. Riddle, let us demonstrate our oneness. Let's forget our differences and just be mothers together. Let's all drink tea." Her eloquent words caused us each to think about our hopes for our children and for the world they would grow up in. This time when tea was served every woman drank. With thankful tears in my eyes, I thought, *Yes, we are all mothers together*.

Before returning to the States on furlough, we discovered that in the new India we had to get permission from the police to leave as well as a "no objection to return" certificate from the central government, records of immunizations, and a statement that our income tax was in order. Documents in hand, we arrived at the airport ready to board our propeller plane, amazed that it would take us from Delhi to London in less than twenty-four hours. As we worked our way through various checkpoints, our paperwork seemed to be in order, but between us and our flight, there was one final desk. The man behind it demanded to see our papers. We handed him our passports, police permits, immunization papers, and income tax documents, but he tossed each one aside angrily. Apparently, they were not what he was looking for. Again, he demanded our papers.

We were desperate, afraid he would refuse to let us through. Chuck opened his briefcase wide and began to leaf through his file folders, pulling out paper after paper, holding each one up just long enough to see the man's response. Suddenly, the man lunged forward and snatched a paper from Chuck's hand. "This is what I was asking for! You may now board the aircraft," he announced, satisfied. We didn't ask questions; we just ran for the plane. When we were safely seated, I asked Chuck, "What did he want?"

"You'll never believe this, but he grabbed a letter from Sardar Gyan Singh, the district commissioner in Ferozepore, saying that the next time he and his wife came through Moga, they would stop and have a cup of tea. The letter had a big, official-looking chop, a seal, on the bottom, and I think that's what caught his eye." We laughed, astonished. Then anxiety began to plague us, and we hoped the plane would leave before he discovered what the "official paper" said. When our flight took off, we silently thanked the district commissioner who had gotten us on the plane with his letter.

When we landed in England, which was still recovering from the war, there was no large airport to receive us. We went through customs in a makeshift Quonset hut with a wooden floor. Our kids, released from the confines of the plane, ran 'round and 'round on its rattly boards, eluding us with glee. The customs officials processed us with alacrity, glad to be rid of the noisy Americans.

After visiting some friends, we crossed the Atlantic on the *SS Queen Mary*, enjoying a few days of leisure and good food. Oddly enough, I had a hard time making the adjustment to life in the U.S. In China, we had survived the Communist takeover, and in India, I had been forced to confront the ghosts of childhood and the deaths of my parents. After the physical and emotional turmoil of the last five years, I thought I'd be glad to be back where I "belonged." But that was precisely the problem: where did I belong?

We landed in New York City on a Sunday, May 1950. When we went to the hotel restaurant for dinner, I was astounded to find that a bowl of soup cost three dollars. In Moga, three dollars fed one of the school's boarders for an entire month. I couldn't eat. How could I pay three dollars or more for a single meal?

Soon after, I went off to Ocean Grove near Atlantic City, New Jersey for the first nationwide assembly of Presbyterian women. The next morning, I was in a drugstore having breakfast when a large bus

The Riddles. Bill, Kittu, Dorothy, Patty, and Chuck, in Boulder, CO, Christmas 1950. The curtains in the background are among the few things that accompanied them out of China.

pulled up outside. A woman emerged and came inside announcing to the world, "We're the women of Texas!" She came over and asked who I was and where I was from. When I told her I had recently arrived from India, her eyes widened with excitement. "Don't tell me! You're a missionary?" When I nodded, she ran out to the bus, yelling, "Girls, girls, you won't believe it! The first person I met is a real, live missionary!" As her friends crowded into the drugstore to see, I wanted to disappear. Her comment made me feel like such an oddity, someone different from ordinary folk.

As the years went by, I was asked to do considerable speaking among Presbyterian women's organizations in the Midwest on each furlough. One spring, I visited Texas for a three-week stint to attend meetings at seven locations across the state. In the town of Paris, not only were there tornado warnings, but we actually saw huge twisters headed our way and the meeting had to be canceled. We spent the next day in Arlington, between Dallas and Fort Worth. The weather was sunny, the tornadoes were over, and everyone seemed in high spirits and enjoyed my morning speech. So, at my afternoon engagement, I decided to tell the story of the warm welcome I had received from the busload of Texan ladies I had encountered in New

Jersey. I was astounded—and confounded—at the response. Never had I managed to so completely crack up an audience. They laughed until they cried, but I couldn't figure out why. I knew the story was funny, but not that funny. Later, I discovered that they all knew the woman who had approached me. In fact, she was in the room. During refreshments, she and I apologized to one another. She hadn't known how her exuberance would sound to me, and I hadn't meant to embarrass her in front of her friends.

On this, our first furlough, Chuck and I weren't sure where we wanted to be, so we bought a Dodge sedan and drove west to Lead, South Dakota where Uncle Paul was pastor at the local Presbyterian church. The children and I spent a month "managing" the church camp for him, showing people to their cabins, playing in the stream, and walking in the woods. It was a calming and nourishing experience. Meanwhile, Chuck drove to Boulder to investigate the University of Colorado, and liking what he found, enrolled in a master's program in vocational guidance. While taking summer courses, he found a house for us and then returned to South Dakota to collect us before the fall semester began.

Dorothy started first grade; Billy and Patty were in nursery school. At age four, Billy was very fond of his sisters' bright dresses and insisted on wearing one made of red corduroy. He dashed outside and showed off to the other little boys on the block. I watched, holding my breath, wondering if they'd make fun of him, but no, each one went home and got a dress of his own. For several days, that was the "after nursery school" fashion on our street. Then the weather turned cold and they were glad to go back to overalls.

Patty had been vulnerable to colds and sore throats, and though I made sure she got plenty of vitamin C-rich foods, at age three it seemed best to have her tonsils taken out. To prepare her for the procedure, we learned what order the shots would be given in and when blood would be drawn before the surgery. Then our whole family rehearsed the process with her many times, taking turns being patient, nurse, and doctor. She was very much at ease when we took her to the hospital, showing the nurse which finger could be poked for blood and calling for a cap before they took her off to the operating room. Within ten minutes she was back, and the surgeon said he had never had such a relaxed patient.

Before Patty's tonsillectomy, I underwent surgery to repair tears from bearing three children. At the same time, I asked that my fallopian tubes be tied. Several weeks later, I developed a sudden pain in my lower left leg and had to go to bed to prevent a blood clot. The timing was serendipitous though, both because my calendar was clear of speaking engagements and because my sister, Clara Jo, her husband, Bob, and their children, Janet and Robbie, were visiting us from Alaska. Clara Jo was a great help and it was a joy to see her and her family.

I had been doing quite a bit of speaking to church groups in Boulder and its surrounding areas. It was hard to accurately describe our life in India knowing that if I mentioned our servants, it would sound overly pampered and lavish, but if I mentioned the lack of modern conveniences, it would sound shockingly deprived. According to our Indian neighbors, we lived in a palace. After all, we had running water: a servant pumped water up to a tank on the roof and it ran down to taps in the bathrooms and kitchen. Every day, we went to the bazaar for fresh food. We didn't have refrigeration and didn't think we needed it. Nevertheless, we had whipped cream made from rich buffalo milk on our cereal each morning. Our children couldn't understand why there was no whipped cream for their cereal in the U.S. and our relatives were shocked that they would ask for it.

The contradictions in our life were difficult to comprehend, even for those who came to visit India. I frequently told audiences about the lunch I'd had with a group of American social workers at the Imperial hotel in Delhi. To me, the food served was extra special because many items were unavailable in the Punjab, and I felt as if I were back in the States. My lunch companions, on the other hand, remarked on the deficiencies of the menu and wondered whether the food was safe.

Dr. Ruth Blair, one of my professors at the University of Chicago, was now head of the home economics department at the University of Colorado. She was interested in the nutritional observations I'd made overseas and enrolled me in independent study so I could research some of the questions that still remained.

For example, I wondered why corn bread and mustard greens are a favorite not only in the Punjab but in the southern U.S. and in parts of Brazil as well. Mustard greens are a rich source of nearly all the essential vitamins, but they contain little protein. Protein is made up of amino acids, eight of which are essential to human life and growth. These essential amino acids are found in meat, dairy products, and eggs, but for those who don't eat animal products, getting all eight can be problematic—nonanimal foods must be eaten in the proper combinations to ensure that all essential amino acids are present. Such combinations are particularly important in a country like India where 85 percent of the population does not consume meat.

I learned that the amino acids found in the small amount of protein contained in mustard greens are complementary to those found in corn. When these two vegetables are eaten together, all the essential amino acids are available. Furthermore, oxalic acid, present in spinach and other greens, which ties up minerals, calcium, and iron and makes them impossible to absorb, is not found in mustard greens or turnip greens. I continually marvel at how people have developed nourishing combinations in their selection of food that not only taste good, but also promote growth and health.

When our furlough drew to an end, I was apprehensive about going back to India and I didn't understand why. I was afraid it might have something to do with the doubts I harbored about my religious calling. Though my reluctance nagged at me, I never thought to turn anywhere for help. I knew little about psychological counseling, but my impression of psychiatry was that it was hostile to religious and spiritual experience. Besides, I was convinced I was far too complex a person for a psychiatrist to understand.

I was still struggling with these feelings when Chuck and I were asked to speak to the Congregational church's couples group. Just as our presentation was about to begin, a psychiatrist from the Boulder Medical Center and his wife arrived. I felt defensive and uneasy, but we went ahead with the presentation. Before we were finished, the psychiatrist and his wife got up to leave. I figured that, at best, we had been terribly boring, at worst, we'd sounded insincere. Yet the next week when I took the children to the Boulder Medical Center for shots, I ran into the psychiatrist in the hall, and he apologized for leaving the lecture early saying that ours was the most interesting and straightforward talk about working in a foreign country that he had ever heard. Amazed at myself, I blurted out, "I need to see you professionally."

He encouraged me to make an appointment. When the day came to see him, I described my puzzling apprehension about returning to India. He asked about family, friends, and coworkers there. When I mentioned a widowed stepmother with children the same ages as mine, he smiled gently. "Kittu, you don't need psychiatric help. You just need to understand a few things about relationships."

His caring and insightful comments during the remainder of our half-hour helped me see that in the wake of my father's death, I was feeling guilty about my stepmother's hard life and felt responsible for her welfare. It was a responsibility I did not have to assume and one that was becoming increasingly burdensome, particularly since Dorothy and her children were doing fine.

In just one brief session, I came to understand that letting go would be freeing. Even more importantly, it would allow me to complete my mourning for Daddy, which I hadn't realized I was still doing—the feelings of guilt and responsibility were simply an outgrowth of my grief. As my perspective shifted, my apprehension dissolved and I found myself eager to get back to India.

Chapter Five
Moving On

We returned to India in late summer 1951 after Chuck completed his master's degree in vocational guidance. He had accepted an offer from United Christian Schools to work in the Punjab promoting the use of aptitude testing among high school students and helping their teachers understand the importance of such testing. We would be living on the new UCS campus in Sura Nussi once our new home was completed. Before Chuck could begin his duties we would need to learn Punjabi, the region's indigenous language, and we moved temporarily to Jullundur, five miles south of Sura Nussi, to begin our studies.

We shared a house with Kaz and Marion Kawata, a couple who would also be moving to Sura Nussi. The house was typical of the spacious, high-ceilinged brick bungalows built all over north India during the time of British rule. The central section included four enormous rooms—a living room, dining room, study, and bedroom, each about twenty-five feet square—that opened into each other and had small windows just beneath the ceiling to let out the hot air that had risen during the day. In warm weather, all doors were left open to improve the airflow and overhead fans hung low in the center of each room to keep the air circulating. Screens or curtains provided privacy. Other, lower-ceilinged rooms—pantry, kitchen, and additional bed, bath, and dressing rooms—had been added around this central square.

By the time we moved in, our trunks and boxes had not yet reached us. We had only our suitcases, and really needed our household belongings that had been stored in Moga. During the festival of Dussehra, which celebrates the end of the fiscal year, we had a break from our studies. So, Chuck and Kaz borrowed the school jeep and trailer and drove the eighty miles to retrieve our possessions. They planned to stay there overnight.

That night I was awakened by stealthy noises that proved to be a burglar in my bedroom. When I sat up, he fled, grabbing a typewriter on his way out. Marion and I called the servants, who found the typewriter in the bushes. The next day, the police were less than helpful. They blamed our husbands for leaving us alone unguarded and said they'd be back to question them about what really had happened. It was clear that they had no faith in a woman's ability to care for herself or to be a reliable witness.

When Woodstock School opened the following spring in March 1952, the children and I moved uphill. Dorothy and Harriet were starting second grade, and Bill and Donald were ready for kindergarten. At a Thursday morning assembly, it was gratifying to hear Principal Rhea Ewing announce, "Today, former principal Allen Parker's son and grandson start school together."

In May, Chuck came uphill and we continued our Punjabi studies at the summer language school held in Kellogg Church. We lived in a small cottage known as The Shanty that sat just below the road that circled the top of Landour Hill. The kitchen and bedrooms were strung along the hillside and connected by a glassed-in verandah that provided dining and living space. Heavy foliage surrounded us and an enormous old oak tree at one end of the building made it feel like a treehouse in the Amazon jungle. Like the other hill houses we had lived in, it was fully furnished, but this one had an oddity that set it apart from the rest: a slide from the top berth of the children's bunk bed to the bathroom door. The kids loved it.

Chuck returned to Jullundur at the end of the language school session. I stayed up in the hills with the children for the full nine months of that school year, consulting in Woodstock's kitchen about meals and menu planning. The staff had trouble getting the foods they wanted in sufficient quantity, and it was difficult to prepare dishes that tasted like home cooking for three hundred or more children. I also became a substitute teacher. For the health curriculum of one fourth grade class, I suggested we plan and carry out a feeding experiment using white rats. One group would be fed a nutritionally adequate diet while the other would, at the students' insistence, get "boarding school food." The students were convinced the latter was terrible and expected the rats to die.

The project proved engrossing for everyone. Each day, boarding students brought samples of their school meals and mixed them up for the test rats. Others fed the control rodents. The students weighed the rats and observed their general appearance with great interest. They were all surprised that those on the boarding school diet did better than those on the regular diet. I never revealed the fact that I planned the boarding school meals, but I did help the children examine how well their diet measured up to guidelines for good nutrition. We talked about how foods that didn't taste familiar might still be nutritious.

I enjoyed staying uphill as the rains ended and summer faded. Not since I'd been in high school had I been in Landour in the fall—these were the loveliest days of the year. The monsoon was over, the days clear and crisp, the air exhilarating. I relished my long walks through the bazaar. Each shop had its goods spread out in front for easy perusal. Many of the shopkeepers were old friends, so I would stop to chat, savoring frequent views of snow that peeked above or between buildings. On weekends, I took the children on long hikes, showing them the places I'd lived and played, talking about my childhood. We adopted a black and white spaniel puppy, named him Spotty, and took him downhill with us.

When we returned to Jullundur that winter, our new house in Sura Nussi still wasn't ready, but Chuck had found us temporary quarters at the edge of the mission compound. Although the house was small—quite a contrast to the huge bungalow we'd lived in before—it fronted a busy city street near the bazaar and was close to several Indian families we knew. There were plenty of children for our kids and Spotty to play with and we were comfortable. We didn't have running water—unless, we joked, we ran to the well in the center of the courtyard to collect it—but we soon discovered that well water is warmer than tap water, a welcome asset during the cold of winter.

Beggars came by each morning asking for food. At first I thought they knocked on our door because they'd heard that "rich" foreigners had moved in. Then I saw that each of our Indian neighbors daily handed out small portions of food to the beggars. I learned that this is how the poor of India are fed—by others nearly as poor. I was humbled, realizing how judgmental and arrogant my initial conclusion had been.

In the spring of 1953, we finally moved to the just-completed campus at Sura Nussi. We were ecstatic. Every staff family, Indian and European alike, was living in a brand-new dwelling, and it felt good to know the entire neighborhood was starting out on equal footing. Our new community was five miles outside Jullundur, so we all had to find ways of shopping and obtaining the services we were used to in the city. I could cycle the distance for shopping, but the Indian women were loath to do so, so we often took the bus together or, on special occasions, used the school jeep.

Chuck and I had an old Maytag washing machine with a square tub and heavy wringers. It sat on the back porch where we set up tin tubs for rinsing. We heated water in a charcoal-fed *hammam* and siphoned the water by rubber hose. Women neighbors came over to watch on wash day and often helped me hang loads of laundry out to dry. Their curiosity made me realize that they were cut off from the services of a *dhobi*, washerman, so I invited them to consider using the washing machine. Different women tried it out, bringing laundry soap and their own charcoal for the water heater. Pretty soon there were one or two families washing every day. We took turns helping each other pull clothes through the wringer and peg them on lines in the yard.

During conversations over the wringer, I learned how difficult it had been for each woman to move into the neighborhood. I frequently heard comments like "Oh, I don't really belong here. I belong in Saharanpur." It was as if they were dipping their toes into an unfamiliar body of water, quite sure they weren't going to like it. It was going to take time and some effort for us to feel like a community.

This realization really hit home for me one day when I saw my neighbor's children playing outside with no clothes on. Thinking their mother might be unwell, I went over to check on her. Embarrassed that I had found her ill in bed, she apologized for the children and the condition of her house. She obviously wanted me to leave and didn't want my help.

I stopped by the house next door and asked the woman there if she knew that Mrs. Patras was sick. "Yes," she replied, "but I haven't gone in because it would embarrass her for me to see her house in disorder."

I was stunned. "But suppose she really needs help?" I asked. "If I were sick, I'd welcome your visit to my house."

"You would?" was her astonished reply. "We thought the polite thing to do was to give her privacy."

Talks like this continued around the washing machine and in other parts of the neighborhood. The women began to plan activities together. Mrs. Jaggu, wife of the school messenger, started a women's Bible study class on Sundays, and others shared their garden produce, took in sewing, or led the neighborhood children on walks. Slowly, we all began to feel a sense of belonging.

I also enjoyed the long philosophical talks I had with our servant Lahori as we washed clothes. A self-confident and dignified Hindu, he asked me questions about Christianity. He believed that Jesus's statement "To him that hath shall more be given and from him that hath not, even that which he hath shall be taken away" seemed to be an unfair judgment on the poor. And yet he pointed out that it applied perfectly to a person's abilities. If someone had a talent and didn't use it, it became useless, whereas when used, it multiplied that person's opportunities.

I've often thought how true that is of nutrition. If we don't use the foods that are available, especially the nourishing ones, we become malnourished and our strength disappears.

Living close to Indian staff members was deeply satisfying and I loved the neighborly atmosphere we'd created together. I felt I belonged in Sura Nussi. But my heart was uneasy. Our welcome by the missionaries now in charge of the United Christian Schools campus had not been warm, and I had an unsettling premonition that we would not be in Sura Nussi for long.

All too soon it was time for Woodstock to open. This year, Dorothy and Patty took the train uphill with the rest of the school party. Dorothy would go into boarding, and Patty would live with our friends, the Alters, and start kindergarten. Bill stayed home and enjoyed having his parents all to himself. We home-schooled him for about six weeks, until mid-April, when it was time to get out of the heat. Chuck remained behind as Bill and Spotty and I made the overnight train journey to Landour. Dorothy and Patty were glad to join us in Stone Ledge, a house built by the Harpers.

The strange feeling I had about our future in educational work at Sura Nussi came uphill with me. The educational philosophy and methodology being espoused was quite different from ours, and I couldn't shake my sense of foreboding. Daily devotions didn't alleviate my unease, which told me that either my faith had let me down or somehow I hadn't worked hard enough and had let it down. This was a crippling thought, and for the first time in my life, I couldn't function. I took to my bed for several weeks.

Friends came to visit me, upset by my depression. One of them brought me Georgia Harkness's book *The Dark Night of the Soul* about Christian saints who experienced deep despondency. It was comforting to know that others had suffered in this way. The words *anxiety neurosis* jolted me into the recognition that this was exactly what I was experiencing. Being able to put a name to my condition helped me greatly. I realized I'd been assuming full responsibility for the fact that those in charge weren't happy with me and Chuck. Once I understood that I couldn't shoulder the entire burden for my family's success and happiness, the clouds seemed to clear, and I summoned the courage to go on. There were still many things I wanted to do in Landour for the sake of the children and for Woodstock.

During the short four-month summer season, the mothers provided as much extracurricular activity as possible for the schoolchildren on the hillside. We planned class parties and hikes, hobby shows, scouting activities, and, most important of all, "The Sale," an annual day-long event organized by the PTA to raise money for the school.

Each of Woodstock's cooperating missions ran a stall. Our Punjab group sold toys. We made doll clothes and brought in handmade toys from different parts of India and the U.S. We stocked puzzles and games, marbles and comic books. It was a day of fierce independence for the children. Clutching their own money, they could go where they wanted and spend it safely. In addition to the colorful, enticing stalls, there were rides and a merry-go-round, ice cream and hot dogs, and other hard-to-get foods. Ever since my own childhood, "The Sale" had been the most exciting day of the year and I wanted it to be that way for my children, too.

That summer I also enjoyed playing my violin, both in the Woodstock school orchestra and in small instrumental groups. A friend and I played Mozart duets for functions at the Community Center and on other occasions. Making music was important because we didn't have the recording instruments that are available today. Those of us who played instruments or sang were always welcome to perform, which, in turn, added to our enjoyment in creating music.

At the end of the season, Dorothy went into boarding, and I took Patty and Bill back to Sura Nussi. Chuck and I had been corresponding over the summer about the changed atmosphere in which he was working. As soon as I arrived, I could see that relations with the leadership had grown distinctly chilly. Before long, they told us that we really didn't fit their expectations and suggested we move back to Moga. My premonition had proved correct.

When word got out that we were being asked to leave, our Indian friends dropped by to tell us they would sorely miss us. They didn't understand why we were considered misfits. Their friendship was encouraging and gratifying because we didn't understand our dismissal either. It was hard to leave the new home we had enjoyed fixing up to suit our family. It was painful for me to give up my emotional investment in the community we had helped create.

The warm welcome we received in Moga upon our return in early 1954 did much to dispel the ache of breaking up the household that had seemed so promising. We were moving back into a familiar old house that we would share with friends and it would be easy for me to find ways to be useful. Though maintaining the home and caring for guests and family was usually the primary role of a missionary wife, I knew that there were many ways for us to put our training and talents to work—being involved in literacy projects and women's study groups and volunteering in church schools and hospitals. I was bolstered by the certainty that my life would become what I made of it. Making choices, I realized, nourishes the spirit.

This was an important lesson and one I was able to impart to my son the following year. At the end of the next summer season, when it came time to go downhill, nine-year-old Bill adamantly refused to go into boarding for the remainder of the school year, insisting he'd come back to Moga and study at home. I reminded him that he'd done many difficult things before and had enjoyed them because he had chosen to do them. Explaining that returning to Moga was not an option, I told him, "You *have* to go into boarding. Your only choice is in how you do it. You can be the kicking, screaming boy you say you're going to be, and that's how I'll remember you. Or you can choose some other way to act. My hunch is that boarding will be a happier place if you give it a chance than if you're determined not to be happy."

The next morning he was wearing the most pained smile I've ever seen. His brave effort tore at my heart, but I was thankful that he'd chosen to say goodbye with as much cheer as he could muster.

Our dismissal from Sura Nussi was a blessing in certain respects, freeing us to consider opportunities that otherwise would not have been available. In Moga, Chuck slipped easily into his former role of advisor to the principal, and each of us assumed responsibilities that would lighten the load of key administrators. Chuck also used his background in vocational guidance, as many organizations and institutions were interested in the training he could give. The central government's Youth Programs Department invited him to lecture and participate in many of their conferences.

Then, in the fall of 1955, we were asked by Church World Service to visit Anglo-Indian high schools in Calcutta and to consider moving there in order to widen the options of the young people enrolled there. While our three children were in boarding, we traveled to India's largest city to size up the situation. If interested, we would have to first secure permission from the church and then move there.

On our visit to Calcutta, we began to see a crucial need for Chuck's services in the Anglo-Indian community. Children of mixed English and Indian parentage were looked down upon by both groups as products of miscegenation, and jobs were hard for them to come by. For many years, the British had given Anglo-Indian youths special status that assured them employment in the rail, telegraph, and telephone systems. With the advent of Indian rule in 1947, however, this practice was extended only until 1957. After that, Anglo-Indian youths had to fend for themselves. Chuck was being invited to set up vocational guidance programs to acquaint the students with more occupational possibilities.

We headed home, eager to talk with church officials about our new project. But we ran into an unanticipated obstacle. Even though it was October and the rainy season was supposedly over, heavy rains and flooding had inundated our area of the Punjab. At Ludhiana, where we had to change trains for Moga, we discovered that no trains were running. It took us an entire day to traverse the last sixty miles by bus. Large bridges had been washed out and highway traffic was virtually at a standstill. As the male passengers got out and waded through the rivers, the women sat gingerly by the windows waiting to see whether the bus would sink into a hole.

Arriving in Moga, we found that the flood had washed through our house and left standing water three feet deep. Though the water had subsided, our furniture still showed the flood lines. The piano was ruined and the whole house smelled of decomposing matter. Kishan, our servant, had stacked clothing and perishable items on tables and carried some things up a ladder to the flat roof, covering them as best he could. We arrived just after he had put them back in place.

Village folk who lived in mud houses lost everything—even, in some instances, the seed for next year's crops stored in urns buried in the ground. The flood had been so widespread and merciless that it had crept into items that were supposedly waterproof.

Chuck worked with the local government in distributing relief goods and money. I hired a tailor to sit on our porch and make children's clothes out of all the scraps of fabric and old clothing I could find. The tailor was delighted to be given the freedom to design whatever he could out of the materials at hand. In one of the piles I gave him was an old elastic girdle. He cut off the garters and sewed on a top with sleeves and a collar. Holding it up with pride he said, "This will surely keep a child warm. And it stretches to fit any size!"

When we had a sufficiently large pile of clothes, I invited women from the school and the villages near us to select what they wanted. To make the process as fair as possible, I handed out six tickets to each, one ticket marked for a woolen piece of clothing. When they had picked out what they wanted, they redeemed their tickets for the garments. It proved to be a lighthearted day of fun, and one which brought encouragement to the women and their families.

After we had done what we could towards flood relief efforts, Chuck and I approached the Church committee with our plans to go to Calcutta for the five or six months that remained before our next furlough, scheduled for 1956. They agreed. Once the children came back downhill at the end of the school year, we set out for Calcutta, stopping in Etawah to spend Christmas with Dorothy, Harriet, and Donald.

We took up residence in an apartment across the hall from Ed and Helen Benedict, who were in charge of Church World Service relief work. Though there was no furniture, to our surprise, a furniture rental warehouse provided what we needed and delivered it to us on handcarts by nightfall.

We couldn't close the windows in our apartment, which were covered with iron bars, so we soon got used to hearing blaring radios, noisy traffic, and the calls of street vendors. The only sound we dreaded was the screech of the gorillas caged on a porch across the street. They screamed when our rented piano was played too long or too loud.

The apartment had gas burners in the kitchen and because food was easy to get, I did the cooking. But I couldn't do all the cleaning as well and asked the Church World Service office to send a woman who needed employment.

To my amazement, the woman who showed up was physically disabled. I was aghast at the thought of her getting up and down, especially when she had to scrub the floor. I was concerned for her welfare and shared my misgivings with her to which she responded, "If you don't employ me, I won't have anything to eat." She was right, but it was hard to watch her work.

In Calcutta, Chuck and I did aptitude testing in eleven high schools. Chuck worked in the boys' schools, and after he trained me, I worked with the girls. The teacher training sessions we held usually included some time for participants to get acquainted. Once, a nun from one of the Catholic schools begged me not to call it a social occasion or she and her sisters would not be allowed to attend. I also remember learning that Loretta Convent School nuns were prohibited from eating or imbibing any liquid outside their residence hall. They generously served me lemonade and cookies, but took none for themselves despite the very hot weather. I was impressed by such selflessness.

We found Calcutta's Anglo-Indian community to be a unique social unit. Its members spoke English as well as Bengali. They were all Christian, loyal to England, and among the poorest residents of the city. Those that did not get an education were forced into prostitution or some other form of vice.

Calcutta offered more culture than what we had experienced in the Punjab, including theater, concerts, museums, and historical sites. We learned how to use the bus system but marveled that anyone got anywhere with the crowded traffic lanes. This transition was hard on our children. They had never lived in a city, they didn't speak Bengali, and their friends were now scattered. So we decided to join the Calcutta Swimming Club where they would have a place to swim and play. The process of becoming members compromised many of our most important values. For example, to join, we had to show our faces and prove that we were white. Looking back, I am ashamed that we did this. I must say though, that I, who had never previously belonged to a club and knew nothing of its conveniences, had little objection to lolling luxuriously in the sun near a pool instead of riding my bicycle on a windswept road in the Punjab.

In the spring of 1956, Billy Graham's evangelistic campaign swept through Calcutta bringing together the whole Christian Community—Indian, Anglo-Indian, European, American, Catholic, and Protestant—in a way that no other Christian leader had ever done. More than 15,000 people joined in open-air evening meetings in front of the large cathedral and thousands who wished to lead a more Christian life signed up for counseling. Other Woodstock parents from mission stations outside Calcutta attended these meetings and signed up as counselors. Before they went home, several of them nonchalantly handed me cards with names and addresses of those seeking counseling, saying, "Here, Kittu, you can follow up on these. You'll be here longer than we will."

I was stunned. Certainly, people who had signed up for spiritual help deserved better. Chuck and I had not volunteered to be counselors because we knew we would be leaving in a few weeks. Still, during my time remaining there, I attempted to follow through responsibly with the cards I'd been given. Out of eight names, I located only four. Of these, only one person was sincerely interested in changing his life. This experience gave me much food for thought about evangelistic crusades.

There was a large Chinese community in Calcutta and we were eager to meet some of its members. It turned out there were three distinct groups: shopkeepers and businesspeople who had lived in India for a long time and had or were trying to get Indian citizenship; Chinese who had left their homeland and were either headquartered in Taiwan or were building another identity, taking on French, British, or Dutch citizenship; and mainland Chinese who were representing their Communist government abroad. Even families were divided in their loyalties, and I was reminded of the American Civil War where brother fought brother.

Despite these divisions, Calcutta had an Evangelical Chinese Christian church that met in an office building and offered two sets of

Sunday services—one in the morning for Chinese businesspeople and expatriates and one in the afternoon for Communist Chinese. Pastor Lam walked a razor's edge ministering to both congregations, but he was a good mediator and was trusted by everyone.

He set up projects he hoped would serve the needs of and foster goodwill among Calcutta's entire Chinese population. One of them was a night school for children who worked days in Chinatown's laundries and restaurants. He asked me to teach English two nights a week. I was happy to oblige. I could tell which children were from Communist Chinese families because they wouldn't look at me nor respond to my questions, having been instructed by their parents not to communicate with Europeans. I could only hope they were getting something out of my lessons.

After one evening class, I joined Chuck at a party hosted by a U.N. representative. The guests looked interesting and I enjoyed mingling. Among them, I spotted a Chinese woman I hoped to meet. Yet my heart sank when I realized I didn't know what "kind" of Chinese she was. I was telling someone about the night school and raised my voice so that she might hear me say I taught Chinese students. She rose to the bait and came over to ask me more about it. It turned out that she and her husband were American-born Chinese working in Calcutta for the National Geographic Society. She asked whether I could help her meet the "right kind" of Chinese—in her mind, non-Communists. So I introduced her to the Dutch couple we knew and discovered that the two couples had recently sat next to each other at the movies but had been afraid to speak, not knowing which group the other belonged to.

In May 1956, we set out for the States on furlough. Our route this time took us through Paris to Copenhagen. We'd been told that hotel rooms in the Danish capital were scarce, so we agreed to take rooms in a private home.

Our hostess, Mrs. Barfred, met us in a taxi, which magically turned into a pumpkin coach delivering us to her palace. Cannons at the door, parquet floors, beautiful ceiling murals, and glimmering chandeliers transported us to another world. Even the children stepped lightly and looked respectfully at the resplendent surroundings.

As soon as we settled in, Mrs. Barfred regaled us with fascinating stories. Though she was related to the Danish royal family, she didn't like to spend summers at the beach with them, preferring instead to invite guests from the travel agency lists to stay with her. She vowed that George Washington himself had slept in the big bed in her room. But my favorite memory of our delightful stay is coming in after a long, dusty day of sightseeing to be served tea from her silver tea set. We hated to say farewell.

When we arrived in Boulder, Colorado, Chuck enrolled in a doctoral program in vocational guidance. Because he was a graduate student, we were allotted a small cabin, cheap and not insulated, in Chautauqua Park, not far from the University of Colorado campus. Now that Dorothy was in junior high and Bill and Patty were both in elementary school, I knew they'd need chauffeuring to various sports and social activities. Like it or not, I'd have to learn to drive again. It had been many years since I'd driven a car. I was nervous at the prospect and procrastinated about taking lessons, telling myself we could ill-afford the $35 fee for drivers' education. But when friends sent us a $35 check designated for child care expenses, I knew the time had come.

When my driving instructor suggested we start out on country roads, I was quite worried, as my grandfather had taught me to drive in the middle of a field. But, as my instructor pointed out, how often would I be driving in a field?

Finally, I graduated to city driving. When we headed downtown, I made a momentous error in taking a left turn, tying up traffic on all sides. Panic-stricken, I begged him to bail me out of my predicament, but he forced me to do it myself, saying, "This way, you'll never do it again."

My confidence was shaken, and as the date for my driver's test approached, I grew more and more anxious. I went down to the Department of Motor Vehicles to ask a few questions, and to my delight, they took one look at my old Ohio license and issued me a new one without administering a test. My instructor was furious. For the rest of my life, I've somehow managed to avoid taking a road test. I never made that same mistake again though.

We stayed on furlough an extra year so Chuck could complete his degree. Moving to a larger cabin helped us feel less cramped, but we had to swathe the back porch with plastic sheeting so Dorothy could sleep there in winter; even so, the snow drifted in on her. I don't quite know how we managed financially, for it was a year without salary. To make ends meet, Chuck and I did Christian education work in the Congregational Church. I spoke frequently, in Colorado and its neighboring states, earning $5 to $10 per talk. Even the children pitched in—Dorothy babysat, Bill mowed lawns and shoveled snow, and Patty sold greeting cards. We ate frugally. I discovered that frozen chicken hearts were only 29 cents a pound so I used them frequently.

That Christmas, we couldn't afford a tree, but when Patty and Bill noticed that the school janitor had thrown out the tree from the

Christmas program, they dragged it home and set it up to surprise the rest of us. We were all delighted. When the church sent us a basket of groceries though, the children were offended that others considered us worthy of charity. They pointed to food they had wrapped themselves, saying indignantly, "We're not poor! We gave those cans to feed the hungry."

At the end of our second year, we had to take stock. Chuck would not complete his degree until August, but the children wanted to return to Woodstock as soon as their Boulder school session ended. We agreed that Chuck would stay on in Colorado while the children and I returned to India.

In June 1958, we bade Chuck a tearful farewell and flew to Delhi, stopping in New York and Paris on the way. From Delhi, we went straight to Mussoorie where Chuck joined us three months later. We put the children in boarding and went downhill to Jullundur, a central location from which Chuck could carry out his work in vocational guidance.

Chuck visited high schools across the Punjab and collected data on the Christian students, but what he really wanted to do was hold teacher training seminars in our home. He had a coworker make contact with various schools and he began planning. By extending our table, we could seat fifteen, providing an excellent opportunity for conversation that would bring the diverse attendees together. This all seemed fine with me at the time. I would have a chance to participate informally in the training process and get to know the teachers.

Yet I soon found myself worn out. It was all too easy for me to respond to calls for help from Chuck and others, neglecting my own needs in the process. I woke one morning without any interest in the day's events and was tempted to stay in bed. Instead, I began thinking about little projects I'd enjoy working on even though they seemed trivial. Then it occurred to me that if I got even one of them done, the day would not be wasted.

I launched into making covers for the toaster oven and other appliances, and magically, my listlessness vanished. Ever since, those pretty covers have reminded me that it is all right to take enjoyment in small pastimes. The day's most important lesson, however, was that I needed to pursue my own interests, nurture my own dreams. Though this seed took root that day, it would take many years to fully flower.

I also took great pleasure in visiting members of the Dutt family, who lived nearby, dropping in to take tea. In cool weather, it was served outside and a stream of people came and went. Mrs. Dutt, a motherly figure, was always willing to lend an ear and offer good advice.

The United Church of Northern India's synod meetings were held annually on our compound in Jullundur, and because our children were in boarding at Woodstock, our extra rooms were earmarked for delegates. Dr. Nazir Tallubudin, one of the church's respected leaders and a good friend of my father's, was usually billeted to our home. When I brought him morning tea, he would pat my head and tell me I was a good daughter. But he got angry at me when I didn't agree with some of the conference proceedings and told me my father would be disappointed. It was a strange, conflicted relationship. I loved him as one who had been meaningful to Daddy, but he seemed to care only whether I upheld what my father would have believed in and obviously had appointed himself the interpreter of what that might be.

One afternoon, when we were visiting with friends camped in the village of Narangwal near Ludhiana, an American woman doctor at the clinic there asked if I'd like to watch a baby's birth. Though I'd borne three children, I'd never actually witnessed a birth, so I jumped at the chance. She asked the woman's permission and called me in about ten minutes before delivery. I watched transfixed as the baby's head appeared. Then next thing I knew, there was not only new life, but new light in the room. With proper medical care, this new mother had brought a healthy, vibrant child into the world, and viewing the miracle only reaffirmed my commitment to helping women strengthen the next generation through nourishing their own bodies. A precious gift had been given to me and I went away in awe.

Since we first arrived in India in 1948, I'd been in correspondence with Prema. Her husband had been the Maharajah of Orissa until Indian independence, when the native states had been disbanded and the former rulers became members of the Upper House of the Indian Parliament. When Parliament was in session, Prema and her family lived in Delhi. I saw her only once. We chatted for hours about our lives, our mates, and how we had come to marry them. Though her marriage had been arranged and I had been "forced" to find my own husband, we decided we were both happy with the results.

In 1959, we began to hear rumblings of Chinese military activity in Tibet and could hardly believe that China would undermine that great Buddhist country. Yet, that same year, the Dalai Lama was forced to flee. He escaped to India, coming to Mussoorie at the invitation of the Indian government, and set up temporary headquarters. Woodstock School invited him to make an official visit, and Dorothy, now a senior, was among the small group who served him tea. That meeting had a long-lasting, spiritual effect on her.

All too soon it was time for her to graduate. I was terribly proud—she was class salutatorian—yet my heart ached for her. Like me, she had not had an easy time. There were classmates who were envious of the honors she'd won.

When Dorothy left us for college in June 1960, I relived my own heart-wrenching departure as I kissed her fondly and bid her goodbye. She was traveling to the States with the Sauers, a family we'd known since our Sura Nussi days. By mid-July we began looking for cabled confirmation of their arrival. On July 20, we welcomed the telegraph messenger, assuming he brought good news. But once we noticed the envelope had multiple stars, we knew that it contained a message of death. With trembling hands, Chuck opened it and pulled out the telegram. It was from his brother Bill and read, simply, "YOUR DAUGHTER FINE STOP MY SON KILLED."

The news was shocking. And because there were no phone connections, it would be at least ten days before we received any details. Eventually, we learned Bill's son had fallen into a culvert during a flash flood, hit his head and died instantly. His death was devastating for Dorothy, who had been looking forward to getting acquainted with him, and this loss, along with the death of her high school roommate, cast a pall over her first semester at college. I missed her and worried about her as she coped with all the changes in her life, yet there was little I could do.

Though I'd never spent any part of the summer in the heat, I decided to go downhill with Chuck in August. I didn't like being away from him for months on end. Patty and Bill could live temporarily with friends or go into boarding. When I got down to Jullundur, I discovered that summertime custom was liberating; it decreed an extended repose after lunch. It was wonderful to have no callers, no interruptions until tea time. Afternoons stretched out luxuriously, and I spent hours reading beneath the large ceiling fan until it was time to go visit the Dutts. I devoured books about people who had overcome adversity—their inspiring tales influenced my life and later prompted me to write my own story.

While Chuck continued his work in vocational guidance, I served as a nutrition consultant to many institutions. I helped improve home economics and nutrition curricula and offered suggestions about feeding programs. At both the University of Lucknow and Baring Union College in the Punjab, I became an outside examiner for courses in nutrition, setting the exams and grading the papers. In addition, the Christian hospitals in Ferozepore and Ludhiana asked me to teach nutrition to their nurses.

There were several dietary changes people could make to improve nutrition without any additional expenditure—for instance, eating a variety of grains such as rice, corn, millet, and wheat. In addition, combining different types of lentils would make it more likely that all essential amino acids were present in the diet. Choosing orange-colored or leafy green vegetables would increase vitamin A consumption. I particularly encouraged the use of turnip and mustard greens.

Word must have circulated that I had a nutrition message. One day, a zealous woman from the Indian Red Cross drove up to our house with a challenge in mind.

"You're a trained nutritionist, you've been here in the Punjab for many years, and you even know the language. But you've never volunteered to help the Red Cross. How would you like to help us now?"

Indeed, I'd never been approached by her group. She wanted me to help her organize lectures on nutrition for village women.

"Do they really want a lecture?" I asked dubiously.

"You're belittling the village woman," she shot back, misunderstanding the intent of my question. "You're saying she can't understand lectures. I'll show you that she can. The jeep will be here Wednesday at 11:30 A.M. to take us to Goroya. Is that satisfactory?"

It had to be. My only choice lay in how I presented the "lecture." Though I agreed that village women needed information, I didn't think a formal speech was the right way to deliver it. I decided I'd show her something about getting women to listen.

The jeep bounced us along rutted roads, across rough fields, around muddy ponds, and through herds of cattle before we reached the village and stopped under a large, shady banyan tree whose roots hung down from outstretched branches. Cotton rugs had been spread out below for people to sit on. It was about 1 P.M., and the women were arriving from their morning's work in the fields.

"While they're washing up and getting ready, you can set up your lecture materials on this table," instructed my hostess. "Here's a chair for you."

"Thank you, but I'd rather sit on the ground," I replied. "I'll need a *charpai* to hold my materials though."

She told her driver to get one of those portable rope beds from the courtyard of a nearby house, watching with curiosity as I set the cot on its side and created a makeshift demonstration board by draping a white flannel sheet over it.

When the women began to gather, I was seated on the ground dressed in Punjabi attire—baggy pants, long shirt, and a *chadoor*, or veil, around my shoulders. The Red Cross lady introduced me as a missionary from Jullundur and gave my academic credentials. The women, as I expected, were indifferent. They were present in body, wearing clean, full skirts, short bodices, and veils, but they were distracted. Their minds were still on their children, some of whom were nestling up to breast-feed.

But when they found I could speak Punjabi, they started to listen and plied me with questions about where I lived, where my husband was, how many sons I had, what America was like, and whether my daughters were married. I responded in kind then said I was ready to ask *them* some questions.

"What do you eat?" I began.

They laughed. "You know very well what we eat. *Chappatis, dal,* and vegetables. We eat that every day."

As they spoke, I put up pictures I'd cut out or drawn of *chappati, dal,* and vegetables. I checked with the women to make sure each picture correctly depicted the foods they were talking about. Soon we were engrossed in a lively conversation about how they made their bread, which vegetables they raised, and which lentils they ate during which season. India's bazaars are colorfully laden with fifteen or so different kinds of dry lentils. Among them are black, white, green, pink, and yellow lentils. They were pleased when I told them that, nutritionally speaking, the combination of whole grain bread, a variety of lentils, and vegetables is among the best in the world.

Then I asked how much food the women actually consume? I knew that men and boys were fed first, then girls and women. My audience admitted that there were times during the year, especially before spring harvest, when food was scarce and females, younger and older, got very little to eat.

"What can you do about it?" I asked. "You are all mothers and you have babies. And you know that making a baby takes more than sex." Here, there were some titters as a young mother drew her *chadoor* over her mouth and glanced at the other women. "It takes extra food to build the baby, more food than you need for just yourself to keep the baby from draining your body."

They admitted this was true, though they'd never thought about it that way. After talking among themselves, they agreed to remind each other to eat enough. It would take some plotting to withhold food for themselves.

Next we talked about weaning and what they gave their infants when they took them off the breast. Some women had good ideas about using soft-cooked lentils. Others said they waited until the toddler could fend for himself or herself before they were weaned. Again, there was lively discussion, exchange of ideas, and agreement that special effort was needed to make sure the toddler was well fed and had a good start in life.

I knew that an important source of village income came from the sale of surplus milk and that there wasn't much saved for home consumption. The women were probably using as much as they could afford to keep for making yogurt and for their tea. I mentioned that children need milk to grow, but it was no use belaboring the point. So I went back to the topic of vegetables. It was here that the women could make the biggest difference by increasing their use of bright-colored vegetables, thereby upping their intake of vitamin A.

Using two strips of colored cloth, I laid the green strip across the bottom of my flannel board and the orange one across the top, with the white sheet showing between.

"There! What does the board look like now?" I asked.

"Our national flag," they called out.

"So, let's talk about being strong for your country," I suggested, asking them to call out the different vegetables they ate. As they did so, I placed pictures of carrots and pumpkins on the orange section, cauliflower and turnips on the white section, and greens—turnip, mustard, and spinach—on the green section at the bottom of the "flag." I pointed out that the bright green and yellow vegetables were the most nutritious, so it would be a good idea to plant, cook, and eat more of them.

As far as I was concerned, mustard greens were the most valuable vegetable they ate. They laughed. Though they liked mustard greens and ate them with flat unleavened cornbread, they were so common that it was difficult for them to believe this food was anything special. We spent the remainder of our time discussing how they cooked the greens and how often they ate them. My suggestion was to cook them less than three hours to preserve nutrients and to eat them as often as possible.

It was hard to bring the session to a close and get away. They wanted me to come back.

"You were very successful," my hostess commented as the jeep bounced and jolted us back to the city. "Can you go to another village next week?"

Reluctantly, I agreed. I had enjoyed the interaction with the women, but it had taken a whole day out of my busy schedule. I didn't have many free days, and eventually, I think I ended up "lecturing" on six of them.

Some months later we took friends to visit the newly built Nangal-Bakhra Dam. We were without transport but a guide kindly arranged for us to take local transport to the bus station. He put me and our women guests on a "women's" bus and the men on a "men's" bus. As I stood in the aisle, I was surprised to hear the women behind me yelling to get my attention. I wondered what was going on, speculating that they'd never seen a foreigner before. But I was wrong, for just then, one of them grabbed my elbow.

"Turn around and look over here," she said excitedly.

"Well, who are you?" I asked, turning around.

"We're from Goroya," the passengers yelled. Then I knew why they were excited and joined the fun.

"Goroya, where's that?" I teased.

"You know very well. You were there," was the reply.

"I was?" I asked innocently. "Why?"

"To speak about nutrition," they called out in unison.

"Nutrition! What did I say?"

With a single breath they shouted, "Eat mustard greens!"

"How often?" I asked. We were all howling with laughter now as they chanted, "Once a day, twice a day, three times a day!" I have never had such positive confirmation that my "lectures" had been heard and remembered.

I accompanied Chuck to help him with his work when the government Youth Programs department sent him throughout India to speak at youth training camps. Chuck had a wonderful sense of humor and both teachers and young people enjoyed his presentations. Our travels took us to many places, among them Kashmir—I'd never been to the region before and was astounded at its beauty. From Dal Lake, where we spent a few days on a houseboat, to the camp in the high forests just beneath snowy peaks, it was breathtaking. By day, we hiked into the mountains with the campers, enjoying our packed lunches and stunning views of the Himalayas. At night we would sit around the campfire mesmerized by the youth's drumming and singing.

When our third furlough came up in June 1962, Patty and Bill pleaded to remain at Woodstock, so Chuck and I left them in boarding and flew off to the States, stopping first in Thailand and then Hawaii, where we rented a house for several weeks on the leeward side of Oahu. We were looking forward to spending time with my cousin Verlene and her husband, as well as our daughter Dorothy who was flying in for a visit. She had recently hurt her back building a water tank with some college friends at a children's school in Kentucky and she was in a great deal of pain. After our long separation, I found it as difficult to connect with her as it had been for my mother to connect with me when I was in college. I felt awkward and inadequate but took solace in being able to care for her and ease her pain, at least temporarily.

While we were on Oahu, Chuck went to see a former professor who was now head of the Department of Vocational Guidance at the University of Hawaii. When he came back to the car where I was waiting, he had a strange look on his face. He'd been asked to teach there the coming year and didn't know what to make of the invitation. I could tell he was enthused by the possibility but knew we'd have to confer with our mission board before responding.

From Hawaii, we flew to Seattle for a reunion with my sisters and their families. Dorothy accompanied us, but after the first day, she flew on to Berkeley, California to be rehospitalized for her back injury. I worried about her until word came through from the Presbyterian Board that we could accept the job offer in Hawaii. Then I jumped on a plane to join her in California while Chuck headed off to Oklahoma for a brief visit with his mother.

Dorothy and I moved into the missionary courts where we had stayed when she was a baby. Although she was getting daily physiotherapy, her recovery was slow. She couldn't sit properly to play the organ, and if she couldn't perform the mandatory recital, it would be impossible to complete her music degree.

Reluctantly, Dorothy decided to transfer from Western College in Ohio. I suggested she apply to the University of Colorado at Boulder where she might qualify for in-state tuition. When she was accepted, Chuck and I helped her get settled, then flew off to Oahu.

After we had unpacked our belongings at one of the faculty apartments, I bought a muumuu and took long strolls, often stopping to gaze at gardens full of flowers like those in India. Wanting to know more about them, I picked up a book on botany, learned their names, and became more familiar with these beautiful creations of nature. Those blissful days of unstructured wandering remain cherished in my heart as some of the freest I've ever known.

In early December 1962, Patty and Bill sent details about their upcoming flight from Delhi. The last twelve hours before their plane was due to land I couldn't sleep. I cleaned and cooked and baked and thought of them flying over the Pacific. In the morning, when I called to confirm their arrival time, I was told there had been a delay and they hadn't even left Bangkok. We still had a fifteen-hour wait to live through. Even after they'd landed in Honolulu, Chuck and I had to watch them go through customs before we could grab them in our arms and hug them tightly. At Christmas, Dorothy joined us briefly and our family was joyously complete again until each went back to school.

While we were in Honolulu, Dr. A. C. Joshi, chancellor of the University of Punjab, was lecturing at the University of Hawaii. He and Chuck had many lively conversations, and eventually, he invited Chuck to set up a vocational guidance training program in Chandigarh where the university was located. This set off a renewed flurry of conversations with our mission board, but again, they were willing to let us do this.

Before we returned to India, I needed to complete some speaking engagements at our supporting churches on the mainland, so I left Hawaii early in May. My first stop was Boulder, where I would also see Dorothy.

We had left our old Chevy with her and one day, while Dorothy was in class, I drove into Denver. Unfortunately, I lost control of the car due to faulty brakes. As the car swerved left into oncoming traffic, I lay down across the front seat which saved my life when a car crashed into me. Though no one was seriously hurt, the car was totaled. A friend helped me through the police proceedings and drove me back to Boulder.

For some reason, I didn't want to tell Dorothy about the accident. That evening I simply said that I'd left the car in Denver. She insisted on going with me to pick it up, so we played out the whole scenario of taking the bus to Denver and a taxi to the junkyard where the true situation finally became clear.

We still talk about that day and why I felt compelled to hide the truth. Many years later, all I can conclude is that I was pained at having so little time with her and distressed that we were unable to communicate easily. Perhaps I was afraid she would think me even more incompetent. It was heartwrenching to leave her knowing it would be two more years before I saw her again.

Back in India, I went to Woodstock to take Bill, now a senior and Patty, a junior, out of boarding. Bill was on the basketball team and a member of the school orchestra. His graduation was postponed for a few days due to the death of Prime Minister Jawaharlal Nehru on June 5, 1964. When Bill left for Swarthmore College in Pennsylvania at the end of the summer, Patty was the only chick left in the nest and she missed her brother terribly. She threw herself into track and field, representing the school and the district in the Indian Olympics where she acquitted herself very well.

Down on the plains, Chuck and I moved to Chandigarh, the then-new capital city of Punjab built by the famous French architect Le Corbusier. Chandigarh snuggles up to the first rise of the Himalayas and is on the train line from Delhi to Simla, the former summer capital of the British. Dr. Joshi arranged staff housing for us in the university sector and asked me to act as hostess for visitors to the nearby guest house, where I found the cook had previously worked at Woodstock and had known my father. In the guest house garden, I could enjoy roses as well as gorgeous bougainvillea cascading from the roof. We could also use the facility when guests overflowed our own lodgings, which were small though the floor space was augmented by four private patios.

We purchased an Indian car with the money the Presbyterian Board had set aside from our furlough salary during Chuck's tenure in Hawaii. We now really needed this mode of travel. The city had been planned in sectors, some of which had been completed, but there were still miles of empty space in between. With a car, we'd be able to drive our many guests around to see the beautiful government buildings and the overall plan of the new city.

When we ordered the car, the dealer told us we'd have to wait for it to be driven up from Calcutta. I went to claim it as soon as I heard that a new fleet of vehicles had been driven in only to be told that ours had not yet arrived. But I had anticipated such an obstacle. The dealer knew we were paying in dollars and had highest priority, and he thought that, by delay, he could get an impatient American to offer a tip. He was not prepared for me to sit down, take out my knitting, and wait. Finally, by the end of the afternoon, he admitted that there was an unclaimed car and told me I could have it.

Our servant Lahori, who had worked for us in Sura Nussi, moved to Chandigarh to be with us. One day, when I saw him fixing his usual *chappati* and *dal* on our stove, I suggested he eat some of the leftover food he had prepared for us. He replied firmly, "Memsahib, you don't understand. If I eat your food and get sick, I can't work and can't support my family. We who are poor can't afford to take chances." That made me pause. I thought my offer might help, but it didn't seem that way to him. In his view, eating the unfamiliar foods he cooked for us might be risky.

Oddly enough, there was another family of Riddles in Chandigarh and we were good friends: Doug, the son of New Zealand Presbyterian missionaries had gone to Woodstock with me. His wife, Marion, was recovering from breast cancer surgery. They had three young daughters. The Riddles were preparing to go on furlough, and when Chuck received an invitation to lecture in Hawaii, he arranged his travel plans so he could accompany them as far as Delhi. A series of mix-ups soon began. At the bank in Chandigarh, Chuck asked for traveler's checks and was presented with checks in English pounds. He had to wave Doug over to his window to claim them and then insist on checks in dollars for himself. At Delhi's YMCA guest house, they got each other's calls. To the general public, it just didn't seem possible that there could be two foreign men bearing the same last name, answering to the same description, and living in the same Indian city.

Sending Chuck off, I felt uneasy. He was going halfway around the world—how did I know if he would return in two weeks as he said he would? I heard nothing from him during his absence but went down to the station to meet the bus he'd said he'd be on. When he stepped off it, I was so relieved, I cried. It seemed miraculous that he'd actually made all the right connections. The date was November 23, 1962, and we had no inkling of the news that would greet us the next morning.

We slept late. Finally, Lahori knocked on the door and handed us the paper. Huge headlines shouted "PRESIDENT KENNEDY SHOT." We could hardly take in the tragedy. Then Lahori told us that people had come to offer their sympathy. We were seemingly the last to know. A university official called a few moments later to tell us that a minute of silence would be observed in President Kennedy's honor on the parade ground at 11 A.M., but he said he'd understand if we were too grief-stricken to attend. Of course we attended, both amazed that the entire university was mourning the death of our president and abashed at being the recipients of condolences.

The next year, Doug and Marion Riddle returned to Chandigarh and their work in the United Church. Marion was sure she was in remission from her cancer and we planned many outings with our girls. Then in early March, we put them on the train to Woodstock with the rest of the school party. After kissing them goodbye, Marion turned to me and explained that she'd been coughing recently but didn't think much of it. Within a few days, however, she was admitted to the hospital. When I went to visit her, she was on oxygen but seemed all right. A few hours later, Marion died.

Completely unprepared for the news, weeping and mournful, I went to their house and experienced something I'd never encountered: the whole house shone. In the living room, the brass and copper pieces she had polished so lovingly now gave off light. I could feel her presence as if she were touching each piece and saying goodbye, leaving behind a special illumination and radiance. I told her girls about it when I drove with a friend up to Woodstock to get them for the funeral.

As with all deaths in India, Marion's funeral and burial had to be held within twenty-four hours. The church was overflowing with high government dignitaries, the whole foreign community, and, of course, all the Christians. In death, Marion had brought together under one roof a melange of people who under other circumstances would never have mixed. I wasn't ready for the shock on their faces when they saw me. Evidently, the Riddle wives were mixed up in people's minds and many thought it was I who had died.

In his visits to high schools around the Punjab, Chuck had identified a boy, Victor Masih, who needed medical attention, so he brought him to the Post-Graduate Medical College in Chandigarh for examination. It turned out that Victor needed a corneal transplant. When the time came for his surgery, he went into the hospital, and his mother, Sardaran, came to stay with us. One morning, she asked for oil for her hair, and I, busy with chores, snapped, "If you'd only asked a few minutes ago before Lahori went to the bazaar, he could have gotten it." She replied, "You have no reason to be angry at me. I have nothing."

Her reproof struck home. With all the bounty of my own life, I had no cause to be cross. And though she had little in terms of material wealth, she possessed a clarity and a fearlessness I envied.

Several days later, Sardaran showed an American student where to catch the bus and returned to tell me that the woman needed a chaperone to prevent the catcalls and rude remarks of Indian men. The American thought she had been brave and independent in facing the streets alone, not realizing that in Indian culture, young, unattended females are considered deserving targets of lewd talk and behavior. After her husband was killed building a railway bridge, the meager allotment she got didn't go far. Bravely, she took her boys back to her own village (it was unheard of for a widow to leave her in-laws) and worked hard in the fields to raise them. In the hospital situation, though she didn't understand surgery, she followed instructions meticulously, holding her son's bandaged head still and keeping him amused. But, one day she told me, "The operation didn't work." Amazed, I asked how she knew. "I can sense it," was her reply. She was right and the transplant didn't take, but she was able to say to Victor, "Never fear, God's will for your healing *will* be done. We'll bring you back." The next surgery was successful. Her firm, Christian faith kept her steady throughout.

Shortly after becoming active in the Faculty Wives Club, I found I was the subject of some controversy. A new female faculty member from Russia was expected and the other members wondered whether I, as an American, would snub her. Of course, I was as glad as they were to welcome her and we became friends. On the day Russia first put a man into space, I braved the cold rain to walk over to her house and congratulate her. She was delighted that I had come and invited me into her home, offering me vodka.

Our last winter in India, I put together the fifth edition of *The Landour Cookbook of International Recipes* that had first been printed in my mother's time for the reading club at Landour Community Center. It was published by the mission press, ten miles away at Kharar. Their messenger would cycle over with the proofs and wait patiently while I corrected them. It got dark early, and sometimes when electricity was out, I had to work by candlelight. Though the recipes are wonderful, the errors are many.

When Chuck and I were getting ready to leave Chandigarh in May 1965, the faculty women gave me a farewell lunch and each prepared something from the cookbook. I nearly fainted when I was asked to identify the dishes—they all looked so unfamiliar. I saw a large, flat, circular, green and white, crusty concoction, and I guessed wildly, asking, "Who made pizza?"

A woman ran up to me and said, "Oh, I'm so glad you recognized it. Your cookbook included information about making substitutions. I couldn't find your kind of cheese, so I used cottage cheese, and there were no tomatoes, so I used peas. Does it taste like pizza?" I assured her that though her pizza was good it was not Italian pizza without tomatoes.

In 1965 we left India for the last time. Some years later, I came upon these sentences in my journal. "The hardest thing I do each day is to go out the gate of our house. I walk to the bazaar for supplies, or run other errands, but sometimes I ride a cycle rickshaw or take my own bicycle. Any way I do it puts me face to face with beggars, with dire poverty, with the homeless who live in the open. That is the India I both love and find hard to live in."

Chuck and I felt that the work we had started there was left in good hands. The Indian Church definitely had a stronger leadership, not because of what we had done, but because it had wrestled successfully and realistically with its own internal problems. Chuck and I said our farewells to friends and coworkers in Chandigarh, Jullundur, and Moga, then headed up to Landour to be with Patty in the last few weeks before her graduation.

When the great day came and the seniors began marching down the aisle to the "Pilgrims' March" from Mendelssohn's Italian symphony, I sat lost in nostalgia. Thirty years ago, I had marched with my class down this same aisle, taking steps to the same music. As it was three decades ago, graduation was held in Parker Hall, named after my father. Mother herself had supervised the making of the brown velvet stage curtains and had them embroidered in gold. Now

Chuck and I would be leaving India, leaving behind this heritage that stretched back a full generation.

As much as I would miss India, however, I realized it was time to go, not only for our sake, but for Woodstock's and India's as well. As long as there were foreign missionaries, even fraternal worker relationships such as ours, India would never become truly independent. I, too, needed to move on—to seek out new challenges and dreams, to fully become myself. Now that my children were grown, I could finally, tentatively, take some steps out on my own.

When the graduation ceremony was over, I received elated hugs from Patty and her classmates who whispered in my ear the joyful refrain, "We made it!"

I looked at them fondly, proud of their accomplishment, and smiled to myself, thinking, *Yes. I made it, too.*

Chapter Six
Home Economics Specialist to the World

This was my second farewell to the land of my birth. I wept with dear friends whom I probably would never see again and drank in familiar scenes, storing up memories. Exhausted from packing our belongings, selling our household goods, and making provisions for servants, I realized I desperately needed rest.

I urged Chuck and Patty to begin sightseeing in the Middle East while I holed up in Ankara, Turkey at the home of some dear friends from China days. I spent several lazy days on a lawn chair in their beautiful garden allowing my spirit to catch up with my body. Soon, I was ready to join Chuck and Patty in Greece for the remainder of our journey across Europe and on to the U.S.

When we arrived in New York, Bill and Dorothy met us and we all spent several weeks in Boston while Chuck taught summer classes at Northeastern University. He suggested I find an apartment on Long Island, New York near Queens College, where he would begin teaching in September. Because we'd resigned from the Presbyterian Board when we decided to stay in the States permanently, the church would no longer be making arrangements for us as it had for the past twenty years. With no experience at house hunting, I found the prospect somewhat intimidating, yet I welcomed the challenge.

I decided on a two-bedroom unit in LeFrak City, a huge apartment complex between LaGuardia Airport and Queens College. Soon after we moved in, Chuck and I debated how we would care for his aging mother who needed help with her daily activities. Should we invite her to live with us, or should I get a job and use the extra money to support her in an assisted-care facility? The choice wasn't easy, but ultimately the decision was mine—either way my life would change substantially. I knew that if she moved in with us, I'd spend most of my time cooped up in the apartment, an idea I didn't relish. So I opted to find a job.

Like many women, I didn't know the value of my own skills. I didn't realize that my master's degree and my years of experience might be valuable in the marketplace. All I could see was that my teaching certificate was out of date and my only experience was in Chinese and Indian schools.

The most logical place for me to start job hunting was the Interchurch Center on Riverside Drive in Manhattan where the National Council of Churches and many Protestant overseas missionary endeavors were headquartered. I planned to ask about a secretarial position, but Gertrude Nyce, a friend from India, told me that the Council's Agricultural Missions was seeking a home economist with my qualifications and background. Members of the Agricultural Missions department worked to improve agricultural and home science practices in church projects around the world, which was something that interested me.

Excited that my talents might actually be put to use, I interviewed with Benton Rhoades, the Agricultural Missions' pleasant and energetic director. He explained the growing need worldwide to strengthen services for rural women to help them provision their families with food. He asked how I would respond to this need and, after listening to my recommendations, offered me the job. I immediately accepted. I was thrilled! I knew that what I'd be doing there would both challenge and fascinate me.

I looked forward to consulting with church-based women's projects in developing nations and traveling to those countries to help secure funding and resources from international or government agencies and educational institutions. It would be an opportunity to work across denominational lines, and, as it turned out, across ecumenical lines—as we worked closely with Maryknoll, an overseas mission arm of the Catholic Church.

First, I was asked to conduct a survey for the Division of Overseas Ministries of the National Council of Churches. They wanted to know how much money the Protestant churches invested to eliminate hunger. For several months, I worked with the research department, creating and discarding version after version of the survey questionnaire. I was delighted—and amazed—when the copy I sent to the department's director for critique was approved to go to press. I breathed a huge sigh of relief. We were ready to proceed.

It didn't take long to mail out the questionnaire and results soon began pouring in. We heard from more than 90 percent of the denominations and found that the average budgetary allocation for alleviating hunger was 5 percent, about what we'd expected. There were, of course, many other interesting findings. The results of this survey were published under the title *Food with Dignity* and distributed by the Council to all its member churches. Later, the

Catholic Church used this same questionnaire to survey its own missionary groups.

Agricultural Missions worked closely with the International Extension Service Division of the U.S. Department of Agriculture (USDA) and I found myself in frequent contact with two wonderful home economists there, Helen Strow and Sue Murray. Benton Rhoades suggested I talk to Helen and Sue about ways we could use the information gathered in the hunger survey to improve the delivery of nutritional health services to church institutions abroad.

Getting to Washington, D.C. to consult with Sue and Helen was easy. LaGuardia Airport, where I caught the Eastern Airlines shuttle, was closer than my Manhattan office. Within an hour, I was in Washington and a taxi to the USDA's offices took five minutes. Many a workday found me there rather than Riverside Drive.

At this time, Dr. Charles Glenn King, past president of the International Union of Nutrition Sciences and one of the discoverers of vitamin C, serendipitously approached Benton, asking if he could help us in our work. Dr. King suggested forming an advisory Task Force on Women's Participation in Rural Development. Dr. King would serve as chair, and top nutritionists with international experience would be invited to join. Three were from United Nations agencies: Dr. Mary Ross of the FAO (Food and Agriculture Organization), Dr. Bertlyn Bosley of WHO (World Health Organization), and Dr. Les Tepley of UNICEF (United Nations International Children's Education Fund). Helen and Sue suggested inviting Dr. Mary Eagan, a nutritionist with the U.S. Children's Bureau, and Martha Sismanedes, a nutritionist with USAID (U.S. Agency for International Development). I, in turn, invited Dr. Ruth Leverton, who was now associate director of the USDA, Dr. Clara Mae Taylor, a nutrition educator at Teacher's College, Columbia University, and Dr. Mary Wood from Cornell University. Sister Mary Alma Erhardt, who had been appointed by Maryknoll to work with me on projects to improve women's lives, served with me as staff personnel.

At each meeting, I shared requests for help I'd received from different parts of the world and Task Force members made suggest-ions, pointing out their common needs and suggesting specific ways to meet them. We drew up plans for my work and travel and lined up contacts in each country. Overall, it was a matter of putting grassroots projects in touch with local, academic, governmental or international assistance.

Our meetings were exhilarating and so well attended that I wondered whether there was some other reason these conclave-hardened professionals came together. One day, it dawned on me that there was no other regular, informal gathering where nutritionists of their caliber and experience could meet to discuss the worldwide implications of their discipline. The atmosphere of the Task Force meetings afforded opportunities that, given the rigidity of prevailing international protocol, couldn't be found elsewhere. Here, it was possible to introduce important plans and possibilities, find support, and discuss objections and suggestions.

Clara Mae Taylor and I agreed early on to compile a bibliography of nutrition education materials published by each nation and in many different languages to let people know what was available in their own country. We felt that this would meet local needs better than circulating pamphlets translated and prepared in the U.S. It was published by Columbia University.

In early 1966, my first overseas journey took me to Italy, then on to West Africa for several weeks. I visited the FAO in Rome, meeting nutritionists who worked in different parts of the world. A Dutch home economist gave me some sound advice. She said, "When you go to a new country, call on the various government ministries concerned with nutrition—for example, health, agriculture, and education. Find out which one funds the delivery of nutrition services. Then, talk only to them—the others are powerless to help you." In each country, I did exactly as she said and ferreted out exactly which of the ministries could offer assistance to the local projects I'd visit.

From Rome I flew to Kano, Nigeria to represent Agricultural Missions at the Conference on Church and Rural Development. It was hosted in conjunction with Amadhu Bello University in Zaria. The atmosphere at the conference was optimistic and we truly thought the country was ready to move ahead with peaceful development. Little did we know how much bloodshed lay ahead. Participants from rural projects in other West African countries had come to see the rural work in Nigeria, to share the results of their own efforts, and to hear about similar projects in other countries.

I was fortunate to room with the main speaker, Mrs. Ransome Kuti, president of the organization of Nigerian rural women's groups. She was an assertive-looking woman who spoke convincingly about how home life and child development would improve if there were peace and if women were informed, trained, and encouraged. I learned a great deal from her about organizational skills and about Nigeria's needs.

Jessie Taylor, a faculty member at Amadhu Bello University and director of the Women's Training Center, was able to illustrate Mrs.

Kuti's words by taking delegates through the Center where homemaking skills were taught in domestic settings. Their model rural houses showed village women how to use the resources available to them in the countryside as they labored to feed their children and increase family income. Their urban models demonstrated to rural women considering moving the sophisticated skills required to be an urban mother and hostess.

My continuing travels took me to the various home countries of the conference delegates so I could see their work firsthand. West Cameroon, formerly a British dominion and therefore English-speaking, was endeavoring to make its home science courses relevant to young women who came in from the rural areas. In the one school I visited, we had lengthy conversations about locating resources and I encouraged the school to call on consultants from other African countries through the All-Africa Home Economics Association.

In French-speaking East Cameroon, the women I met—wives of men upwardly mobile in government and business—faced a different challenge: their husbands were dissatisfied in their marriages because the women were not socially sophisticated. As we talked, I described the two-level training center in Nigeria. Realizing that they needed similar training, the women began planning a visit to the facility in Zaria and hoped to set up a similar training center in Yaounde.

My next stop was Accra in Ghana, where I was met by Presbyterian Ghanaian women and taken to a building with the large sign "Presbyterian Center of Ghana" on its front. Their work there was impressive. Their child care centers, assistance programs for working mothers, schools, and informal classes were models for women in other countries.

Next, I flew along the African coast, over Liberia and Cote d'Ivoire, to Freetown, Sierra Leone where an extension home economist demonstrated a smokeless stove just like the ones used in India. What a wonderful example of cross-cultural sharing of useful ideas.

A small local plane took me inland, hopping over jungles dotted with hundreds of open places in the center of which were red pits—gold mines. I stayed for a few days with a missionary family in their jungle home. I loved the feeling of being sheltered by trees and enjoyed bathing under their sun-heated outdoor shower. The mother of the family, a doctor, saw patients in her kitchen. I sat with her and listened as she gave health talks, made recommendations about feeding the babies, and chatted with the women who came and went. The father was one of our Agricultural Missions contacts, and he too had several demonstration projects to show me.

Upon my return to New York, I began documenting the projects I had learned about that significantly improved the lives of women, reporting my findings to the Task Force and writing about them for our Agricultural Missions newsletter that was mailed to nearly 1,000 people. The response to my articles led to a number of speaking engagements for church groups of all denominations. Overseas church workers would stop by my office to discuss possibilities for work in their respective countries. Both the need to enhance the lives and health of women and families and the means to achieve this, were becoming more widely recognized and better understood.

Our second year in New York, we bought into a Manhattan co-op on 121st Street only three blocks from my office so I no longer had to commute. This was an exciting time for me. Opportunities to expand my contacts and broaden my knowledge of nutrition services opened up. I was meeting people with similar visions—those who saw the importance of large-scale nutrition planning and programming. I could now devote all my energies to this newfound interest, as I no longer had children at home and Chuck's teaching position in Queens made no demands on me. I was discovering new dimensions and abilities within myself including a talent for getting people to think and plan together, to expand their horizons. Plus, I was exercising authority I never dreamed of having.

My next major trip took me to Asia in early January 1967. I spent New Year's Eve in Hawaii with Abe Akaka, chaplain of the state senate, and his wife Mary Lou. From the balcony of their home above Honolulu, we watched the fireworks, both those in the city and the special display out on Diamond Head. The next morning, they took me to Kawaihao Church, where Abe was pastor, and he told the congregation I was headed across the Pacific on a special mission for the church. Deaconesses put special leis around my neck and the beautiful voices in the choir sang a benediction.

After a last swim on Queen's Surf Beach, I headed to the airport and caught a plane to South Korea. Seoul, a city I had passed through with Florence and Sarah thirty years earlier, filled me with memories. I was glad it had survived the Korean War and could see it had grown enormously. I was also aware that we were just across the Yellow Sea from Peiping, now called Beijing. Though my thoughts flew there frequently, I knew China was still closed to foreigners.

Scheduled to visit rural villages and observe home economics extension work, I was unprepared for the signs hanging over the road at our first stop that proclaimed, "Welcome, Mrs. Riddle." Evidently, since I was coming from the National Council of Churches of Christ in wealthy America, it was expected that I would bring gifts and donations. I felt like a fraud. I admitted that I had nothing to share but my interest, experience, and questions. My words were a terrible disappointment. Things improved, though, once I was introduced to the extension agents and assured them that the information they provided would be disseminated in other countries.

From Korea I flew to Hong Kong where I would have a day of rest. Barbara Gepford, a home economist, took me to the Maryknoll Convent to relay greetings from Sister Mary Erhardt to the dietician there. The three of us soon began discussing how to promote nutritional change in the city. I suggested that they gather together all of Hong Kong's nutrition professionals and spend six months reviewing possible approaches before deciding on any action. I later learned that, by doing just that, they were able to secure an increase in the government allowance to Chinese refugees, an amount that covered the cost of an adequate diet. I've chuckled to myself many times about how productive this "day of rest" turned out to be.

In Thailand, I visited the worksites of home economist Jean Johnson and met faculty members in several women's training institutions. When word got out that I was going to India by way of Burma, I was besieged with requests from Burmese refugees in Thailand who wanted me to take clothes and other supplies to their relatives at home. Since I'd be there only twenty-four hours, I hesitated. How could I deliver these items? I was told not to worry, that someone would meet me. Knowing that Burma was under a repressive military government, I agreed to do what I could.

By the time I boarded my plane in Bangkok, I was loaded down with bags and parcels. Before getting off in Rangoon, I put on dark glasses and prepared to play the part of innocent visitor looking for a tour guide. I sat down on a bench with the parcels beside me. Moments later, a man appeared asking if I were Mrs. Riddle. I got up to greet him, fully aware that I was leaving the parcels unguarded. When I looked back, the bench was empty. The man, who turned out to be from the Burma Council of Christian Churches, assured me that the packages had all been taken care of.

At his home, we met with a large group of Christians who were glad to see someone from the "outside." They knew I could stay only a few hours but were anxious to hear about my work and tell me about the restrictions they lived under. They treasured my assurances that they were not forgotten and asked me to tell churches wherever I went that I had witnessed a strong, living Christian community in Burma.

My next stop was India. To my delight, Maryanna Cassady, a dear friend and excellent home economist, was there working on a practical homemaking handbook in conjunction with the All-India Home Science Association. She was very helpful to me on that visit, suggesting valuable contacts and bringing me up to speed on progress and setbacks impacting our work.

Among the many people I met, several stand out. Ramoth Burkholder, also a home economist, told me how she had encouraged the newly literate women of a neighboring village to practice reading and talk over what they had read. She was also concerned about how village children were being fed, so she obtained government pamphlets in Hindi on child nutrition and distributed them to their reading circle. As the women discussed the pamphlets, they recognized ways to better feed their own children using local foods. Then they realized they wanted to share this information with other families in the community. Fourteen of the women teamed up in pairs and each pair visited one family a day, seven days a week. On Saturdays, they came together and shared their experiences. If they had been asked questions they could not answer, they read further and discussed possible solutions.

The teams encouraged pregnant women and breast-feeding mothers to eat well and drink more milk. They also promoted breast-feeding, helped women who were having difficulty nursing, showed mothers how to prepare food for infants ready to be weaned, and talked about serving children a variety of grains and lentils and about how to get and use more vegetables, fruit, milk, and eggs. They visited their families each week, answering questions, seeing how their suggestions were being implemented, and asking if more information was needed. After the pairs had been doing this for about six months, they began weighing and measuring the children and keeping growth charts. After two years, the village people could see a marked difference in how the children grew.

Ramoth's story delighted me. The program, inexpensive and requiring few outside resources, made so much sense. It was a shining example of what women can do when they are encouraged to learn and share their knowledge. This program clearly illustrates the notion that it takes a village to raise a child.

At Vellore Christian Medical College, I listened to Dr. Sheila Pareira speak simply to mothers of children with *kwashiorkor*, a debilitating disease brought on by a nutritional deficiency. Her research indicated that *kwashiorkor* came from not having *enough* to eat, so in her talk, she showed mothers how much food a young child actually needs. Five toddlers were led into the room and seated on the floor. Rice with a sauce was heaped on newspaper in front of each child. As the children began eating with their fingers, the mothers watched in disbelief, saying, "My child won't eat that much." But gradually, each child worked his or her way through the pile. Then the truth came out—the mothers sorrowfully told Dr. Pareira that they didn't have that much rice to give to one child.

I wondered how this problem, which afflicts small children worldwide, would ultimately be solved. It was not a matter of providing nutritionally sound calories but of simply providing enough calories. In many countries, adult males are fed first and the boys second. What is left over goes to the girls, then the mothers. But where do toddlers fit in? And why doesn't the world recognize that young girls need to be better nourished than boys? After all, their bodies will house and nourish infants. It seems as if the world doesn't yet cherish its young and does not yet realize that nourishing children results in healthier, more productive adults.

I returned from my Asia tour enriched and encouraged. Much was being done to inform and empower rural women, and these exciting advances could be disseminated and built upon by Agricultural Missions through its seminars, newsletter, and extensive contacts around the world. Yet simultaneously, my grueling travel schedule had depleted my inner resources. Feeling the need for personal renewal, I decided to attend a human relations seminar in Green Lake, Wisconsin in April 1967.

I'd first heard about sensitivity training in the early 1960s and knew its goal was to help people recognize their feelings and deal with them honestly, to listen to each other and converse in a responsive way. My curiosity was piqued. I thought the training must be almost like learning a new language. I longed to enter into this kind of dialogue.

At Green Lake, I enjoyed being one among several hundred trainees who were not into one-upmanship, false flirting, exclusiveness, or fault-finding. I could be part of a conversation or go off by myself—either was fine.

One evening, Bob, a trainer I had met through Agricultural Missions, approached me and said, "Katharine, I haven't had a chance to tell you that I find your genuineness very attractive."

I hardly knew how to respond, but at that moment, a young man from my training group joined us. Bob turned to him, saying, "Jim, I was just telling Katharine that I find her very attractive. What do you think?"

"Madly in love with her," he replied.

I knew his statement was sincere, if somewhat exaggerated, and was relieved when the two began talking with each other and then bid me goodnight. This brief exchange gave me much food for thought and made me feel good. These men who hardly knew me and had plenty of other interests had spontaneously told me they thought I was attractive and worth knowing—to me, a stunning piece of news. Of course, I had heard as much from Chuck and close friends but was amazed to hear it from virtual strangers. How could this be? And what did it mean to me?

Growing up the daughter of missionaries hadn't been easy. Others simply expected me to be a good and likeable person. I tried my best, but nobody realized what a struggle it was sometimes. I think friends assumed it came naturally to me. As an adult, I was riddled with self-doubt when I failed to meet expectations. I didn't want to let friends and family down. It wasn't until this revelation at Green Lake that I realized the expectations were mostly mine. Bob and his friend, who hadn't known me prior to the seminar and had no preconceived notions about me, held up an unbiased mirror that showed me that indeed I was quite acceptable.

The sensations that rose up in me were so euphoric, I had to go outside. Walking out into the night, I felt as if a self I hadn't yet acknowledged and hardly dared to look at was making itself known. That self was likeable and enjoyable, even to strangers. What had I been overlooking? Perhaps, deep inside, there was a newness I needed to recognize. Would this newness teach me the kind of understanding and the ability to communicate that I longed for?

It seemed as if a new green shoot were pushing up in my body, breaking through layers and barriers to spontaneity. The world suddenly seemed intoxicating. Giddy and laughing aloud, I realized that my longings to be "seen" and appreciated unconditionally were the dream, and this was the reality. The sensations I experienced were those of falling in love, and that was exactly what was happening: I was falling in love with myself, truly glad to be me.

The rest of the week is hazy in my memory. I was on a high and hardly slept. I was conscious of living on two levels, hearing what members of my group were saying with deeper understanding than before and enjoying, almost with disbelief, my newfound self. There were meanings and dimensions in our group discussions that I hadn't recognized before. And I realized that other trainees were having similar, though perhaps not as intense, experiences.

Reentry into the real world was difficult. I had to redirect my thinking and contain my euphoria. Still, I was grateful for the insights, the confidence, and the new sense of being in the world that Green Lake had provided.

Agricultural Missions had for many years provided a week-long training seminar for overseas workers at the National 4-H Center in

Washington, D.C. Foreign missionaries and nationals from countries as diverse as Brazil, Thailand, and Kenya met and talked about their respective nations, focusing on the morés and agriculture programs of each. Through this came a deeper understanding of the obstacles that contributed to poverty and lack of education.

In late spring 1967, the year Jack Keller's book *Yesterday's People* about his work among the poor of Appalachia was published, we invited him to speak to the seminar group. He started out apologetically, saying he didn't know whether his experiences had any relevance to those of us working in foreign countries. But as he described the communities and individuals of Appalachia, their intense family loyalty and their difficulties in becoming part of the larger community, people around the table began saying, "That sounds just like where I work," or "I know exactly what you're talking about." This came as a surprise to each of us and helped us recognize the worldwide phenomenon of poverty brought about by being outside the social mainstream. Enriching conversations on the interrelationships between isolation, food availability, nutrition, and health status followed.

Out of this event came the idea for a similar week-long workshop on nutritional improvement that would cover not only how to meet the nutritional needs of different family members, but also how to grow, prepare, and preserve nutritious foods. Other topics included menu planning which meant comparing meal patterns from different countries, surplus foods and emergency feeding programs, infant and child feeding, and nutrition education. With the help of the Task Force, especially Dr. Ruth Leverton and the nutrition resource experts they suggested, we provided training in nutritional improvement in subsequent years.

The sessions were very practical, offering opportunities to share experiences and ideas. When talking about preserving food, for example, a delegate from Angola told us that guavas, an excellent source of vitamin C, were plentiful but that their season was short. He asked for suggestions about what to do with those fruits that couldn't be eaten fresh. Delegates from India suggested slowly cooking the guavas down into a thick liquid that could be sun-dried. In India, guava leather, or guava "cheese," is very popular.

Agricultural Missions and Maryknoll worked closely together, and I often traveled to meetings and conferences with Father Phil Weaver (not his real name), a gifted, articulate young priest who had spent nine years in Tanzania. We soon became friends. In January 1968, I arrived at the office to find him sitting there, wearing a suit and tie and looking preoccupied. He told me he was leaving the

priesthood, effective immediately, and was here to interview with Ed
Espy, head of the National Council of Churches, for a job.

Further conversation would have to wait until the end of the work
day, so we made plans to have dinner. Unfortunately, the restaurant
I'd suggested didn't serve wine. Phil was noticeably disappointed.

After we'd eaten, on the way back to my apartment he stopped at
his car and got a bottle of Chianti out of his trunk. He set it on my
dining room table and got two glasses from the kitchen cabinet. I was
highly uncomfortable. He asked what was wrong and I told him it
was the first time a bottle of wine had ever been on my table.
Nevertheless, I agreed to join him in a glass as he revealed what had
brought about his profound life change.

"Kittu," he said, "I'm getting married."

I couldn't believe it. Now pensive, we each sipped slowly.
Cautiously, I asked how he and his fiancee had met.

"She's a cloistered nun. I listened to her confession for a year and
found myself so in love with her that I couldn't bear not being near
her."

I smiled and said ruefully, "You and I have each tried to serve the
Lord as best we could. For me, sex has been acceptable, but liquor
hasn't. For you, the opposite is true. What a crazy world."

He gave me a quizzical look, then burst into laughter. "You're
right," he said. "In the name of religion, we tie ourselves in knots!"

He and his fiancée eventually found jobs in another city. They
waited eight months before the Pope granted them permission to
marry. On their honeymoon, Phil and his wife stopped by and I was
distressed to see how down he seemed, no doubt from this long
period of uncertainty. In my mind, this incident raised serious
questions about the church's vision and decision-making abilities. By
depriving Phil of the job he did best, the Catholic Church was clearly
the loser. I recalled similar examples among various Protestant
denominations where insistence on certain religious practices and
beliefs caused such great anguish that some had even left the church.

I had some fine colleagues at the National Council of Churches.
Next door to Agricultural Missions was the Medical Missions office
headed by Bill Nute. Early one Monday, I passed his door and asked
how things were going.

"My wife died this weekend," he responded, then hurriedly
added, "It's okay. We knew it was coming. We're glad she didn't
linger in pain. She didn't want a large funeral, so I just went ahead
with the cremation."

I was floored. How could anyone be so cool and unemotional after losing a wife? "You have daughters. Have you told them? Are they coming?"

"I told them it was no use coming. There's nothing they can do."

At this point I nearly exploded remembering my own experience when my mother died—the loneliness, the sense of uselessness, the lack of closure. "Bill, your daughters need to be here to carry out their grief. They need to go through their mother's things, to cry with you, share with you, and comfort you. I'll bet your Quaker group would organize a memorial meeting if you asked them to. That way we can all express our remembrances."

He looked at me in amazement. "You're right. Of course that's what I should do."

And so it was that his two daughters came to participate in a memorial service and learn things they'd never known about their mother. They later thanked me for helping their father see how he had shut himself off after her death. During this time, my own mother seemed near, comforting me with her gentle presence as I relived my sorrow at losing her and grieved for the pain of Bill's daughters.

Bill and I grew close and I called on him soon after, at a time of personal crisis. One Sunday in September 1968, while Chuck was in Columbus, Ohio on assignment, I was walking home from Church of the Master in south Harlem. As I climbed the stairs to leave Morningside Park, a man caught up to me, put his arm around my shoulders, and began walking alongside me as if we were friends. This all happened so suddenly that, at first, I didn't realize he had a knife to my throat. Saying he didn't want to hurt me, he told me to act normal and not to scream. Then he pulled me into the bushes and raped me.

Stunned, I thought, *Could something this horrible actually be happening on a lovely summer Sunday?* Didn't anyone see us? Isn't there anyone to help? A strong urge to protect myself swept through me and I submitted to the inevitable. But a voice within me directed these thoughts to him, *You can have whatever else you want—pleasure, my purse, my money—but you can't take from me my love of humanity. I won't hate you just because you are a man. You cannot make me cynical. You cannot rob me of my love of human beings.*

Shortly after he finished, he got up and left. But for all I knew, he would come back, perhaps with friends. The voice inside me was urgent, *Get up and run!* I scrambled to my feet, stuffed my panties in my purse, and fled. A policeman stood at the top of the stairs, but I said nothing to him. He must have been nearby during the attack, and I feared he'd known what was going on yet had chosen to look the other way. I just kept walking—fast—though I knew enough not to go straight back to my apartment. When I was sure I wasn't being followed, I went home, threw away the clothes I'd been wearing, and took a long shower before sorting out what to do next.

I called Chuck in Columbus. At first my words didn't register. Once they'd sunk in, he was terribly upset that this had happened to me and that he hadn't been home. I called the church, but the deacons were in session and there was only an answering machine. I called friends, but everyone was either at church or out to lunch. Some help the church turned out to be in my time of need!

Then I called Bill Nute. He reported the rape to the police, took me down to the station for questioning, and accompanied me to the hospital. There, doctors examined me, then asked whether I was in danger of becoming pregnant. I hadn't even thought of that! I told them my tubes had been tied. Then the police drove me around Harlem hoping I could identify my attacker. It was useless—I had hardly looked at him. In fact, all of this activity seemed useless. But having a loyal friend like Bill, who stuck by me throughout my ordeal, made the situation easier to bear.

At the next staff meeting of the Division of Overseas Ministries, I, one of the few women present, shared the story of my rape. These people were my friends so I thought they'd care about my welfare. Instead, they either looked away or got up and left, offering the barest of sympathies. I got the feeling that many thought the rape was my fault, that I had brought it on myself. Bill Nute was as appalled as I was at their response, knowing their rejection was almost as hard for me to bear as the rape itself. Hurt as I was, I still could not hate them or feel vindictive. Eventually, some of them softened, and a few even apologized explaining they hadn't realized that rape could happen to someone like me, a churchgoing wife and mother.

When Chuck got home, we had a long talk. He felt he'd let me down by not being there when I needed him, and he was angry that I'd been violated. After we'd had a chance to express our feelings, resuming physical intimacy brought us close again. In time, I was able to let go of the rape because I'd survived with my self intact.

As I healed, one source of comfort was the staff of Church Women United, an organization devoted to promoting cooperation among women's projects. CWU sponsored interdenominational programs that brought women together for innovative global events such as World Day of Prayer held on the first Friday in Lent. Each year, CWU held a national gathering that felt more like an international gathering because so many women leaders from other countries attended. As a speaker at the 1968 assembly, I shared stories of the women's empowerment I had seen taking place in families and communities around the globe.

Dr. Charles Glenn King had mentioned to our Task Force several times that his son, Dr. Kendall King, had started some highly effective malnutrition prevention clinics in Haiti. I had occasion to visit them when a rural development meeting took me to Hispaniola. There, mothers were taught to make special food for their weaning infants using the formula developed by Dr. Jellife, a recognized authority on the importance of breast milk. Mothers mixed a paste containing three kinds of food in equal quantities—a soft legume such as lentils or soybeans, powdered milk, and a soft animal protein such as egg, fish, or chicken. This paste, which could be prepared fresh each day, was far better for weaning than sucking haphazardly on a crust of bread—the typical fare for many toddlers and usually the reason for their sudden weight loss. I was also impressed that clinic workers helped mothers who had been through the program, therefore, and to understood its value find each other so they could share home duties and child care.

Finally, on a visit to East Africa, I got to see Dr. Jellife's clinic at Makere University Hospital in Kampala. The mothers who brought in malnourished children were superstitious enough to hope for some magic cure from a needle or flashing light. Instead, they had to see for themselves that the children would get well simply by eating nourishing foods—in this case the weaning paste. It sometimes took a month for a child to become strong enough to go home, so the clinic provided accommodations for the mothers. While in residence, they learned how to cook and mix the weaning paste, fed their children with what they had made, and finally, taught classes on paste-making to new mothers. It was a long, tedious, yet rewarding process.

As part of the Agricultural Missions' collaboration with Catholic relief agencies, I went to Nairobi several times to meet with a Belgian priest/nutritionist and draw up plans for mothers-and-children clinics where powdered milk provided by Catholic Relief Services would be distributed. We discussed how best to incorporate nutrition education into the clinic programs. The facilities, to be built all over Africa, would be furnished with scales, measuring equipment, and copies of recently published growth charts showing optimal growth curves. Mothers would be taught how to weigh and measure their children and to plot this information on the chart to see if they were growing well.

The big question was where to keep these growth charts. Should each clinic have a file cabinet? My immediate reaction was that the charts did not belong in the clinic because clinic records are sometimes lost, eaten by white ants, or spoiled by flood. I strongly believed that the growth charts belonged with the mother. Therefore, instead of file cabinets we invested in heavy plastic envelopes that mothers could keep the charts in.

I learned from letters that this plan was implemented, but I lost touch with it after leaving Agricultural Missions. Nearly twenty years later, as a faculty member, I was showing a professor from Zimbabwe around the University of Nebraska campus. When she learned I was a nutritionist, she began telling me about the nutrition program in her country.

"You see," she began, "we have women's clinics. We give the mothers powdered milk, and they weigh and measure their children then plot their growth on growth charts. The mothers consider these charts a prized possession and guard them carefully, for they are a guide to the nutritional status of the child."

I couldn't tell her how happy I was. My eyes welled with tears. I was glad I had insisted that "the chart belongs to the mother."

My time with Agricultural Missions was drawing to a close. Chuck was interviewing with Morehead State University in Kentucky for a position in the education department. We were reluctant to move so far from his mother, whose condition was worsening. Now in a nursing home in Connecticut, she resisted being fed, spoke less and less, and lapsed into a coma much of the time. But on our last visit, she gave me a great gift. Chuck had been stroking her hair and I was holding her hand, musing out loud over what she might be thinking about as she lay there. To our amazement, she spoke, saying, "I think about you all the time." Those words were among her last, for she died soon after.

Just before I left New York in 1969, I accompanied an American delegation of twenty-six church-affiliated, racially diverse home economists to the Conference on Asian Hunger in Bangalore, India. On the way, we stopped in Rome to visit the FAO. That night, we watched Neil Armstrong take his first step on the moon and it struck me as symbolic of what we hoped to achieve in Bangalore. That meeting, too, was a first. Held in Asia, it featured women from six Asian countries who were all professionally involved in alleviating hunger.

Though highly trained, the Americans wondered privately whether they were adequately prepared to respond to questions that might arise. During the conference, their nervousness changed to amazement and delight at the knowledge displayed and the innovative ideas suggested by the Asian delegates.

As events progressed, a Filipina pointed out that nothing had been said about meal planning and the topic wasn't even listed on the program. Since I was leading the session I acknowledged the oversight and proposed we hold the discussion right then. I asked the women to divide themselves into four groups based on the staple food that formed the backbone of their daily diet—rice, wheat, corn, or meat. Then I asked them to share meal plans and food combinations among themselves. The American delegates—the meat eaters—learned a lot by listening in on the other groups.

At the end of the scheduled meetings, the whole conference traveled together to the respective countries of the delegates, visiting the projects that had been described. One of the American delegates remarked, "I didn't know that these problems were already being addressed. And where did all these capable women come from?"

Of course, over the years, women worldwide have been getting college educations and advanced degrees. Each country has its own large corps of home economists and women working in related fields. These women are pioneers in bringing progress to their countries. For them, the conference provided an exciting opportunity to demonstrate what they were doing with their "educations." When I heard our American delegates say, "I can use all of this in my teaching," I knew they'd gotten past the usual know-it-all American stance. This was very satisfying.

While we were in the Philippines, I left the group and returned to the States for Bill's wedding. While excited for my son, I wasn't quite ready to leave this post-conference tour, further evidence of women's resourcefulness. Nor was I eager to say goodbye to this wonderful, exciting period in my professional life knowing that I'd made important contributions to promoting nutritional services worldwide. During my four years with Agricultural Missions, I'd stepped out on my own and earned recognition from my peers. I'd truly begun creating my own life.

Chapter Seven
Stepping Off a Cliff

When Chuck had interviewed in October 1968 for a faculty position at Morehead State University in Kentucky, I'd accompanied him with a heavy heart. It was difficult to imagine abandoning my promising and fulfilling work with Agricultural Missions, but I saw no other choice. We couldn't afford to maintain two separate households and I feared our marriage might not survive if we lived so far apart. At a time when social convention maintained that a man's career took precedence over his wife's, mine would have to be sacrificed. I struggled to swallow my bitterness and keep an open mind as we drove into Morehead.

Together we toured the campus. Though the buildings and student population of 9,000 nearly overwhelmed the small college town, Morehead was charming. Nestled in the rolling Kentucky hills, its blazing autumn colors beckoned me, warming my heart and sparking my resolve. If I had to leave New York, I'd find something engrossing to challenge me here.

When the position was offered, Chuck accepted it and we returned to Morehead to find a place to live. The fireplace in the first house we saw seemed inviting, perhaps because the weather was now damp and dreary, so we decided to buy it. Chuck started work in March and moved in right after the sale closed, but I stayed in Manhattan to complete my contract with Agricultural Missions.

I was deeply touched by the farewell my colleagues gave me and by the wording of the award they presented me for "distinguished service in the advancement of nutrition education among the women of the world." The citation read:

> Katharine, we salute you for your amazing ability to marshal important information, to generate interest, to enlist and train leadership, to foster cooperation and to inspire action on behalf of the hungry and malnourished people of the world. During your three and a half years as Associate Director and Home Economist of the Agricultural Missions Program, you have pioneered an area of action by the Christian Churches which promises to help rural

women realize their true Christian vocation in the development of their families and their communities.

Being valued and recognized for contributing something original and significant to the world was an honor, and I treasured this affirmation of my work.

When I arrived in Morehead, Chuck proudly showed me the house, now filled with our furniture and possessions. For the first time in nearly thirty years of marriage, we owned our home and everything in it. I'd gotten so used to making do with assigned lodgings, turning allotted space and used furnishings into livable dwellings, that I could hardly believe we were free to decorate as we pleased. We looked forward to getting acquainted with our neighbors, planting flowers, and settling into the neighborhood.

I was curious about how this large institution of higher learning fit into Appalachia. Students, many of whom came from the mountains, filled the dorms and spilled over into boarding houses. The academic atmosphere hummed, bringing scholarship, research, and liberal arts into the heart of these valleys.

The quiet beauty of Appalachia soothed my sense of loss over leaving my job. Moving to Kentucky had been like a little death, but I was a survivor and I set about finding my role in this new community. When Dr. Morris Norfleet, the university's vice president for research and development, invited me to join his office and write grant proposals to be carried out by university departments, I jumped at the chance. Though I didn't know much about rural Appalachia, I was well aware that the mountain hollows around us were full of poverty and need.

A mile from our subdivision, I saw squalor as appalling as anything I'd encountered in India. A neighbor had taken me there, warning me never to go into the valleys on my own or I'd be shot. I believed him. These were proud people who didn't want outsiders peering at them. To become the kind of friend and advocate who could make a difference, I'd need to learn a lot more. And it wouldn't be easy.

Hannah, a young woman from the "hollers," came to clean for me. As we ate lunch at the kitchen counter, she told me about her life and her family. She described the excitement of the demolition derbies that echoed through the hills from the track a half mile behind our house. The object was to see which car could run the longest after smashing into other cars. One afternoon, I told her of an incident I'd witnessed on my visit to a neighboring county just a few days earlier.

She listened, nodding, familiar with the story. She'd read about it in the papers.

The local public health nurse, Ellie Holloway, had been asked to carry news of a death to an elderly woman named Rose. Neighbors, fearing Rose would have a heart attack when she learned that her grandson had shot his father, called the hospital to ask that Ellie be the one to deliver the shock. I went along only because Ellie and I were expected in another location that day.

It was a tribute to Ellie that not only was she trusted, but that, on her say-so, I, a stranger, was also accepted. We drove deep into the hills, down a secluded draw, parked the jeep, and waded across a creek. Ellie left me on the porch of an old log cabin and went inside to administer a sedative to Rose before breaking the news. A woman came out and joined me. We rocked a while and she explained that the dead man, with an injunction out against him, had shown up drunk at his estranged wife's house and the son, on his mother's orders, had shot him as he got out of his truck. Horrified, I asked what they'd done with the body.

"Called the fun'ral parlor to cum git him," was her reply. "Only when they cum, he warn't dead yit, so they sent 'em back to git the coroner."

Just then, we heard screams from inside.

"Nurse dun tell Rose. Cum'on," my companion said, rising.

It was now fitting to go inside and "pet on" Rose. Though she was still wailing and shouting out her wonderment at how Jesus expected her to bear all this, Rose welcomed our hugs and assurances that she was brave and that Jesus would help.

Ellie motioned that we could go, but the drama was far from over. People had started streaming into the valley from all directions—down the mountain, down the road, out of the bushes and into the backyard. In a phalanx they moved toward the house and entered it. They'd seen Ellie's jeep come down the hollow and waited until Rose knew the awful truth before coming to comfort the grieving woman. Her screams had been the signal.

We'd seen no one as we came down the draw, but we'd been watched. Ellie had been trusted to make this special trip because she was known in the area. She had come on many occasions the previous winter to nurse a woman dying of cancer. Ellie, in turn, had relied on the local people when her jeep slipped on some ice.

I was shaking as we drove away. I'd never witnessed anything like the raw, powerful drama that had just unfolded.

This incident, unnerving as it was, brought me right into the bosom of Appalachia. It was like a foreign country in the heart of the

U.S. wanting its own autonomy. The denizens of these hills where it was hard so to scratch out a living, wanted to be left alone, but they didn't want to be considered alien. To those of us living on the outside, the culture of rural Appalachia wasn't visible because it didn't want to be seen.

Though I was at loose ends in terms of my career, life in rural Kentucky had its blessings, among them the many opportunities Chuck and I had to enjoy the outdoors. In spring, dogwood and redbud bloomed mysteriously in the forest depths, the hills were dotted with serviceberry bushes, and later on, blue chicory blossoms lined the roadways. We took picnics to Natural Bridge State Park, where we marveled at the tall tulip poplar trees that rose from the canyon floor to branch out in the sunlight at the top. Chuck and I bought a canoe, carried it on the roof of our station wagon, and slid it into a succession of small mountain lakes. When we could get friends to join us, we tried small rivers, leaving one car down river and driving upriver in the second to launch the canoe. Chuck and I also explored hiking paths and I found that the exertion of an all-day hike brought with it a familiar euphoria. It was a singular feeling, a high that replaces worries with a detached glow, similar to what I'd experienced at Green Lake the previous year.

Still, nothing had shown up to replace the fascinating work I'd been doing with Agricultural Missions. The trouble was, I knew what I could do, but no one else did. There was little empathy for a woman who felt she should be able to find work commensurate with her abilities. Rather, my new friends and acquaintances felt I was fortunate enough to have a good husband and a nice home, and besides, I could teach at Morehead State, couldn't I?

Unfortunately, the situation was more complex than that. Working in the same arena as Chuck would put me in a difficult position. As his wife, my primary responsibility was to support him, not compete with him as a fellow faculty member. On political matters where we might disagree, I felt I'd have to bite my tongue. To find my own work and pursue my own interests, I'd have to look elsewhere. It was hard to grab onto that kite, to grab any kind of joy or excitement.

My faith helped sustain me. I joined the local Presbyterian church and was enjoying the warm fellowship of the congregation when I was asked to take ordination as an elder. I agreed to do so mainly because I knew it was hard to get women to take leadership roles. But I had reservations.

About a year after our arrival, we attended the funeral of a theology professor who, amazingly enough, had known my parents in India and remembered my birth. I was awed to hear him eulogized by Catholic, Protestant, and Orthodox Christians alike with representatives of all three branches of the Christian Church standing side by side. This convergence seemed to me to be the purest form of Christianity. Churches express themselves in many ways, but when one of them clings to its own orthodoxy as the only way it misses the richness.

As I sat there I got a glimpse of the tremendous power of love, acceptance and inclusiveness. This, I felt was what Christ conveyed— not individual salvation but a way of enabling all human beings in our living together and relating to each other.

Someone suggested that I volunteer to chair the synod's task force for women. Although this work needed to be done, I knew it was not my job. Most women had grown accustomed to the roles they'd been assigned in the Church and didn't see that their participation could expand. In their minds, church government, like the Scriptures, wasn't open to reinterpretation. They weren't willing to work for the changes necessary to alter their status and make their voices heard. It would take a younger woman than I, with more energy, greater zeal, and closer rapport with Kentucky women, to rally the effort. My awareness of how and why the Church kept women in certain limited slots was growing.

Sadly, there seemed no way for me to combine faith and practice. If a male representative of the National Council of Churches had come to Kentucky, there would have been plenty of requests for his services from various denominations. But I, a woman, and a home economist at that, was not thought of as a resource by the Church. Nor, it seems, were others of my sex. This was vividly played out when I attended a Presbyterian conference on world hunger in Athens, Georgia. It was April 1970 and the program was full of male speakers. When I asked why no women were lecturing, I was told, "We don't know any women experts."

Instead of pulling out my credentials, including those from the recent Bangalore conference on Asian hunger, and saying, "Well, I'm one," I called for a caucus of women and presented the situation to them. We agreed that the refusal to acknowledge women's leadership roles in the home—both at the conference and throughout the world—needed to be addressed. When our caucus protested the lack of women speakers, we were told to prepare our comments for the conference report.

We met each day, confident that our discussions would identify some core issues. We realized that the male planners thought in terms of the logistics of relieving hunger but were completely oblivious to women's expertise in providing food day after day, often in very difficult circumstances. The faithful delivery of nourishment by women, even in the face of war, famine, earthquakes, and floods, was not viewed as significant.

But when our report was read to the entire conference, the conclusions had been condensed into words that didn't accurately reflect our views. I jumped to the microphone and six or seven other women did the same. While waiting to speak, I heard a man say loudly to another seated beside him, "I don't know what these women want!"

Well, what we were calling for was a different interpretation and comprehension of the word 'expertise.' We wanted the following statement inserted into the conference proceedings:

> *"Until and unless the work that women do in providing food for their families is recognized as an expertise, the problems of world hunger will not be solved."*

We were successful in changing the wording of the proceedings but less so at altering the understanding of the male participants.

In 1969, Pat Young, a Presbyterian leader and Republican Party member, told me that newly-elected Richard Nixon planned to hold a White House conference on food, nutrition, and health in 1970. She said she'd call on me if she was asked to help. There were compelling reasons why a conference on this topic was timely. Americans were becoming aware, as never before, of the extent of hunger and malnutrition in the U.S. NBC had broadcast a documentary showing how hunger afflicted four different geographic sectors of the country; Robert Kennedy, then attorney general, had visited Appalachia and reported on the horrific poverty and hunger he found there; and Dr. Arnold Schafer had documented serious malnutrition among poor people in the ten states thus far studied in a national nutrition survey.

In addition, a report titled *Their Daily Bread* was published showing how the National School Lunch Program missed many of the poorest children. I found the study, related as it was to my master's research on the Type A school lunch, compelling and politicizing, revealing how easy it had been to leave out the truly needy. Representing Church Women United, I had participated in the study along with representatives from other national women's groups. We presented our findings to Secretary of Agriculture Orville Freeman and made sure he heard our recommendations on how the school lunch program could become a more effective tool in alleviating hunger.

Kittu meets First Lady Pat Nixon in the White House, 1970, during the White House Conference on Food, Nutrition, and Health.

The White House conference was held in December 1970, presided over by Dr. Jean Mayer, a Harvard nutritionist. Pat Young chaired the Task Force on Women with First Lady Pat Nixon serving as honorary chair. I was invited to join because of my work with Agricultural Missions. Other members included a nutritionist from the American Red Cross and the presidents of a number of national women's organizations including the National Council of Negro Women, National Jewish Women, National Catholic Women, Church Women United, the League of Women Voters, and the Federation of Women's Clubs.

We studied the program materials, took some time to get acquainted, and heard each organization's priorities in overcoming malnutrition and hunger. We then formulated consolidated recommendations for action at different levels of government and among voluntary organizations, planning a cross-organizational strategy. What impressed me most was the cooperation between Democratic and Republican women—it was understood that hunger transcended politics.

One evening, to our surprise, we were told that Mrs. Nixon had invited Task Force members to coffee at the White House the following morning. We were received in the private dining room and asked to stand on one side of the room while Mrs. Nixon emerged from an elevator and stood by the fireplace opposite us. Each of us in turn walked up, shook her hand, and briefly engaged her in conversation. I was tremendously impressed with how quickly she picked up on my being a nutritionist. She described programs for women and children in India, saying ruefully, "If they only had enough to eat." A few days later, she invited all the women conference participants to the East Room. It was exciting to be with such a wide range of American women of all races, both poor and rich, some barely educated and others university professors. Her remarks were candid and to the point. I'll always have a special place in my heart for Pat Nixon.

One feature of the conference—and to me, its strength—was that four hundred poor people were present to speak for themselves. This led to confrontations with some delegates because the poor felt their needs were not being fully heard and the recommendations given were unrealistic. They were upset that delegates were willing to cut corners and make concessions, not understanding that this was part of the political process.

The results were unfortunate. I think this was the first, and maybe only, White House conference to which the poor were invited. And President Nixon, who'd heard about the troublesome episodes, failed to approve the practical recommendations agreed upon by conference members. But our work wasn't fruitless. Our recommendations were printed and circulated to all national, state, and local agencies represented at the gathering and they strongly impacted the direction of nutrition programming nationwide.

With activist Zi Graves, I attended the Appalachian caucus, the only white minority caucus at the White House conference. Although Lyndon Johnson's Great Society programs had brought much work to Appalachia, there'd been little actual improvement in income, employment, or well-being. And now, under a Republican administration, the money and workers were gone. Caucus members debated how to reverse this discouraging situation and secure long-term funding for health and nutrition programs.

Zi worked closely with Representative Carl Perkins of Kentucky, Appalachia's staunchest champion in Congress. She introduced me to him and the three of us discussed the soon-to-be-launched Women, Infants, and Children (WIC) program—one of the most positive outcomes of the conference. Targeting pregnant women and children from infancy through age four, WIC provided monthly vouchers for highly nutritious foods such as milk, cheese, enriched cereal, citrus juice, and eggs. Through Carl's recommendation, I became a state health department nutritionist for Rowan County, my county in Kentucky, and was able to initiate the WIC program there.

WIC eventually became quite popular, but I wished that its designers had paid more attention to a successful experiment in northeastern Kentucky. For several years, nutrition paraprofessionals had taken USDA allotments of surplus foods into the homes of welfare recipients and demonstrated how to use them—training that proved quite valuable to homemakers. Instead, a second program was implemented. The Expanded Food and Nutrition program taught homemakers how to use foods available through the Food Stamp program, but trainers couldn't actually take food into the home, and thereby lost some of their effectiveness.

Our county health department staff worked long hours to complete admissions and instruct five hundred mothers about WIC. The program reached out to all women, regardless of economic status. Affluence, after all, didn't guarantee a knowledge of good nutrition. Some faculty wives who came said haughtily, "This is the first government program that benefits us." Their unkind words implied that the government did too much for poor people who didn't pay taxes. Some women even suggested I let them through ahead of the other mothers as if they were somehow superior.

But with WIC, every woman was treated alike. Each time the faculty wives returned, they too had to attend group discussions and consult with me or the other nutritionist before receiving new vouchers. Some began chatting with the poorer women in the waiting room and soon realized that these welfare mothers were not lazy women looking for a handout, but people with real problems struggling to make ends meet and learning how to improve their health by using nutritional supplements.

Through listening to the local women, I learned some of the difficulties they faced. The water in many of the county's wells and public water supplies wasn't potable because of its nitrate content. This posed a real danger to pregnant women and to infants in their first six months. So the women bought their children soda pop instead. But soda wasn't good for children's teeth and also led to unnecessary weight gain. WIC provided several free alternative liquids, among them orange juice and milk. By using National Dairy Council comparison cards containing the nutrient profile of each food or beverage, we could show the mothers nutritional alternatives to expensive sodas. One woman with three young children studied the charts of orange juice, milk, and pop—the latter contributing nothing but empty calories—then looked at me and shook her head, saying, "Hain't nobody never tole me that."

She joined a group of mothers who were trying to get their children to drink water. Several of the women worried that their kids were so hooked on pop that they'd refuse. After a few meetings, one delighted mother could hardly wait to tell her story. "We was all out of sodies, and I just tole 'em they cud drink cole water from the fridge."

"What'd they do? What'd they say?" came the questions.

"They didn't say nuthin'. They drunk it!"

We crowed over her success. What she'd done seemed miraculous to some in the group, but after that breakthrough, her method seemed to catch on. Women on the street would stop to tell me their kids were now drinking water instead of pop.

Marion Wightman, the county's extension home economist, told me of extension clubs that were emphasizing home gardens and food preservation. One group volunteered time in grocery stores to help food stamp recipients shop for nutritious food. In fact, there were many different agencies in Rowan County attempting to alleviate poverty, raise nutritional levels, and improve health. It was heartening to be involved with these diverse programs for nutritional improvement. WIC aimed to break the cycle of poorly nourished mothers producing sickly children. I know it succeeded for many.

Several county agencies were talking about training and hiring paraprofessionals from the rural communities for health-related work. This was encouraging, for it would engage the residents of the hollows in their own health care, nutritional support, and empowerment. I gladly joined the training effort.

The first group of women were initially reserved, watching the procedures warily and no doubt wondering what would be expected of them. I tried drawing them out by describing a situation of an elderly woman, bedridden, and asked how they'd care for her if they were called upon to work with her. But they were unwilling to suggest ideas. Subsequent discussion revealed that they felt being trained meant learning to do things in ways completely different from those familiar to them. Once I'd reassured them, they began to realize that their ideas might have merit and might serve as a basis for building new concepts.

Through my job with Rowan County, I found the engrossing challenge I was looking for. My work was effective in helping women. I pondered the reasons why certain community services were more productive than others. Reenergized, I began thinking about pursuing a Ph.D. in delivery planning for nutritional health services. A doctorate was mandatory if I wanted to further my career or teach at the college level. I'd finally grabbed hold of that kite again and was eager to see where it would take me.

I found that one way of deepening my understanding of spiritual purpose was to memorize the words of certain hymns, and sing them while driving or doing housework. It kept my mind centered. Then, my sister Barbara told me she was enrolled in the School for Esoteric Studies and was learning about the Ageless Wisdom that has inspired all spiritual teaching. Deciding to enroll, I began a formal path of study and meditation beginning with a deeper comprehension that there is one beneficent life pervading all existence.

The step came at just the right time. Suddenly everything changed. I was scheduled for a routine physical exam on Friday, September 3, 1971. At the last minute, I almost called to postpone it because my brother Donald, who had been in India for two years, arrived unexpectedly. I knew my doctor was booked for the next six weeks though, so I decided to leave Don on his own for the short time I'd be gone.

Dr. Louise Caudill, short, energetic, and Appalachian to the core, chatted about the mountain communities while she performed her exam. I enjoyed her breezy, straightforward manner. Then suddenly, she stopped talking. She bent over me and focused her total attention on my right breast. I knew instantly that she'd discovered something serious.

She felt the breast from many angles, compared it with the other breast, and sucked in her breath. For a long time, she said nothing.

"It's a lump," she said at last. "A very small lump, but very hard. Did you know?"

"No," I responded numbly. My life whirled in front of me. What did this mean? Surgery? Was it imperative? How soon? I could hardly feel the lump when she showed it to me, but my heart screamed, *Get it out—now.*

Maybe the surgeon won't think it's urgent, my rational mind countered. But he did. Urgent enough to schedule a lumpectomy the following Tuesday. Stumbling over my words, I shared the news with Chuck, Don, and other family members. Moments seemed precious. Time which had always been my enemy seemed even more so now.

I was terrified of having cancer and all it entailed. *But wait,* I thought. *There's a way out, if you don't survive the surgery.* My throat constricted. I cried inside as I thought of dying. I wept for the beautiful world and all I'd miss, and for Chuck, who'd miss me.

I couldn't concentrate on details, the things that might need to be done. They weren't worth the effort. I lived in the moment just enjoying Chuck and Don and the world around me. I drove down to the stream and walked out under the sky, among the trees, gazing at the clouds and scanning the hills and valleys. In my heart, I was saying goodbye.

After the lumpectomy, there was an agonizing two-day wait for the laboratory report. The surgeon's face, as he approached my hospital bed, revealed that I had cancer. My breast would have to be removed.

I hadn't allowed myself to think about this possibility, but this painful reality now hammered into my consciousness focusing my whole attention, my whole being, on the fact that within twenty-four hours, I'd lose my right breast. Protest boiled up inside me. I didn't want to be maimed and didn't think I could bear the indignity or the public exposure of a matter so private.

As I waited for surgery, a nurse sensing my rage and panic, moved me into a quiet room, laid her hand on my shoulder, and told me to cry it out. What else could I do? I had to release my emotions, look my situation in the face, weep, moan, and mourn the loss of my breast. Great wrenching sobs overtook me as I grieved for myself, my own flesh.

It was so unfair. I liked my breasts, their shape and their feel. They'd suckled three infants and nourished them. They were an important part of me, of my body, of my being a woman. Chuck liked my breasts, too. I didn't know how I, or he, would feel with one of them gone.

Don't worry, that little inner voice said, *you won't have to face this after all. It's cancer and you're going to die.* Tears flowed as I thought about it. *Yes, I'll choke under the anesthetic. That'll be the end of the whole situation.* This outcome was not unappealing. After all, the only woman I'd known who had breast cancer, Marion Riddle, had died. Her surgery and treatment, spoken of only in whispers, seemed secretive, invasive, dangerous. If I were to live, I'd join the same ranks—those of suffering cancer patients.

While contemplating mortality, I realized that I'd already accomplished what I wanted to in life. Several months before, I had read somewhere the question "What is the one thing you would regret not having done if you were to die soon?" I thought and thought, and decided I would regret not having seen the Grand Canyon. So in May of that year, I had taken a rafting trip down the Grand Canyon. So logically, it must be time to die. But inwardly, I protested. Life was beautiful. I didn't *want* to die! I grieved at the thought of being taken from those I loved. Nobody realized how alone I was. I'd had a rich life, but now it was over, and no one knew it except me. Finally, the sobs subsided and I came back to myself, calm. I didn't weep again. I'd faced it all.

Three days after surgery, I was still alive and ready to be discharged the following day. To my surprise, the operation had gone smoothly. The mastectomy had been simple. Apparently, the cancer was only in the original lump, not the rest of the breast tissue, which, in Dr. Caudill's graphic language, was "no use anyway, 'cept to toss in the garbage," shocking words, but I knew she was only being pragmatic. A lumpectomy would have been sufficient.

At the time, I didn't question the decision to perform a mastectomy. I was just grateful that the ordeal was *over*, the cancer was gone, and I wouldn't have to undergo radiation or chemotherapy.

To some extent, I was actually chagrined and disappointed that I hadn't died during the operation. Now I'd have to confront even more uncertainty and change. What would others think when they saw me maimed? Would they be repelled? Would my husband still find me attractive? What would I wear? And how could I face myself? How could I live with the permanent reminder of my cancer? I looked at the diagonal scar across my right chest. It would take some doing to get used to the disfigurement. And I'd have to accept the tightness of my chest, at least until exercise stretched the remaining muscles of my shoulder.

It was hard to sleep on my right side—I needed a pillow. That last night in the hospital, I tossed restlessly, thinking about all that had happened to me in less than a week. Part of me wanted to stay in the hospital and hide, but another part wanted to reach out to a whole new life. I slept and woke and slept again. Each time I woke, I was more excited about the chance to change my life. I knew that if I'd died, my obituary would say, "She lived a fabulous life." That could never be taken from me. So now I was free to make a fresh start. I could break off unnecessary involvements, reshape my use of time, and concentrate on deepening the meaning of my life.

In the morning, I was deliriously happy. I'd been given a precious opportunity—I could start a new incarnation without having to die first. I went down to Ellie Holloway's office and told her what I'd been experiencing. When I shared how unprepared I'd felt to cope with losing a breast, she put up her hand and said, "Wait. Our head nurse should hear this."

She took me into a larger office and there the two of them listened to an amplified version of the ups and downs and searching of my past few days. There were tears in their eyes when I finished. They turned to each other and said with wonder, "We're nurses, but we're also women. Why haven't we recognized what a woman goes through when she loses a breast?" They realized that aside from the nurse who'd comforted me and urged me to cry, no one had prepared me for what I'd face in the world outside or told me where I could turn for resources and help.

As a result of that conversation, the hospital changed the way patients were informed about their breast cancer treatments. Through the American Cancer Society's Reach-to-Recovery program, breast cancer survivors, including myself, visited patients before and after their surgery and shared our experiences and listened to their questions. Later, we even scheduled Bosom Buddy luncheons so we could stay in touch.

I was feeling fresh vigor inside—a desire to meet each person as a unique individual, to start again with no preconceptions or expectations, to let my own uniqueness express itself. I wavered at first about what to wear over the scar on my chest. I tried a cotton-filled pad, but it wouldn't stay aligned with my left breast. Then I bought a prosthesis, but it was uncomfortable and it moved around too much. Finally, I decided that I wanted no falseness—or falsies, except with dress clothes. People who knew I was maimed would accept this, and those meeting me for the first time would just have to deal with it.

Chuck grew accustomed to my new look and feel. I knew that in his eyes, losing a breast did not detract from my womanliness. I've come to grips with the fact that part of me did indeed die during my hospital stay. The person who left was not the same person who had entered with a lump in her breast. The excision simultaneously removed the old and yet opened a whole new life.

During the years we anchored in Kentucky, our grown children changed locations and vocations. Bill and Nancy, whose wedding I'd attended after the Bangalore conference, moved to Tempe, Arizona and worked on master's degrees in social work. Patty graduated from Trinity University in San Antonio, Texas and went on to get a master's degree in physical education at the University of Illinois in Champaign-Urbana.

Dorothy was teaching at the College of William and Mary in Williamsburg, Virginia and becoming increasingly concerned about gender disparities. She told me that in her honors seminar of ten seniors, all of the men, but none of the women, were planning to do graduate work. As she became more active in the women's movement, she received an offer to start women's studies courses at Richmond College, at the City University of New York. So she and her partner, Greg, moved to Staten Island in late summer 1970 and then Greg went off to graduate school at Rochester.

Several months later, Dorothy was in constant abdominal pain. By the following spring, she'd been diagnosed with endometriosis and ordered to absolute bed rest. With no financial cushion, Dorothy insisted that she had to keep teaching. She gave up her lodging and moved onto a daybed in the front room of a friend's apartment, a block from the college. Students came there for lectures, as did her women's consciousness-raising group. I drew up a series of simple menus that would provide variety without making her gain weight, since she had to stay completely still. Her colleagues in the community took turns shopping, cooking, and doing her errands.

By summer 1971, Dorothy was no better. Greg transferred to New York University and they moved into an apartment next to Richmond College so Dorothy could continue working. That summer was a pivotal period for her. Her women's group split into lesbian feminists and Maoists who were anti-gay. Despite her illness, Dorothy had been successful in starting the first B.A.-granting women's studies program in the U.S. But now that program was being torn apart by the political divisions among the women. Because Dorothy insisted that lesbian faculty and students be part of the women's studies program, she came under vicious attack by the Maoist group, some of whom had been her closest friends.

Meanwhile, I'd gone to New York to help with Dorothy's care. At that point, I knew nothing about lesbians. I didn't know whether their attraction to women was something they couldn't help—in which case I felt sorry for them—or whether they had a predatory sexual interest in women, a desire to touch and fondle women as men did—in which case I felt afraid. There in Dorothy's apartment, I couldn't at first identify which of the women who came and went were lesbians. They greeted me and interacted as women everywhere do. Then one day, while talking with her friends in the living room as Dorothy rested in the bedroom, I realized that every woman present had in some way identified herself to me as a lesbian.

Uncertain how to react and fearful that I'd say something offensive, I was confounded. My instinct was to run. Still, nothing had changed except my perspective—these were the same kind women I'd been around for several days. I didn't want to cut them off and couldn't deny how thankful I was for the loving way they cared for Dorothy. This gratitude rose to the surface, helping me see their kindness and their commonness, and my fear evaporated.

Eventually, Dorothy had to take a medical leave of absence and find a place to heal. She asked Chuck and me whether she could stay with us. Thinking she'd be a burden, Dorothy wanted the weight to fall equally on each of us and insisted that Chuck assume half her care. We were willing. This meant that Chuck would cook and do housekeeping—duties he'd never done before.

When she arrived, I took her to my surgeon. He confirmed her endometriosis and recommended a hysterectomy, which meant that at age twenty-eight, Dorothy would be postmenopausal. The only other treatment involved steroids. It was a tough decision, but she opted for surgery. It was a difficult time for all of us. Dorothy's highly successful teaching career was being cut short, her relationship with Greg had ended in the midst of her illness, and she had nowhere to go.

While Dorothy's body was healing, so was our shaky relationship. Through the years, I'd longed to be reconciled with her. The previous spring, we'd finally talked about her rejection of me as a "traditional woman" who pushed aside my own interests and skills for the sake of my family. We had started to bridge the gap. While sitting in the living room one day, Dorothy asked me about the difficult period when Chuck was ill with jaundice. As I finished speaking, she said in amazement, "But you were younger than I am now . . . and you had a husband almost dying and three young children as well. So, no matter whether you were with Daddy or with us, you were always letting someone down. That must have been so hard!" And suddenly, the distance between us was gone.

Searching for a place to recuperate, Dorothy began corresponding with Grailville, a Catholic lay women's community in Loveland, Ohio. I was intrigued that rather than "living the intensity of the spirit," as they put it, in a convent, they chose to do this in the world. By late summer 1971, Dorothy had gone there to recover her strength and her spirit. I joined her briefly on several occasions and these visits drew me into an event that would change my life.

Through Dorothy, I met Janet Kalven and others in the Grailville community. Dorothy, Janet, and I became a three-generation team working on a weekend event that featured Mary Daly, a Catholic theologian and author. The weekend was followed by five more days of workshops for those who could stay. The intent of the program was to empower women to speak up for themselves, to voice their needs, to take a leadership role in their own lives.

The weekend was transforming. In Mary Daly's speech, I heard the words I'd been waiting for all my life: "We cannot feel the new ground rise up under our feet until we have stepped off the cliff."

She considered herself an alumna of the Christian Church and when I said I'd been a Christian missionary, I spontaneously added, "And considering graduation." I didn't deny my upbringing or my training, but I was ready to leave that schooling and move on. I wanted to keep learning in other ways.

After her speech, I sat outside on the lawn, stunned by the knowledge of what I had to do in the near future. A woman, sitting a short distance away, called over to ask, "What are you thinking about?"

I replied, "The cliffs I have to step off of." I knew at that point that I had to leave the Church and my marriage. I suspected there might be additional cliffs ahead. The truth both excited me and filled me with dread.

On Sunday night, I had to shake free the thoughts that preoccupied me. That evening, I was to facilitate a session in which workshop participants would plan the next five days. I hoped that all seventy-five women would help design the week's framework—an exercise in leadership itself.

I opened the session with the question, "Are we going to work together in one large group or several small groups?" When the decision was made for small groups, I asked, "How are we going to select them?"

After considerable discussion, we decided to draw straws, leaving group composition completely to chance. But when Dorothy and I landed in the same group, some women grumbled and wanted to draw straws again, complaining, "We can't have all the power in one group."

"Who says all the power is where Dorothy and Kittu are?" others retorted.

In this way, we arrived at five groups, randomly selected and completely free to do as they pleased. It finally sank in for each woman that it was up to her to outline what she wanted to accomplish and to get her agenda on the table. At lunch I'd sit in a certain place, and if there was discontent, individuals or group representatives could come to me to discuss their dissatisfactions. But even then, I turned the complaints back to the individuals or groups and asked what they intended do about the problem.

One issue our planning group hadn't foreseen arose when lesbians began leaving their respective groups to join the one that Dorothy and I were leading, feeling somehow more comfortable there. The groups that had been deserted brought this to our attention at the next noon conversation, wondering what had provoked it and why our group was special. Further conversation revealed that in discussing personal leadership, many groups habitually referred to husbands, boyfriends, and children, unintentionally alienating women whose sexual preference and lifestyle were different. Those who joined our group knew that Dorothy had lesbian friends in New York and they assumed her world view would be more inclusive, embracing all women.

Out of this came an evening circle session during which our group gathered in the center and talked about what had happened in our group and how it felt. The rest of the women sat around us and, at intervals, asked questions. It was an educational experience, deepening my understanding of minority/majority issues and we/they relationships and helping me feel more at home with people whose lifestyles are different from mine.

At the end of the week, I went home to Kentucky knowing that the first cliff I had to step off of was leaving the Church. But on Sunday, I couldn't bring myself to get dressed and go to services. I decided to wait for the committee meeting held afterward. I got in the car and started down the road, only to realize that I was heading in the wrong direction. So I came home and wrote a letter to the minister announcing my resignation and asking that my name be struck from church rolls and my ordination as an elder be demitted. Then I got back in the car, drove into town, and mailed it.

The minister came out the next day to see me and I welcomed his visit. It gave me the chance to explain that my decision was not based on any dissatisfaction with his ministry or the warm fellowship of the Church, but on the fact that I could no longer say I believed in Jesus Christ as my savior. I felt it was important to take responsibility for my words and actions—in other words, I had to save myself. My faith was no longer based in a spiritual hierarchy presided over by a supreme being who metes out love and forgiveness. Rather, I saw myself as part of a system whose members all circulated these energies, nourishing and being nourished.

"Well, Kittu," he said, "That's pretty basic."

"Yes," I agreed, "what I'm saying hits at the very core of Christian theology. So I can't call myself a Christian anymore. It feels like graduation—I'm out on my own but grateful for all that my faith community has given me."

Once I stepped off this cliff, many possibilities began converging, forming new ground beneath my feet. At Grailville, I'd seen women embrace their own power. This was exciting fodder to bring to meetings with United Presbyterian Women, who'd retained me as an outside planning consultant for their area meeting in western Pennsylvania. UPW was sincerely searching for a more powerful role for women in the Church. To my surprise, I found myself suggesting that women cut off their giving if their requests weren't met since more than half of the Church's support came from women, but this suggestion was seen as too drastic.

The Pennsylvania event we planned exceeded my wildest hopes. One thousand women had the freedom to get in touch with what they wanted from themselves and their church. The last session in the auditorium had the crowd bouncing beach balls back and forth and singing and hugging in satisfaction. I sat down by a dear friend, a retired missionary to India who'd known my family since I was a child, and asked her how she thought the meeting had gone.

"Kittu," she said, "you've wasted your chance to present the gospel in Bible study to these women."

I was shocked and hurt by her complete blindness to what had just happened there. But moments later, a woman standing in the aisle reached down, took my hand, and said, "This conference has changed my life."

It was up to me to decide which words to take to heart. I chose the latter.

Healing was evident in many areas of my life. I'd recovered from the loss of a rewarding job in New York and found meaningful nutrition work in Appalachia. I'd survived breast cancer, graduated from the Christian Church, and been reconciled with my firstborn daughter. Best of all, I'd decided to pursue a Ph.D. in the independent studies program of Union Graduate School in Yellow Springs, Ohio. The future beckoned, and I was ready to meet it.

Chapter Eight
New Ground Rising

Union Graduate School, located in Yellow Springs, Ohio, was a member of the Union for Experimenting Colleges and Universities, associated with Antioch College, and had recently applied for accreditation. I'd heard about UGS at a conference in Maryland where Goodwin Watson, one of the school's founders, described its innovative graduate program to a circle of prospective learners. When I asked what disciplines the degrees were offered in, he replied, "What area would you like one in?"

His answer was so unexpected that I blurted out, "I want to study how living systems are nourished. But it'll take study in biological development, behavioral sciences, biochemistry, nutrition, and even systems analysis."

"There you have an interdisciplinary investigation," Goodwin said. "What would you call it?"

I responded without hesitation, "Nourishment."

Chuck was supportive of the idea and urged me to apply.

I knew that the program would require a great deal of motivation and discipline. I'd have to chart my own way to define my goals and figure out how to achieve them. But I welcomed the chance to tackle this independent study, to discuss with other inquisitive scholars the new ideas churning inside me. Through my work in Appalachia and with Agricultural Missions, I saw that social groups were either nourished or malnourished, just as human bodies are. I wasn't sure this observation was obvious to others though and didn't know what extrapolations could be made from it. Surely someone had already blazed this trail and formulated the relevant hypotheses.

Other doubts nagged at me as well. I knew I was bright, but an internal voice warned against appearing too smart. I didn't want to be seen as competing with Chuck, or worse yet, showing him up. Besides, I really didn't know what I'd do with the information I gathered. And why wasn't I considering a doctoral program at a mainstream university? Was I a snob thinking I already knew more than the professors who'd teach me? I had to admit that in the area I wanted to study, I *did* know more and had more field experience than many academics. I simply needed a chance to review current research, reflect on my experiences, and frame a new view of nourishment— but free from the pressures of a structured curriculum and regularly scheduled courses.

This was exactly what UGS offered. So, I put aside my fears, mailed in my application, and, much to my delight, was accepted.

In June 1972, I participated in a six-week introductory seminar in Kennebunkport, Maine along with thirty or so other UGS students. We listened to the degree requirements, then divided into small groups and presented our study ideas for feedback. The clearer we could be, the more help UGS could provide as we worked toward our goals.

On a fundamental level, I wanted to build on my life's experiences and broaden my understanding of how the world is nourished, or can be nourished. As the seminar progressed, my thoughts coalesced into specific hypotheses and questions: Can the word 'nourishment' be used in different ways? Can the concept of nourishment also be applied to organizations, communities, and nations? Is it possible to describe a *process* of nourishment? Could I discover an all-encompassing model for how nourishment functions in the physical, intellectual, and spiritual realms as well as in social systems?

I'd be pursuing my studies at home in Kentucky, but before they could begin, I had to line up an advisory committee of peer learners, adjunct professors who lived near enough to access easily, and a core faculty member who would serve as a liaison between my advisory committee and UGS. I selected my committee of peers and we worked out a contract that included a schedule for periodic reviews of my work and the feedback I could expect as I focused my research and prepared my dissertation.

Two professors at the University of Kentucky in Lexington agreed to advise me—my friend, nutritionist Dr. Abby Marlatt, and Dr. Ray Wilkie, a behavioral psychologist. I described my preliminary notions about nourishment and living systems, and they offered me a reading list, pointed out applicable research, and suggested topics for further investigation. Dr. Chuck Martin, the leader of the seminar, agreed to be my UGS core faculty member.

The next two years of study were joyous and productive. I reflected on my experiences with Agricultural Missions—my role as an extension nutritionist to the world—and thought about how those experiences had nourished me—and how the world, in turn, had been nourished by what we had accomplished. From there, I envisioned how the nourishment of people relates to the nourishment of social systems. Nations and communities, like individuals, are entities that must be fed, whose health depends on the economy, the success of the crops, and the courage of its members. It wasn't long before I realized that just as bodies and social systems need nourishment, so do intellectual and religious systems.

An American agriculturalist who took young farmers around the world to observe cultivation practices, told me a story that elucidated my understanding of nourishment in its relational forms. His group visited a rural community in northern India where everyone participated in the harvest. The men, women, and children each had their respective tasks and were busy all day long. The American observers had never seen such intense collective labor, and one of the group members remarked that it would be much easier just to bring in a tractor and show the people how to do the same work in only a few hours.

But the agriculturalist then asked the group to share their observations on community morale. Were these people enjoying themselves? Did they feel good about their work? Did the community look reasonably prosperous? This last question raised the issue of the relative importance of nourishing the community versus nourishing the pocketbook. The entire group agreed that the community they'd observed was flourishing. Every person was a useful part of the whole.

I worked with these revelations, struggling to develop a model of how nourishment functions, and I began thinking about the cyclical nature of life. We are born, and the quality and length of our life is determined by how well we are nourished. When nourishment is unavailable, we stop growing and eventually we die. But death is not an ending in itself—it merely marks the end of one cycle of nourishment and the beginning of another. For when an organism dies, it is no longer taking in nourishment, but providing nourishment for other organisms. Some organisms also nourish the life cycle by producing offspring.

During this period, health planning was growing in prominence and Rowan County, Kentucky became part of the five-county Gateway Area Development District. I decided to ally myself with this new system at my doorstep, work with it, and document its nourishment as part of my dissertation. To do this, I signed up for an internship with the Health Development Association to learn systems analysis. At the members' recommendation, I also joined the Gateway Area Health Planning Council, which certified qualified new hospitals, clinics, and nursing homes.

While becoming familiar with systems analysis, I thought about nutrition programs and how nutritionists in particular have an excellent perspective for understanding the way systems operate. If we examine the nutritional processes of the body and the circulation of energies within it, we have a meaningful conceptual framework for observing and understanding all living systems.

Finally, the structure of the nourishment model became clear. Living systems take in resources, process what's usable, eliminate what isn't, and arrive at an end product different from and, ideally, better nourished than the original. On the physical level, for example, human bodies take in food, extract and use nutrients, expel waste, and emerge reenergized. On a sociological level, communities and nations utilize human and natural resources, arrive at successful methodologies to use them for the benefit of the whole, discard unsuccessful or outmoded methodologies, and emerge stronger and more vibrant. The same model holds true for interpersonal, intellectual, and spiritual development as well, benefiting both individuals and social systems.

The more I thought about the nourishment process in all its forms, the more I understood that I was attempting to describe the wholeness—or holiness—of life itself.

What is easily overlooked in this model is the importance of elimination. When I was battling cancer, I read about how cancer cells function. Their early growth is parasitic, using the body's systems to bring in nourishment and expel waste as the cancer cells multiply. But if these cells can't establish their own systems for taking in nourishment and eliminating waste, they die, drowning in their own waste products.

The same can be said of the way we handle emotions. If we don't rid ourselves of toxic feelings, we, too, will drown—in unhappiness, listlessness, even illness. To remain emotionally healthy and happy, we must be spiritually nourished.

As a member of the Health Planning Council, I worked to strengthen the delivery of nutrition services in the Gateway Area. I shared my new concepts with fellow members and together we reviewed our nutritional delivery system, examining the wide variety of services available and identifying needs that had not yet been met. We agreed on how best to aid and supplement each other's work, thereby enlarging our personal visions of what we could accomplish.

Our meetings resulted in a multiorganizational system that ensured the provision of nutritional services. We tied this new system into the existing professional structure, making it more responsive to the needs of nutrition workers. The implications were exciting—we'd developed a power base from which to launch collaborative projects, challenge the overall health system, and affect change. As I carried out my own work in Rowan County, I, like everyone else in the system, now had a wider network of professional contacts and was better able to point out collaborative opportunities and offer support. This made my last months in the area very satisfying. Even after I left Kentucky, I continued to hear about the successes of the enlarged network we'd created.

The time had come to write up the theory I'd developed and the practical applications of that theory as documented in my work for the Health Planning Council. The excitement of this exploration had opened me wide. But as I strove to put words to my thoughts, to explain all I had learned, the scope of the discussion kept getting bigger and bigger, and I wondered whether it would ever come together. Piles of notes were stacked all over the study—I'd even begun using the ironing board and card tables to hold essential bits of information. But one day, in what was probably the biggest surprise of the entire two years, the complete picture jumped out at me with all of the different pieces pulled together into a meaningful whole and I was able to complete my dissertation. I wrote:

> *The nourishment process can best be described in systems terminology. That is, it operates within a given environment, using resources available to it as input to feed the activities of the system and to produce an expected outcome. The amount or nature of the input is adjusted or determined by a decision-making center, using feedback from the satisfactoriness of the expected outcome. It is this process by which systems function.*

Elated, I finished the paper, *Nourishment of Living Systems*, and sent it to my committee. They agreed that once I'd completed my oral examination, I'd be ready to graduate.

In keeping with the school's emphasis on self-motivation, UGS encouraged me to design my own graduation process, or terminar. I asked my committee and adjunct professors to come to Morehead, Kentucky on April 6, 1974 and invited all the people I'd worked with in the Health Development Association and the Gateway Area Development District to join us for the celebratory lunch Chuck had arranged. For this part of the day, I was not on the griddle and could enjoy the lively exchange of questions and answers.

After lunch came the time for my orals. My advisory committee, including my two faculty advisors from the University of Kentucky, would ply me with challenging questions. My stomach tightened in apprehension. Their grilling, though, was quickly stalled by Chuck

Martin, who said, simply, "Kittu, I think there's really only one question. Are you aware of the importance of what you've done?"

I went limp with relief, "No, I guess I'm not."

He and the others began describing what they saw as the significance of my study. My vision of the nourishment process in all its applications, they explained, was unique, compelling, and thought-provoking, and it had enlarged the perspective and understanding of the entire committee. Our two years together had been meaningful, both personally and professionally. These welcome and unexpected words of praise helped me comprehend that my work was successful—and now complete.

As I look back on that day, I realize we were spelling out universal concepts, collectively realizing how systems nourish each other, how each living system becomes nourishment—magnificent food—for other systems.

When the terminar ended, so did the study. The high that had sustained me for two years quickly faded. Fear sprang up in its place. It was now up to me to get a job, to use the degree I'd worked so hard for, to earn money to repay tuition costs. I was more qualified than ever to apply to Morehead State University, but my reasons for not doing so remained unchanged. How, then, would I find work? My best chance would be through my connections in Washington, but it had been five years since I'd walked through the doors of the Department of Agriculture and the thought of knocking on those doors and asking for a job was terrifying.

Nevertheless, I went. The first few days in the city, I dragged my heels, not quite ready to approach my contacts. I needed time to gather courage. One morning, I went to the Kennedy Center to hear Yehudi Menuhin speak. I drank in his words about creativity and the knowing that lies within us. Wanting time to reflect on these moving ideas, I decided to have a leisurely lunch at the Kennedy Center's restaurant. As I savored the delicious French cuisine, words from a poem my teacher Miss Frances used to quote floated into my mind:

> I stay my heart, I make delays
> For what avails this eager pace?
> I stand amidst eternal ways
> And what is mine will know my face.*

These words were transforming—my reluctance suddenly turned to eagerness. I was ready to knock on some doors.

I immediately took a taxi to the Department of Agriculture. The first person I encountered was Helen Strow who took me along to a retirement party for Ruth Leverton, then second-in-command at the

*Poem appears as recollected by the author.

USDA. Ruth asked why I was there, and when I explained that I'd just completed my Ph.D. and was looking for work, she turned to the crowd, called for quiet, rattled off my qualifications, and asked, "Who has a job for her?"

Being on this particular auction block not only felt good, it saved me hours of interviews and secured for me a faculty position in the nutrition department at The Pennsylvania State University in State College, Pennsylvania.

Chuck was proud of me, my new degree, and my new job. He knew how thrilled I was to dive into academia and the fresh challenges it would bring. In late August 1974, we drove up to State College and found a duplex that I rented for a year. We'd discussed the strains that living apart might place on our marriage and decided that the relationship could survive if we saw each other as often as possible. That year, we managed many weekend visits, either in Morehead or State College.

I was teaching two Introduction to Nutrition classes, each with nearly a hundred students, many of them first-year. They didn't realize it was a freshman experience for me, too, as I prepared lectures, learned names, and administered tests. Fortunately, we had an excellent text written by the head of the department, Dr. Helen Guthrie, who was willing to go over the approach I would use. She also arranged for me to teach upper-division classes on world nutrition.

There was much I could bring to my classes from my work overseas and in Appalachia. Specifically, I could show students that nourishment involves more than just consuming particular nutrients. I could help them understand nourishment as a process impacting all living systems.

I loved teaching and getting acquainted with fellow faculty members. Many were doing fascinating research and listened with interest to my recent studies. It was an exciting atmosphere to teach in, and I was pleased I'd made the move.

Outside the university, I made many friends, including Esther Pashek, who'd spent three months driving around the U.S. alone. Her independence impressed me. Women seldom had the courage to take responsibility for their own nourishment—instead, they nourished others. She, however, had embraced her responsibility and undertaken an empowering and nurturing journey.

As we grew closer, I shared my hopes of establishing a place where women could learn to nourish themselves. Esther was intrigued by the idea. She offered to let me run nourishment workshops in her home, helping me earn the money I needed to implement my dream.

Being on my own was exhilarating. I'd never lived this way before. In India, even when I was apart from Chuck, I was still responsible for making a home for the children. Here, I was discovering that I liked independence and making my own plans. Life was full and rewarding, blossoming in many new directions.

But things weren't going as well for Chuck. He was getting discouraged about himself. At Morehead State, the demands of teaching had only increased and a younger, more competitive member of the education department was making his professional life difficult. In terms of our personal life, Chuck felt that it was I who reached out and made contacts, initiated new activities, and kept in touch with the children. He felt that Dorothy, Bill, and Patty were interested mainly in their relationships with me. And, of course, he missed me and our companionship.

Chuck seemed to depend on me more and more to keep up our social contacts and this became progressively more difficult for me to cope with, especially now that I was realizing and fulfilling my own potential. I told him that as an outgrowth of my doctoral studies, I was thinking of establishing a place where women could gather to nourish themselves, and we discussed the fact that our lives might be diverging. If I immersed myself in this women's service project, I'd be moving in a direction that he probably wouldn't want to follow.

I wished with all my heart that Chuck and I could continue to relate intimately and still do what was of compelling interest to each of us. Yet deep inside, I suspected that to live my own life, I'd have to jump off yet another cliff. I'd have to leave my marriage.

But I didn't want to hurt the man I loved. We'd been happily married for thirty-five years and had nourished each other well. It was through this nourishment that I'd found my own strength. I had to trust that it would give Chuck the strength he needed, too, if the time came for us to part.

Earlier that fall, Dorothy had relocated to Tucson, Arizona, finding both the climate and the contacts she'd made in the women's community there welcoming. She urged Chuck and me to visit and we did during Christmas 1974.

We both loved Tucson. Even though it was a colder-than-usual winter, the clear air, beautiful desert and mountain views were very appealing. Chuck even considered moving there if things at Morehead State didn't work out. The fact that he was thinking about alternatives to our life together was encouraging. Even though our future was uncertain, we still wanted the best for each other and hoped we could remain close friends. The new ground was rising.

Chapter Nine
Nourishing Space for Women

The idea for a "Nourishing Space for Women," grew out of my experiences at Grailville. I wanted to create an informal, secluded place where women could come and go freely, pitch tents, and share life stories around a campfire, a safe place where we could be by ourselves or with other women, a nurturing environment where we could come together, transcending differences in background, race, age, socioeconomic status, and sexual preference. For married women, taking time off from daily cares and family responsibilities to simply be with other women in a beautiful location would be rejuvenating. And for lesbians, who by and large lived closeted lives, the chance to retreat to a private place where women could rest and play together would be appealing.

I was recognizing my own personal need to be with other women, both like and unlike myself, and come face to face with who I was without having to relate to men. I needed a place where I could tap into my own personal sources of nourishment and not be dependent on the secondhand satisfaction of nurturing others. And if I needed this, if I needed to learn how to nourish myself, as well as or instead of others, perhaps other women did too. Only in this way, I realized, could we begin to honor our real selves and experience the strength within us. Maybe, if we had our own space, we could find ways to face the quandaries we felt trapped in.

I shared my ideas with Dorothy, and while Chuck and I were in Tucson over Christmas, she introduced me to two women, Lavina and Leslie, who were interested in my vision. Though they had no money to invest, they helped me look for a site outside the city where a nourishing space for women could be created.

My ideas were still rudimentary. But as we rode around, we shared thoughts on what we were looking for, what a women's space should be like. Lavina was paying attention to the general aura of the land we visited. Leslie was interested in a space where women could gather for rituals or games. A more nebulous goal for all three of us was to find a place where women could dream and where those dreams could be brought into being.

On a more practical level, we'd need land that was private. At each spot we visited, we looked for a reliable source of water but usually found none. Most of the year, women could camp out beneath the stars, pitching tents or sleeping in campers, but we'd need one or two structures for permanent shelter. Unfortunately, many of the buildings we saw were dilapidated.

The roads we traveled were dry and dusty, the rides long and hard. After visiting about twenty places, none of which measured up, we became discouraged. But one afternoon, our luck changed. We went to see Cave Canyon Ranch, down a sandy road that followed a creek through a ravine in the Rincon Mountains east of Tucson. It had rained and there was light fog ahead. Suddenly, two magnificent rainbows appeared in front of us, right over the gate to the ranch. Surely this was a sign.

Daring to hope again, we inspected the two small residences, an A-frame the owners had lived in while crafting the second, more permanent cedar dwelling. There were sheds, a large watering tank, and a well dug right beside the creek—an excellent water source. Tall cottonwood trees shaded part of the stream. To our delight, the sheltering slopes of the 160-acre slice of desert canyon provided both privacy and awe-inspiring beauty.

Still, there were drawbacks. Neighbors to the north had a right-of-way through the property, which lessened its privacy. And there was a cave on the land which would be noted on the maps of every spelunker in the country. It was close to the west property line, and we knew nothing, not even 'No Trespassing' signs, would keep eager cavers from fence-hopping. We could at least put up signs asking them to respect the privacy of the rest of the property.

These deterrents we could live with. Now it was up to me to decide whether to buy the land. I was certain that this was the place, but I hadn't expected to find it so quickly. Was I really ready? Taking a deep breath, I put down a deposit. Four months later, in April 1975, I became the owner of Cave Canyon Ranch.

After saying goodbye to Dorothy in early January 1975, Chuck returned to Kentucky, put our house on the market, and made plans to move to Arizona. I'd gone back to State College to finish out the academic year. When spring semester was over, I joined Chuck in Morehead and we sorted through our belongings, deciding which pieces would go to Nourishing Space and which would stay with him if we parted. For the time being, we'd decided to live together in the cedar house, the larger of the two dwellings on the property. We drove out to take possession in early June.

As soon as we arrived, I faced a dilemma. During the spring, word had circulated through the Tucson women's community about the nourishing space for women I planned to create. Many women were eager to help bring the project into being. Chuck and I had barely settled into our house when several of them confronted me demanding to know how the ranch could be women's land with a man living on it.

Torn between honoring my relationship with Chuck and implementing my most cherished vision, I scrambled for a solution. Chuck was very upset about the situation, but he agreed to move off the property and set up a tent in the campground next door. This way we could still be together without jeopardizing my dream.

Over the summer, Lavina and other women came and went, helping improve the land and getting a feel for what it would take to transform it into Nourishing Space for Women. I decided that the loan payments would remain my responsibility, but women who wanted to live on the land or participate in its development would have to raise money for everyday running expenses.

Those first few months were extremely difficult for me emotionally. I wished the women would allow me some leeway as I struggled over what to do about my marriage. Chuck and I realized we'd be better off if we didn't try to live together during this period of uncertainty, so he took an apartment in Tucson and contacted Presbytery headquarters about employment possibilities. Several months later, he became pastor of the Presbyterian church in Apache Junction. Decisions about our future were put on hold.

In September, I returned to State College for a second year, visiting Nourishing Space briefly over Christmas. That winter, I reached a difficult conclusion: even though I loved Chuck, there was no way to go forward without causing pain for each of us. For me, my personhood was at stake. The issues involved were my issues as a woman. I wanted the freedom to determine my own direction without having it be contingent on my husband's desires, needs, and actions. I wanted to spend time with women, to work with women for our empowerment. And as much as I wished it were possible, I couldn't do this and stay married.

During our years together, we had functioned well as a team, helping each other adjust to living in different places and cultures and raising a family. We'd nurtured our relationship and improved our communication skills to better understand each other. But now things were different. We were no longer working together. Our careers had taken us to separate locations, and while we were apart, I'd begun developing new interests and new aspects of myself. This was an important period in my life and I had to take things slowly, one step at a time. I moved back to the ranch permanently in June 1976, driving west with Esther Pashek, who now had a position on the faculty of Arizona State University in Tempe.

Throughout my personal transformation, Chuck had been supportive and encouraging, but now that we were both in Arizona, relating to him and the newness of Nourishing Space was more than I could handle. I didn't want to be tied to him—or to anyone. I was finally ready to step off that second cliff and leave my marriage. I dreaded making the break. Chuck was a fine, honorable person and I didn't want to say the words that would deeply wound him: "I love you. And at the same time, I don't want to be married to you. My interest in the women's land is taking me in new directions where you can't go." We met to talk about our future and agreed that it might be best if we separated and gave each other the freedom to fulfill ourselves as individuals. Chuck was reluctant to make the separation permanent, but he agreed to initiate legal proceedings, and in September 1976, our divorce was finalized.

I couldn't tell at first whether I'd done the right thing. After all, I was breaking a promise I'd made sincerely—given my background and beliefs, not something to be taken lightly. I desperately wanted to talk to my mother, to someone more experienced than I who could tell me how a couple parted. But I was on my own. It was up to me to find the new path, take new steps, find new words. No one, not even I, could predict the outcome.

When Chuck and I split up, most of our friends and family were understanding. But a few friends said scornfully, "We could see this coming when you became so independent." What they had really seen was budding independence where society disallowed it and their judgmental words hurt. It was painful to realize that they laid all the blame on me and refused to take into account the love I still felt for Chuck. They couldn't see how difficult the divorce was for me. I had to accept the fact that they completely overlooked my agony.

As I reflect on that struggle, I realize it was the "shoulds" that society puts on marriage that were oppressive and malnourishing to me—I "should" put Chuck's needs first, "should" take his advice. I'd accepted these "shoulds" when we were working together in China and India, but here in the States, we were seeking personal and professional growth independently. Where my searches were venturesome, his were cautious. When he saw me taking risks, he warned me of the consequences. And like a rebellious teenager, I didn't want that kind of advice. Now that we were no longer a couple, I was free to make my own mistakes—and achieve my own triumphs.

Chuck and I spoke by phone and even saw each other occasionally. I knew he'd been hurt by the divorce and my heart ached for him. But as he settled into his work at the church, he began finding new friends and interests and things between us became more comfortable again.

When I'd gone back to State College in September 1975, Lavina had moved onto Nourishing Space. During this formative period, she knew I wanted women to work together to bring Nourishing Space into being. Friends often came out to discuss ideas for use of the land, and in early 1976, six or seven women, including Lavina, established a collective. While living at the Space, they took time to study the land and think about organized activities that would benefit the women while not overusing the fragile desert terrain. There was also plenty of work to do. They started a vegetable garden, repaired old buildings, and established safe fire rings where women could camp.

One of the first things they agreed on was that Nourishing Space would be for women only. Those who wanted to bring a male companion, even one they defended as being supportive and understanding of women, would be told, "There are few places where women can be by themselves. Women who come for that purpose expect to find a place without men. The man who seems 'nice' to you may not appear that way to other women."

Before I returned in June 1976, women in Tucson had designed and published a brochure about Nourishing Space and mailed it out to women's publications across the U.S. News of the Space also passed through the area by word-of-mouth. As we prepared to welcome visitors, I prepared materials for responding to mounting inquiries with explicit descriptions of the desert land, instructions on how to reach the space, what time of day to arrive, what to bring, and what to expect. Life in the desert wasn't easy and had its dangers. Even so, once Nourishing Space opened, many women came completely unprepared. A few were angry and disgusted by the terrain, but most grew to honor it. In the process, they learned about taking care of themselves.

I recognized that most of the women who invested themselves in organizing fundraising events, workshops, hikes, potlucks, and weekend work parties were lesbians. I was still naive about lesbians but was impressed that their energy was so clearly their own, not directed by a man. I was glad they responded well to the women's space and liked to initiate projects to work on together.

Cathy, who didn't live at the Space but had a sense of what it needed, spoke to the collective about building a ramada—an open, covered shelter for gatherings. The group agreed to help. They carried stones from the stream to build it and finished the structure with materials Cathy brought from the city.

Another project the women took on was replacing the piping in our water system. Lavina, who'd become a compassionate and devoted caretaker, organized the whole thing. She rented a Ditch Witch and located women with plumbing experience who were willing to pitch in. It was fun to see women working together, driving the equipment and laying down pipe. Our male neighbors in the desert were surprised we didn't need help—women experts were on the job and everything was under control.

Women repaired, cleaned, and filled an old stock tank so we could swim. It soon became a popular gathering place for sunbathing and cooling off on summer days. To me it was a spiritual haven. I'd go out there at night, slip into the water, and float beneath the stars. I felt cradled in the arms of the universe and knew that life could be trusted.

Lavina and some of the other women rigged up a tent near the stream where they could heat rocks and pour water on them to make a sauna. After steaming inside the tent, they could cool off in the stream—that is, when we had a stream. The bed was often dry.

With no men around, we didn't need to wear bathing suits, so I had the privilege of looking at women's bodies and appreciating their beauty for the first time. Here I became more comfortable with my own maimed body. Our privacy was a joy to women who liked to walk the land unclothed. Nudity didn't bother me, but I did suggest that those who wanted the freedom of going naked stay away from the right-of-way where outsiders had permission to drive. After all, we didn't want voyeurs.

Organizing the rules we would live by on the land proved more complicated than I'd anticipated. As the population of women who came and went grew, those living at the Space became the decision-making body which was fair and logical but also problematic, as its membership—and therefore its goals—constantly shifted. So I recommended we invite women who didn't live at the Space to form a panel that would offer advice and help keep the larger goals of Nourishing Space on track. Names were suggested and a formal advisory group convened to work on long-term projects, possibilities, and procedures. Both groups operated on a consensus-building basis which meant we spent hours coming to agreements. Every woman interested in guiding the decision-making process was asked to attend meetings and help shoulder responsibilities that arose from them.

We welcomed all types of women as long as they were willing to respect the rules. After asking new arrivals to sign in at the cedar house, we took turns orienting them to the Space and how it operated, explaining what had gone into our decision-making. I was constantly amazed that just when the group had reached consensus on an issue and things were working well, some newcomer would announce that she didn't have to abide by the decision because she hadn't been part of the consensus. I hadn't known there were women that brash but realized that this was a prime example of women learning to be more assertive.

Some decisions were fairly simple, like how much we'd charge for an overnight stay or a long-term visit. But the use of tobacco, alcohol, and drugs elicited a wide difference of opinion. We finally agreed that outside of residences, tobacco would be allowed if the women were careful about picking up cigarette butts, and alcohol would be imbibed only at specified social occasions. Drugs were prohibited. These agreements worked fairly well, although when new arrivals challenged them, they had to be explained over and over again.

Then there was the matter of work. Litter had to be picked up and garbage carried off the land. Living spaces needed to be cleaned. Someone had to greet newcomers and talk to them about nourishment. Expenses had to be entered into the ledger and records had to be updated. Keeping track of who was living where and what activities were taking place was essential.

We had to determine how much was expected of the women who lived on the land—both those who could pay and those who couldn't. I wanted work efforts to be elective so that women could contribute as they wished. A wonderful example of a successful collective endeavor was the garden we started. Some tilled it, others tended it, and we all benefited from the vegetables that grew there. No one refused to work, but some women were more skilled than others, and a few had little knowledge of the basic cooperation that keeps a community going.

Many ideas emerged from our discussions about fundraising. Phoenix women, including Esther, wanted to host a women's outdoor concert. Even though the thought of women's music echoing through our canyon was terribly appealing, we had to face the fact that having hundreds of women milling around the land would be hazardous to the soil and plants. However, we did implement another money-making suggestion from the Phoenix women—raising earthworms and selling them to aerate gardens. For years, we had earthworm beds near the main house that were tended daily. As the worms grew and multiplied, they did wonders for our vegetable plots, but the worm market became glutted and we never did seem to sell any.

Despite its rigors, life on the land wasn't all work. We gathered to watch the full moon rise over the ridge to our east. We celebrated the solstices. The circle gatherings we held at these times made me aware that a deep spirituality permeated the lives of the women who came there. It became a common concern, a personal involvement that drew us together and led us to share insights. Many of the women kept journals and helped newcomers develop their own spiritual disciplines. I held steady in the trust that we were all on the land for a purpose—to discover new meaning in our lives.

Being on the land brought me closer to Mother Earth. I was beginning to see how basic the eternal feminine is, and that I, as a woman, am part of that archetype. In daily meditation, I reflected on the natural processes taking place all around me, awed by their complexity and, at the same time, their elegant simplicity. Understanding the interconnectedness of all living things, all living systems, everything in the universe, I realized, is the ultimate learning. Every single human being is an integral part of the whole.

We had informal community potlucks whenever the spirit moved us. On Thanksgiving, fifty or more women would bring food, music, and games. We had workshops on such skills as how to camp in the heat of the desert. Here, all that I'd learned while living in India's hot weather without a refrigerator came into play.

We often hiked up under the cliffs and sometimes saw mountain lions. Deer were frequent visitors. On occasion, javelinas, or wild pigs, and iguanas were sighted. There were many snakes—some quite harmless, like the colorful racers, but we tried to avoid rattlers. The birds were cheerful neighbors. Hawks soared overhead, and cactus wrens who lived in the saguaros were chatty.

The torrential rains of August, often preceded by thunder and lightning, poured straight down from what had been, just minutes before, a clear sky. They were dramatic and their power altered the landscape. As soon as I felt it was safe, I'd run out and climb up the ravine, splashing in the rivulets that were still cascading and reshaping the vertical streambeds.

At one of our advisory group discussions about the future of Nourishing Space, we decided that we should find out what was happening on other women's land. Four of us drove up to Oregon to explore the many acres owned by women, each organized somewhat differently. In one place, women were building snug cabins. In another, they were gardening extensively. Owners were glad to have us visit. In fact, we were invited to a weekend retreat at one of the locales.

After participants shared how things were progressing on each site, conversation turned to Oregon Women's Land (OWL), common land purchased collectively by the property owners in response to the trespassing problem they faced: women simply came and parked themselves on private land without permission. The landowners felt taken advantage of, yet they realized that most of these women intruders had nowhere else to go. The solution was to create OWL—common land where all women were welcome, a long-held dream of many of the property owners.

OWL, purchased in early 1976, had been in operation only a few months and the retreat provided an opportunity to evaluate its success. What the owners were finding was that many women who came to OWL didn't know how to take on leadership. Without someone to make sure that residents had food and shelter and took responsibility for chores, it operated dysfunctionally. Homeless women were that way for a number of reasons, one being that they didn't know how to care for themselves. OWL's owners were beginning to realize that simply making land available to women was not the entire answer.

Although this had not yet been an issue at Nourishing Space, I knew it was something we would undoubtedly face. Women would come because they had nowhere else to go. It seemed more important than ever to engage women in thinking about their own nourishment and about caring for themselves. I came away from the retreat with a deep sense that there are skills we must gain to create true community, among them recognizing and respecting our diversity, honoring and being patient with our differences of opinion, and trusting each other.

Though I never asked about the sexual preference of the women who came to Nourishing Space, I knew that some were lesbians. Homosexuality had once mystified and frightened me—I remembered how perplexed I'd been when a male college classmate committed suicide over a broken relationship with his roommate—but I'd overcome those fears. Now, here at the Space, I was having a good time with women no matter what their orientation. The fun we were sharing was far more enjoyable than any I'd experienced in heterosexual social life. As we talked, worked, and played, I saw myself as an asexual bridge connecting heterosexual and homosexual women. I had no thought of becoming involved in further romantic relationships.

Then life's kaleidoscope shifted and something completely new happened. Cathy, the ramada builder, a woman whom I admired a great deal, told me she had a crush on me. I was stunned—surprised that she felt as she did, amazed at her courage in telling a straight woman, and touched because I didn't think of myself as appealing to women. Moved by the directness of her admission, I was able to recognize my attraction to her. To my surprise, I found myself in love—not with women in general, but with one special woman.

I was deliriously happy in the close connection that developed. The sweet intimacies we exchanged were heady. The exhilaration I felt must have been apparent to everyone I met. For the next few months, my feet scarcely touched the ground.

It was quite a challenge for me to put this turn of events into a framework I could understand. It was one thing to be friendly with lesbians; it was quite another to identify with them. To admit to myself and others that I was in love with a woman meant identifying myself as a lesbian or bisexual—a person whose lifestyle was, in many places, still illegal. I'd be leaving the straight world, the only world I'd ever known, and the only way I'd ever thought about myself. It was *metanoia*, an earth-shaking change in knowing, akin to changing religion or nationality.

I had to become circumspect in what I said and who I talked about because I could easily expose closeted friends. I learned what it meant to "pass" in a society that, for homosexuals, was tantamount to a police state. I felt fear but knew that every aspect of what I was experiencing was familiar to my lover. She told me about the lesbian community, sharing herself, her life, her interests, helping me to know her. She took me to lesbian events in the Tucson area, and as I got acquainted with her friends, I was gently guided, instructed, and upheld by women. What joy. My time with Cathy wasn't long—we separated several months later—but it was intense. I'll always be grateful to her for bringing me out and for being, through thick and thin, a soulmate.

Women continued flocking to the Space—alone, in couples, and in groups. Their reasons for coming ranged from sheer curiosity to needing a place to stay, from wanting to get away from family headaches to wanting to find community. Some spent a day or two. Some remained for months, camping out on the land or sleeping in a shelter.

During the three-and-a-half years I lived there, my friends and relatives came, too. I arranged times with the residents when it would be okay for male family members to visit. My children stopped by, as did my stepmother, and Chuck brought Jean Day (whom he later married), a friend from our India days. I was glad the two had found each other and that I felt comfortable around them.

It was important to me that my heterosexual friends and family visit the land. My new sexuality wasn't obvious outside Nourishing Space or the Tucson lesbian community—and I chose not to share it with my family for some time—but those friends and relatives who came could see that my relationship with women had somehow changed. Being at the Space gave them an opportunity to meet and have fun with women who just happened to be lesbians. Only through exposure to that which we fear can we receive enlightenment and overcome our prejudices.

Barb Armstrong, a member of the advisory group, brought women grant writers to Nourishing Space. We applied for and received federal block grant funds that made it possible to employ three part-time workers from among the residents as a way of helping them care for themselves. One checked to see that everything on the land was in good shape. Another welcomed and briefed new women about living on the desert and protecting the environment. A third answered the phone, responded to inquiries, and kept records. I did the accounts myself because I was ultimately responsible for the financial support of the Space. We met frequently to talk about the health of the land, guests, and pocketbook.

Early one morning, the FBI arrived unexpectedly. Though I was scared by their bold raid, I knew they had no right to be on my land without authorization. They admitted they had no search warrant but argued that they were simply looking for a fugitive named Bonnie and had heard she might be at the Space. I told them that not only was there no Bonnie, but they had no right to be on my land. I ordered them to leave immediately.

Asserting my prerogative as a landowner was empowering. The FBI officials apologized and left, but they parked outside the south gate and questioned everyone who came and went. The discussion this raid provoked helped those of us on the land realize how easily and unnecessarily we were intimidated, so we developed coping strategies for similar situations that might arise in the future.

In September 1976, a Tucson friend invited me to a potluck supper hosted by her Shalom group that was made up of women in church-related professions. I knew few of the women or their guests, but I was intrigued by one of them, a builder named Margot Kostenbader. She was almost as tall as I was with short brown wavy hair, brown eyes, and an unpretentious expression on her attractive face. Outdoor work had tanned her and roughened her hands. I discovered later that she was married but was looking for a way out of the relationship.

I sat next to her while we ate and told her about Nourishing Space. I described a problem we'd recently encountered when a violent storm tore the roof off our ramada and set it down, intact, fifty feet away. I asked whether she'd be willing to come out and help us put the roof back on. She agreed. A week or so later, she arrived in her blue Ford truck to assess the situation. She said the old roof was too crumpled to repair, but that she'd help put on a new one if we'd buy the materials she specified, have them delivered to the site, and get some women ready to help.

Roofing day dawned bright. Margot arrived and women gathered. But before the women climbed up to place the rafters, they took off their blouses and T-shirts and started lathering sunscreen on themselves and each other. I watched Margot's reaction, pretty sure she'd never bossed a topless all-woman crew. She took it in stride but afterward admitted she'd been concerned that some of the nails being hammered into the roof might snag a pendulous breast.

Groups of gypsies visited us at different times. One group, traveling in a large pickup truck, was looking for a place to unload, sort out their belongings, and work on the truck motor. They brought with them a problem that until then had been hypothetical: would we welcome a male child onto the land? We were discussing it quietly when a car drove up and a writer for lesbian newspapers emerged. She'd come from Los Angeles to see Nourishing Space.

The timing of her arrival was unfortunate and dramatic. No sooner had she introduced herself than she saw the boy in our midst and screamed, "Kittu, you've completely disillusioned me! I never dreamed that the first thing I'd see here is a male!" She jumped back into her car, roared off, and later expressed her feelings in a negative review of the Space. Her upsetting behavior had a decisive effect. We immediately agreed that we'd welcome male children who were part of a family.

Many women passed through Nourishing Space and I soon discovered how many were battered and bitter, how many were homeless out in the world on their own, how many had suffered sexual abuse from brothers and fathers. It was important to converse with these women, important to divert their anger into constructive action, lest it be taken out against the land or other women. But I wasn't always sure what to do when they arrived asking to stay. One woman with two children appeared and promised me that she'd soon have a job, wouldn't be any trouble, and wouldn't ask for shelter. Then it started raining.

In all of our literature, we stated clearly that we didn't serve food or have stores of food and that women who came should be self-supporting. Even so, women arrived with nothing and I occasionally found myself making a big pot of soup and ladling it out. We drew on the resources of social service agencies in Tucson and Phoenix to find shelter and employment for those in need. Many social workers, knowing we didn't want to become a homeless shelter, advised us and were willing to come to the Space and talk directly to our residents about their options.

The women who came had differing political opinions and philosophies. Some women lectured me on being an oppressive capitalist landowner and suggested I turn the land over to women. When I asked who would sign the papers and pay the monthly mortgage, they asked how much it was, gasping when they heard the amount and demanding to know how I expected them to pay it. That was the whole point—I didn't. But I also knew that if it wasn't paid, we'd lose the land. In the early days, their challenges might have felt like a slap in the face, but I'd grown used to the leftist talk of young newcomers and was ready to engage them about the realities of finance.

As the landowner, I felt it was important to stay on good terms with neighbors. We were all living in the wilderness and needed to help each other. I made it a point to talk with people who drove through the land, explaining, "There are many places where men can go to be together, but there are few such places for women. This is one of them." A particular frustration was that newcomers who had corresponded with us and supposedly read the literature often paid no attention to our careful maps and instructions about what time to arrive. Disgruntled neighbors told me about being wakened in the night with inquiries about how to find us.

The postal worker at Vail, where we picked up our mail, was frequently called upon to give directions. I encouraged her to visit the land, but on Saturdays and Sundays, her days off, she had family to attend to. Knowing she was the main source of information for curious people in the area, I spent time with her trying to explain our mission. After Nourishing Space closed, I heard that for years she'd been saying, "Dr. Riddle takes in women and turns their heads around." Though her statement credits me with something I didn't do—the women turned their own heads around—this is actually what happened. By nourishing ourselves, we saw our lives differently.

Since the Space first came into being, I'd been interested in issues related to building a community. When I heard about a seminar on women in architecture being held at the University of California in San Jose, I eagerly attended, and in the process, opened up more possibilities for Nourishing Space. In mid-December 1976, the Tucson City Planning Council invited two women who had served on that seminar's faculty to come to Arizona to talk about sexism in architecture. Along with the Tucson Women's Commission, we cosponsored the event. Among other things, the speakers discussed and showed slides to illustrate phallic and feminine structures.

After the lecture, they came out to the Space and stayed overnight with me in the cedar house. The next day, they toured the land with the site-planning group I'd called together early on to help outline the physical development of Nourishing Space. The main outcome of this exchange was the development of a grant proposal around the site plan, which now could be used as a tool for teaching women nontraditional skills.

We approached the Federal Initiative for Post-Secondary Education (FIPSE) for funding to build an alternative secondary education site where women could enrich their understanding of the land and of themselves. The course work would prepare them for professions women usually didn't think of entering. This project became central to our planning. Though they didn't fund this first proposal, FIPSE's feedback was positive. They suggested we proceed as far as we could on our own, then submit another proposal as the project matured, indicating that they would consider it seriously.

Nourishing Space was an entity in the process of becoming an organism requiring a great deal of attention. Daily, we experienced the tension of working for her emergence while maintaining the land, making it possible for women to come and camp, hike, and participate in celebrations and workshops. Keeping the show going was a difficult juggling act. We were like the root of a plant developing new cells as it reaches into the ground while simultaneously transporting nutrients from the ground to the rest of the organism. The analogy was not lost on us as women—we talked about it often. This uncertainty, the transition implied in growth, is found in any well-nourished entity.

Being in transition ourselves, the questions we faced related to conflicting demands on our energy. What takes priority when we are exhausted—the needs of the Space, the needs of other women, or our own needs? We wanted to be available to those who came—other women in transition—but we also needed to improve the living facilities, raise money, and develop possibilities for the future. Plus, we needed to take care of ourselves.

The land itself helped us keep our perspective. Her austerity and seeming barrenness veiled a beauty and spiritual energy divulged only to those who sought to see it. As we took care in preserving her ecological balance, she, in turn, provided us the same. She offered both rest and challenge, nourishing our inward and outward journeys and providing a good place in which to experience transition. She was a third party to all our communications. Listening to the land, in all her infinite power, helped us put our struggles into perspective, cope patiently with uncertainties, and clarify our goals.

We ultimately realized that the canyon, large as she was, was not a place for a sizable population of women. Her voice called us to reexamine not only how we thought about living on the land, but also about our own personal values. She helped us experience ourselves in new ways. In her presence, each woman had to come to terms with her limitations and gifts. Women who found the land nourishing came back. Others moved on. Recognition of the land's special qualities formed a bond across generations of the occupants.

Margot had visited the Space several times since replacing the ramada's roof. When the Sexism in Architecture speakers visited the land, she drove out to meet them. During that weekend, she and I discovered a strong mutual attraction. In fact, it was hard to keep our minds on the business at hand, showing the guests around and hearing the site-planning committee's report. By the time Margot left for Tucson, we were sure we'd see each other again, as frequently as possible.

Meanwhile, I'd planned to drive to San Francisco to see a friend. From there, I'd visit my stepmother at the Missionary Courts in Berkeley, then return to Tucson via Los Angeles. Margot offered to fly out to Los Angeles, meet me at the airport, and help me with the drive back to Arizona. I happily agreed.

On the day she was due to arrive in Los Angeles at midnight, I started south from Berkeley at 4 P.M. There were rainstorms and other delays along Interstate 5 and I realized I hadn't allowed enough time to meet her. Not only that, I'd forgotten to get Margot's flight number. I knew she was flying in on TWA but had no idea where in the terminal the airline was located.

The evening wore on and I didn't reach L.A. until 11:45 P.M., just fifteen minutes before her plane was due. Luckily, I found the airport and TWA without much trouble. I pulled up to the curb, parked illegally, and ran up to the entrance. Just then, Margot walked out. What a miracle! Tired but happy, we took a room in the nearest motel. After several idyllic days in southern California, we headed back to Tucson.

Afterward, she came out to Nourishing Space as often as she could. I knew she was trying to figure out what to do about her marriage. At one point she told me she couldn't leave until her youngest daughter was out of high school, six years hence. I found this difficult to comprehend. If we were considering a serious relationship, as I knew we were, six years seemed a long time to wait. But until she decided differently, there was nothing I could do except enjoy our time together.

When she could she brought her daughters, Laurie and Debbie, out to the land. She showed them the ramada she'd helped repair. She even introduced me to her parents, who owned a small ranch not far from the Space, and they welcomed me as her friend. Several years later, however, when they realized we were lovers, that welcome was withdrawn. Unable to understand our relationship, they refused to acknowledge it. Their unwillingness to discuss our partnership was very difficult for us.

In March 1977, Margot arrived on the land early one evening and announced that she wasn't going back. I was glad to have her move in, though we had to reorganize the furniture and figure out how to live together in this new arrangement. There was no place for her girls to stay, or go to school, so she decided they would stay with their father in their family home in the Tucson Foothills. That way, they could remain in their current school systems and be near their friends. Margot completed her jobs in the city and began looking for work closer to the Space. She and her husband divorced later that year.

It was an unsettled time for everyone. Margot and I took things one day at a time, choosing to remain quiet about our new relationship. Margot saw her family at church and brought the girls to visit us as often as she could. Fortunately, Laurie and Debbie were excellent students, and to their credit, they continued to do well in their studies despite the distress they were experiencing over their parents' divorce.

When I told Margot that I'd received an invitation to Park College's 1977 graduation ceremonies to accept a Distinguished Alumna award, she insisted we go together. She wanted to see the campus and then drive back through Colorado to see the places that had been important to me there. The ceremony was held on my birthday, May 21, and the award was signed by the president of the Alumni Association, Jonathan Hawley, whose grandfather had been president of the college during my student days. My classmates, especially my old roommate Jeanne Allison Dawson, were proud of me, and all concurred that the words of the tribute were appropriate:

With uncommon zeal Kittu has translated theories about nutrition into practical programs which not only sustain life but also nourish the total person. Actively involving herself in an impressive number of humanitarian projects, Kittu has discharged the obligations of her college experience with creative courage. She has demonstrated a pioneering spirit in seeking original solutions to nutritional needs, whether individual or global in scope. Her Park College friends recognize Katharine's contributions to the human race with gratitude.

Before she moved in, Margot had participated in a special event at Nourishing Space—the first formal gathering in the U.S. of lesbians over age fifty. We didn't know then that a group called Old Lesbians Organizing for Change (OLOC) would be created ten years later or that I'd be one of its founders. Our definition of 'old' was elastic enough to include any woman over thirty-five who considered herself so but it was comforting and affirming to have women my age lending perspective to what was happening on the land. We discussed the need for older women's communities. I valued this idea and hoped, based on experience, such communities would include a mix of generations for the richness that brings.

Two weddings took place back-to-back in October 1977. Patty married Terry Dutton in Illinois and Chuck married Jean Day in Michigan. Margot, Dorothy, and I flew to Chicago, rented a car, and drove down to Champaign-Urbana. It was the first time that all five Riddle nuclear family members had been together in a long time. We celebrated Patty's birthday on October 28 and her wedding the next day.

On October 30, Bill and Patty and their spouses drove off to East Lansing, Michigan, for Chuck's ceremony. The day was foggy and rainy, so flights were canceled, leaving Chuck stranded at the Champaign-Urbana airport wondering how to get to his own wedding. Dorothy, Margot, and I were able to drive him to Chicago where we had our own flights to catch. I joked, "I won't be at your wedding to give you away, but at least I can see that you get to the church on time." He and Dorothy flew from Chicago to East Lansing and we waited for her to return before flying back to Arizona.

In witnessing two couples making lifelong commitments, Margot and I realized that we, too, were building a lifetime partnership even though there would be no public ceremony acknowledging that fact.

That Christmas, Margot's first away from her girls, was going to be hard, so we elected to go away. We drove to Santa Fe, New Mexico, and celebrated there with Pat Hill and her children. I'd met Pat at one of my "Nourishment" workshops in Esther's home in Pennsylvania and we had kept in touch. In the spring we returned to New Mexico to Ghost Ranch to attend an adobe building workshop hoping to use some of what we learned at Nourishing Space.

But that same year, 1978, the spring rains were unusually heavy. It was cold and too wet for women to camp. We were miserable. For the first time since I'd been on the land, the streambed was full, almost too full to drive across. There was no bridge and the A-frame and cedar houses were cut off from each other. Vehicles got stuck in the mud. Sometimes it was impossible to get into Tucson. We had to wait hours for the water racing across the road to die down. Heavy-hearted, I realized that before another such rain we'd have to build a bridge. We also needed more spacious and substantial shelters. Even though the rain brought a spectacular display of desert flowers, the somber memory of how it felt to live through that wet and uncomfortable spring remained with us.

About the same time we were dealing with this oppressive weather, we were facing the fact that money was getting short. Not only money, but energy. We knew we'd probably get funding from FIPSE, and many women were contributing to the ongoing upkeep of Nourishing Space, but we were tired. We'd worked hard for three-and-a-half years and no longer had the vigor required to carry out our plans. Regretfully, I admitted that the mortgage payments had become an impossible burden so I'd have to sell the land.

At first I felt like a failure. Then a dear friend from Tucson showed up one Sunday morning and suggested a hike up the canyon. We climbed to an overlook and surveyed the hills around us and the tiny encampment of buildings down below. She wanted to know how I felt about giving up the land. I was deeply touched by her sensitivity and care for me. She listened as I shared how much I'd grown and how wonderful it had been to live on the land and be with women. Talking about it helped me realize that I'd achieved everything I wanted from the land and the project—I had learned to nourish. Neither I nor the Space could be called a failure.

By the time we returned to the cedar house, I was at peace. I was ready to tell the advisory group that within a few months, my resources would be exhausted and I'd have to put the land up for sale. Unless they could come up with a way to buy me out, we'd have to set a date to close Nourishing Space for Women.

The land had been available to women for over three years. More than 1,000 women had found their way to the canyon and I'd witnessed a great deal of personal growth. The isolated location threw women back on themselves—the desert forced them to examine their lives. Martha Courtot wrote a chapter about Nourishing Space in the book, *Lesbian Land* (of course it was not just for lesbians but for all women). I quote:

> *Although the land could not be sustained for women, we cannot judge it to be a failure in women's land. Much that happened at Nourishing Space was powerful in the spiritual sense. Solstice rituals, the empowerment of women in their spiritual selves, the connections that many of us made there cannot be lost because the land is gone. Rather, we might consider that the land came to be lived within us: we moved, we scattered. Some went to cities, some went to country land. We took what the land and the women there had given us, and we made new things come into being. We cannot consider Nourishing Space a failure. The double rainbow still lives in us.*

For me, the most important lesson was that it's all right to start something and have it end. I'd promised nothing. Any woman who came to Nourishing Space did so for her own reasons and took care of herself. That way, there was no disillusionment. The projects that were undertaken, whether planting a vegetable garden or replacing pipes, were initiated, financed, and carried out by those who saw a need and wanted to meet it. Each woman was allowed to nourish herself and to keep track of what that process meant for her.

I learned a great deal about human interactions and building self-esteem. I found that in most situations, women are united in wanting the best for the world. When we are not competing for the attention of men, we unite in a powerful way and support each other. I, myself, became more assertive and confident as a result of Nourishing Space. I also gained more understanding of what women have to endure in the world. When the Space closed, some people said to me, "It's a shame it didn't work out," to which I replied, "Who says it didn't?"

We named a date shortly after Thanksgiving 1978 when the land would no longer be Nourishing Space for Women. We had a closing ceremony before the women left. Some wanted to stay on and rent from me until the land sold, but I decided it wouldn't be possible. We shed tears, gave thanks for what we'd gained, and said goodbye. Then Margot and I returned to the cedar house to work out what to do next now that the property was on the market.

Eventually, the land sold. Only once did I gather the courage to go back there. I parked by the north gate and slipped over the fence. I sat down high above the stream and took a good look around me. The camping circles we'd established were still there, but the vegetable garden was gone, and no new buildings had been erected. I talked to the land and asked how she was doing. "Waiting for women to come back" was her response.

Margot and I still have the records, the site plan, the files of accounts and decisions, the workshop outlines, and many names of those who visited the Space. We've lugged them with us to Tucson, Lincoln, and San Antonio. They are the tangible remains of a dream that was important to me and my own nourishment. Perhaps they may someday be useful to others planning to carry out a similar project. They are a reminder that we can make a Nourishing Space for ourselves wherever we live.

Chapter Ten
Budding Opportunities

Margot and I remained on the land, waiting for a buyer, but being on the huge 160-acre expanse was often lonely. Each time I walked out along the streambed and looked up at the cliffs, ghostly echoes of the bustle and laughter that had been Nourishing Space haunted me. Still, all that had happened here remained to nourish us as we rested a while, wondering what to do next.

Living with a woman was a new experience for both of us. We'd been together about a year. Margot had nourished me through the dissolution of my relationship with Cathy and was now nurturing me through the sale of the land. As we grew closer, we discovered each other's talents and nuances of character, which deepened our understanding of ourselves as a couple. We each expressed surprise at how much we enjoyed being together.

For fun, we made a quilt using scraps of fabric from our previous lives, explaining the significance of each bit of cloth. Margot was as talented a seamstress as she was a builder. "They're really the same thing," she said. "You just follow the directions." When she showed me the house she'd finished just before meeting me, I was struck by its beauty and impressed by the care she had lavished on details.

An excellent housekeeper, Margot somehow managed to keep our home and our clothes clean despite desert dust that found its way everywhere. She liked my cooking and enjoyed being cooked for. When the house needed maintenance, Margot took care of it, which was satisfying for her and a great relief to me. Margot, the doer, was the perfect foil for me, the visionary.

She was pleased that I'd bought land in "her" desert. She knew its color and magnificence far better than I and she was eager to share it with me. Though I've looked at and loved the sky all my life, she helped me see its grays and whites and blues in a whole new way.

Margot wasn't jealous of the many women friends I had, for she had a strong network of her own in Tucson. Fortunately, her women friends were supportive of our relationship and included me in their companionship. We continued attending the Shalom group whose members welcomed spending time with us, two women without husbands. That and the fact that we were also romantic partners created subtle shifts in our conversations, which revolved around values and women's strengths rather than on marriage or relationships with men.

Margot and I had our differences and we learned to accept this. I didn't like her smoking and she didn't like my nagging. At first, I'd run away from a quarrel, just get in the car and drive off. She'd jump in her blue Ford truck and give chase. When we stopped long enough to look at what was happening, we could see the humor in it. Eventually we decided that we were together, a couple, and no matter how many angry things were said, we'd stick it out and work through the hard spots. Leaving the relationship was not an option.

Before the land sold in 1979, we rented a temporary apartment in Tucson. Margot's faithful truck, which had made many trips out to the land, now carried us and all our belongings back to the city. Margot knew Tucson well and we drove all over looking for a new place to live. We recognized a small adobe house on Roger Road in the middle of a large grove of tamarisk trees and tall pink oleander bushes as our next home. Its wonderful picture window afforded views of the Catalina Mountains, whose 8,000-foot peaks reminded me of the Himalayas.

After buying it, we celebrated with a big open house. Margot's family and friends all came, glad she had "come to her senses" and moved back to town. Women from both our Shalom group and Nourishing Space brought their spouses, lovers, and children. It was a diverse crew sharing good food and lots of fun.

Though Tucson had been Margot's home since she was a little girl, she was now discovering facets of the city she'd never known about. I was familiar with the women's community, its bars and parties, but didn't yet know Tucson as my home. For both of us, individually and as a couple, the city revealed itself in a new light and we shared our discoveries with each other.

One of the nicest places we could go together was Casa Nuestra, a women's club Cathy had opened around the same time Nourishing Space closed. We thoroughly enjoyed the club as a place to relax, play games, have a meal, swim, and meet friends. There were discussion groups and programs, dances, and other planned activities.

Now that we were settled in, we had to figure out how to support ourselves. Margot was loath to return to piecemeal construction work. She wanted a long-term project she could devote all her energies to. Then she heard that the YWCA was looking for a plant manager to care for its various facilities, including a beautiful building in Tucson, several other locations where child care was provided, and a camp in the desert. She applied for the job and was offered the position as assistant director for the YWCA.

I was reluctant to slip back into the harness of professorial duties, so I took odd jobs—servicing fruit juice machines in a dozen or so locations around the city and serving summons for a lawyer friend. But these jobs were getting me nowhere. I had to start earning real money. Selling the land would bring in a nice sum but not nearly enough to cover my retirement. And there were living expenses to consider. More importantly, I needed to find fulfilling work again— something that utilized my background in nutrition and promoted women's empowerment.

The University of Arizona Health Science Center seemed a likely place to start looking because Dr. Gail Harrison, one of the authors of *Nutrition, Behavior and Change* and a faculty member in the Department of Community and Family Medicine, had many interesting projects in progress. Sure enough, she put me to work right away teaching international nutrition. I also helped her design nutrition units that were inserted into the medical school curriculum as a part of the regular coursework in areas such as pediatrics.

On behalf of the Department of Community and Family Medicine, I responded to a request from the USDA to submit a proposal on promoting breast-feeding at the Papago Indian Reservation in southern Arizona. If funded, the program promised to be a long-term project on a topic I was very interested in pursuing.

Through her connections, Margot found some part-time consulting work for me. Problems sometimes arose in the YWCA-sponsored feeding programs. One mother insisted that her child was eating too much, getting too greedy. Her responses to a few leading questions revealed that she thought her three-year-old should follow the same spiritual discipline of fasting and restraint that she and her husband espoused. Instead, the little girl was sneaking food, thereby, in her mother's mind, putting herself in spiritual jeopardy.

Once I realized that the parents were actually withholding food, I gasped inwardly—this bordered on child abuse. I gently but firmly explained that because the girl's body was still growing, it couldn't sustain itself without enough nutrients. In sneaking food, the child was assuaging a very natural need. Much to my relief, she was able to change her frame of reference and make allowances for her girl, allowing her to grow. Years later, at a women's conference, the mother recognized me. Catching her lovely, healthy, ten-year-old daughter's hand, she led her to me and thanked me for insisting she not force the child to fast. That was welcome, positive feedback indeed.

Soon, my life in Tucson was rich and busy. I was asked to join the Tucson Women's Commission, whose members I'd gotten acquainted with during the Sexism in Architecture project, and I quickly became involved in many local issues. For example, in 1979, the commission did something nearly unheard of at the time. It held public hearings on domestic violence. Victims came forward and spoke to city council officials about this form of abuse. I was not alone in my shock at its prevalence.

Though I found my new job and other involvements rewarding, I missed Nourishing Space—the beautiful desert environment and the daily contact with women who were learning to nourish themselves. It would take time and effort to replace the creative and original work I'd done there. Still, my new schedule allowed me to spend more time with family, a great blessing.

Margot and I didn't expect our two sets of children, or their lives, to mesh, so we devoted attention to each individually. During our first year in Tucson, Laurie graduated from high school with honors and received a scholarship to the University of Arizona. After the party we threw in her honor, she moved into a small apartment on our property. Debbie, her sister, still attending high school, was living with her father and learning to drive.

Dorothy had set up a counseling business in Tucson, then started work on an MBA. When that was complete, she moved to Phoenix and joined the faculty of the American Graduate School of International Management. After earning a Ph.D. from the University of Illinois, Patty moved to Lincoln, Nebraska with Terry and was now teaching in the Health and Physical Education Department at the University of Nebraska. After Bill finished his master's degree in social work, he and Nancy moved to the Seattle area and got jobs. When Nancy inherited some money and wanted to enroll in graduate study, Bill became a house husband. He now had time to pursue his love of carpentry, but as an unemployed male, he found himself ignored and sometimes denigrated by others—an experience familiar to many unemployed women.

I was saddened when Bill and Nancy divorced in 1978, but the following year he married Barbara Lumpkin. He invited both Margot and me to the wedding, a lovely occasion held in a beautiful mansion in downtown Seattle. Chuck performed the ceremony and his wife Jean was present. It was the first time Margot and I had appeared together at one of my family's celebrations. Everyone was very accepting of us, but I was uncomfortable and defensive for reasons I didn't understand. Margot bore the brunt of my unease—I failed to insist that she be included in the family photographs that were taken.

Later, after some discussion, I recognized that my behavior was rooted in fear, fear that I'd relinquished my status as family matriarch by stepping outside of social convention. I didn't want to be a wife, but I was forced to confront the sense of identity and social position that being one confers. It was a humbling revelation.

When Margot's ex-husband sold their house and split the proceeds with her, she wanted to use part of the money to go to India. It was important to her to see the land I loved and understand the culture I'd grown up in. I was delighted. I began arranging our trip, attempting to provide a favorable introduction to India for Margot while still affording myself opportunities for nutrition consulting.

We set out in early 1980, planning to visit from mid-March to mid-April, before it got too hot on the plains but after it had warmed up a bit in the mountains. Our first stop was Bombay. Arriving late at night, we made our way from the airport to a mission guest house. We slept a few hours before India's early morning noises reached into our third-floor windows and drew us out onto the balcony where we watched the comings and goings of workers purchasing morning tea, vendors stoking stoves, and children brushing teeth as they readied themselves for school.

When we were ready to sight-see, we began with the India Gate, which for more than a century had been the official docking point for ocean vessels carrying English royalty and important visitors. Then we went up to Malabar Hill overlooking the huge curving bay now lined with miles of tall apartment buildings spilling hordes of people onto the sand. Along the way, we peeked briefly at the bazaars with their endless tempting wares.

Early evening found us at Bombay's enormous Queen Victoria Railway Station looking for our berths on an express train to Miraj in Maharastra. Trays of rice, lentils, vegetable curry, and *chappatis* were passed to us through the compartment window. We'd brought boiled drinking water with us.

A few stations down the line, Margot, intrigued by the vendors calling out their wares as they passed, wanted to buy a bottle of Coca-Cola. She made the transaction and started drinking the Coke. But, as the train began to pull slowly out of the station, the salesman came running alongside the train calling for the bottle—he needed it to claim his deposit. We hastily found a cup to pour the soda into and he gratefully snatched the bottle when she held it out the window.

Our friends Maryanna and Mel Cassady met us at Miraj the next morning, fed us papayas, *chappatis* with whipped cream and treacle, and hot steaming tea—a wonderful breakfast, taking me back to the years I'd lived in India. They announced that we were headed out to a village to see a feeding program for children there. Margot decided she'd rather spend the day wandering around the compound, which housed a school and other residences. She ended up taking a chair out to the main road to watch the endless stream of buses, horse-drawn vehicles, cars, and cycle-rickshaws. She could hardly take in the numbers of people carrying loads on their heads or pushing produce on carts. By spending several days observing in this way, and meandering in the bazaar, she really saw India.

From Miraj, we hastened north to Agra to visit the Taj Mahal during the full moon. Its jeweled surfaces sparkled in the moonlight. The Methodist guest house we stayed in was a huge mansion, even larger than the ones I'd lived in. Inside, Margot smelled the ancient mustiness of overhead fans and experienced sleeping beneath mosquito nets as I had so many years ago. When we awoke the next morning, Palm Sunday, breakfast appeared from an outdoor kitchen, built to keep heat out of the dwelling. As we ate, we watched children waving palms and singing as they marched into the church next door.

Late that afternoon, we strolled through the gardens of the Taj Mahal, took off our shoes, and entered the palatial tomb. The Muslim call to prayer echoed around the octagonal interior. A carved, lacy marble screen protected the bejeweled sepulchres. Outside, we walked around on the elevated platform supporting the building and craned our necks up at the four protecting towers.

The sun was setting as we gazed down at the Jumna River flowing past to the east. We returned to the garden, found seats under some banyan trees, and watched the glowing orb of the full moon rise behind the Taj. Once it grew dark, we watched the moonlight wink from the precious stones adorning the marble walls.

Reluctantly, we left the grounds and took a night train to Delhi and flew on to Chandigarh the following day to be with the Dutts, old friends from my Jullundur days. Mrs. Dutt and I happily reminisced about our many afternoons of tea and badminton. Nearly 100 years old, she had moved to Chandigarh to be with her son Monu and his wife, Sharda. The latter had established a highly successful private school for girls. I enjoyed seeing the campus and the hundreds of colorfully dressed schoolchildren.

On Easter Sunday, Margot and I made enchiladas using sauce and corn tortillas we brought with us from Tucson and cheese purchased in the local bazaar. The Dutts greatly enjoyed this new dish. Sharda confirmed what I had experienced. The red pepper used in the enchilada sauce tasted quite different from Indian red pepper.

I'd been asked to lecture at the Home Science College on the nutrition work I'd been doing in different countries. The women faculty members welcomed me warmly and joined in an extended discussion afterward. They described their research and I was highly impressed with the important information they'd gathered about village family life.

Then I began to realize their plight as professional women. They had no way to publish what they'd discovered. Not only were they loaded down with domestic activities, leaving little time to write up their findings, they didn't even own typewriters. The college was scant help, short-staffed as it was with stenographers. An idea began taking shape in my mind. I knew similar research was being conducted in other home science colleges in India. Perhaps I could find a way to return to India with the funding to pull this research together and get it published. It was an idea I'd later pursue by applying for a Fulbright Scholarship.

From Chandigarh, we headed for Woodstock School. I wanted us to follow the same route I'd taken uphill when living in the Punjab, but I wasn't sure if this was still possible. Margot, willing to put up with some discomfort and uncertainty, agreed to try. We caught an afternoon bus to Ludhiana hoping to catch the night train to Saharanpur.

When we arrived at the train station, I was daunted to learn that it was the time of the Kumbh Mela—a national festival held once every twelve years when devotees traveled to holy places to bathe. The crush of people getting on and off our train was unbelievable. We finally managed to secure an upper berth in an air-conditioned second-class car and we cuddled together to keep warm.

At Saharanpur, we learned that there was indeed a 2 A.M. bus to Mussoorie. Shortly thereafter, we slid gratefully into our seats and settled in for the journey. The bus climbed through the Siwalik Hills and, at daybreak, emerged into the doon valley. As we crossed the twenty miles to Dehra Dun, we rode through paddies of basmati rice. From there, the road snaked back and forth into the rising alps.

When we stepped off the bus at Mussoorie, we breathed in the brisk mountain air and watched coolies scramble for our suitcases. A rickshaw, pulled by two men and pushed by three, delivered us to the top of the Landour bazaar where a familiar vista appeared before me—the precipitous hillside sprinkled with cottages and the graceful curve of red-roofed school buildings, all against the hazy blue backdrop of the Tehri Hills. My heart filled with joy. I hadn't realized how much I'd yearned for this sight.

We paid the rickshaw crew and began walking the fairly level path to the guest house at Edgehill. From there, the view back across the doon to the Siwaliks was even more breathtaking.

Enchanted, Margot said, "Let's stay a week!"

She was even more delighted when the hostess came out to greet us and told us breakfast was ready and hot bath water was waiting. After we'd enjoyed some delicious *dalhiya*, or hot cereal, scrambled eggs, toast, and coffee accompanied by plump loose-skinned tangerines and bananas, Margot decided to have a long soak before taking a nap. In our bathroom, she was amused to find a kerosene tin full of steaming water beneath a padded cover. She sloshed it into a portable tin tub, added some cold water, and sat in it with her knees bent—a different kind of bath indeed.

I was too excited to sleep. The sun was already high in the sky shining down on scenery very dear to me. In the bazaar earlier that morning, I'd greeted old friends, shopkeepers, and vendors and heard them spread the news, "Parker Sahib's daughter has come!" *Chaukidars*, watchmen from nearby houses, men whom I'd known for many years, were already arriving at Edgehill asking about my family and wondering how long I'd be here. I sent a note off by coolie to Woodstock's alumni office to let them know that we had arrived. By return note we were invited to a dinner there the following night.

While Margot was sleeping, *wallahs* brought their wares and spread them out on the verandah. She awoke to an entire market that had appeared as if by magic—Kashmiri shawls, embroidered bedspreads, brass candlesticks, copper bowls, and many trinkets.

On this beautiful day, I hoped that the 19,000-foot peaks north of Landour would be visible. Taking a narrow path past the community center my father had built, past Zig Zag where I was born, Margot and I climbed to the road encircling the hilltop. I glimpsed the snow-capped summits before I expected to and gasped in wonderment. At first, Margot thought something was wrong, but seconds later, she, too, witnessed the glorious view before us—austere white mountains marching across the clear blue horizon, their ridges glistening in the sunlight, plumes of wind-driven snow streaming from jagged summits. Their pristine beauty and remote majesty were spellbinding.

We had reached the *chakkar*, the road around the top of the hill, where we bought tins of fruit juice from nearby shops. We strolled along gazing at the red rhododendrons and long-needled pines around us. Villages dotted the nearby hills to the north and the towering sunlit peaks stood in the distance.

Our days here were filled with long walks along the Tehri Road, a winding ribbon connecting us to the border of Tibet, strolls through the Woodstock campus and to the cottages of friends where we visited and drank tea. Along the way, I told Margot stories of picnics in special places, of terrible tumbles down the mountainside, of the monsoon rains that washed out roads but also carpeted the hillsides in orchids and dahlias.

When the time came for us to leave, the Woodstock staff helped us get a taxi—a luxury I still wasn't used to—all the way to Delhi, two hundred miles south. On our way we stopped in Rajpur for lunch at the home of Mrs. Vijaya Lakshmi Pandit, now retired from diplomatic service. I wanted to thank her in person for her kind words about my father in her book *The Scope of Happiness* and for what her daughter Tara said about him in her other book, *From Fear Set Free*.

Mrs. Pandit told us about the estrangement between herself and her niece, Prime Minister Indira Gandhi. Apparently, Indira's younger son, Sanjit, who was being groomed to succeed his mother, had told her to be more supportive of Indira, adding, "Otherwise, you know, there are such things as accidents." Similar threats had been made against Tara and her husband. It was difficult for me to believe that within the Nehru family—so united on the issue of Indian independence—there could be such animosity.

Not long after our visit, Sanjit was killed while flying his plane. Then his mother, my friend Indira, was assassinated. I watched her cremation on television and saw her oldest son, Rajiv, officiate at the funeral pyre. He greeted his aunt, Mrs. Pandit, with great love and respect, which warmed my heart. Much later, Rajiv himself was elected prime minister. He, too, was assassinated. I was saddened to see this three-generation political dynasty, whose members were close to my heart, come to such a violent end.

During our last days in India, the YWCA of India graciously invited Margot to view its work among village women and send its greetings to the YWCA in Tucson. Our homeward departure, with its long lines and overbooked planes, proved tedious and tiring. We arrived in Arizona absolutely exhausted and bursting with purchases. Once we'd recovered from the journey, we recounted stories of our trip to friends and audiences at churches, schools, and the YWCA.

Margot told me that the trip changed her life and altered the way she viewed the world. In India, she'd immersed herself in the culture and developed a deeper understanding of the people and their way of life. Now, when we talked about India and other countries I'd worked in, I knew we were on the same wavelength. This brought us even closer together.

And to my delight, while traveling in India, the proposal I'd submitted to the USDA for a breast-feeding project on the Papago Indian Reservation was funded. I'd be working under the reservation's tribal government.

Until 1920, every Papago mother had breast-fed her babies. But as baby formula became available, fewer and fewer mothers bothered to try it. Young mothers who worked or attended school found it easier to simply leave the baby and the bottle with grandma. Formula is a wonderful supplement to breast milk, but it can't do everything breast milk can to provide nourishment and promote health. Unlike breast milk, it does nothing to strengthen the immune system. But to make matters worse, it was causing intestinal problems among many Papago newborns.

The tribe's administrative offices were based in Sells, a 70-mile drive from Tucson. I was lucky to be able to share the drive with Judy Seoldo, a nutritionist with WIC. Judy participated in all the planning meetings for the new project and introduced me to mothers who wanted to make breast-feeding a way of life again. My job was to listen to these volunteers' ideas and enlist their help in carrying out educational programs.

We designed interventions to encourage breast-feeding. An area was set up in Sells, staffed by volunteers, where breast-feeding babies could receive day care while their mothers worked or went to school. Working mothers were called when their infant was hungry and the infants of those attending classes were brought to school so the mothers could nurse between classes. We hired and trained two women who spoke to pregnant women in the reservation's clinics urging them to consider breast-feeding. They also went to the hospital after babies were born to help new mothers start breast-feeding.

Best of all, the volunteers held conferences in which the older, experienced mothers talked about both the joys and challenges of breast-feeding. One mother told of her difficulty in weaning her four-year-old son who still insisted on nursing. When she asked him to bring in wood from the woodpile one day, he said defiantly, "No breast, no wood."

We encouraged young women to attend these meetings even before marriage. Fathers who wanted to participate were also invited. As the women shared stories and their hopes and dreams for their children and the tribe, breast-feeding came to be seen as a way to pass on tribal culture. We seized upon this notion of breast milk as a tribal resource and used the slogan "Breast milk is tribal food" on all our posters and promotional materials.

I kept track of mothers who gave birth and how they fed their children. Within a year, the practice of breast-feeding had more than doubled, rising from 20% to nearly 50%. The growing number of women who experienced the benefits of breast-feeding were eager to tell their friends and help other women who wanted to try it.

By April 1981, the documentation of all our work was in order. However, the tribal administration made clear that writing the report was to be done by the tribal office. It was a jolt to realize my job there was over. During the months I'd spent on the reservation, I'd made many good friends. But I also felt weary. The long drives and work hours had taken a toll and I realized I needed rest.

When my daughter Patty, at the University of Nebraska, told me that positions were available in the nutrition department of the College of Home Economics, I sent in my resume.

That summer, I met the search committee and talked about a position as a nutrition specialist in the home economics extension service. The job description was very similar to what I'd done with Agricultural Missions. I also learned that Dr. Robert Kleis in their International Programs division was interested in interviewing me for a part-time position on an advocate for women's roles in international development. The two positions seemed to dovetail nicely and I grew more and more excited about the possibilities. But afterwards, weeks dragged by without a word from them. Then, I learned from the Fulbright office that my proposal for the publishing project in India was being seriously considered.

I soon had a difficult choice to make. Just as I was offered a position in Nebraska, my Fulbright proposal was granted. The University of Nebraska offered a secure, long-term affiliation that would take me into retirement. I'd be doing nutrition education work, which I loved, and promoting women's involvement in agriculture, which I found challenging. The Fulbright grant would take me back to India for a year or two—a compelling reason to accept it. But while I still strongly supported helping Indian women publish their nutrition research, I knew that others could pursue that goal—its success was not dependent on me. Also, though both job offers entailed long separations from Margot, her new work with Neighborhood Housing Services might allow her to relocate to Nebraska, an important consideration.

Reluctantly, I turned Fulbright down and went to Lincoln instead.

Chapter Eleven
Nebraska in the World

In late summer 1981, Margot and I loaded up my car and readied ourselves for the long drive to Lincoln. I was thrilled about the opportunities that were opening up professionally but devastated by the separation I'd have to endure. Margot would stay in Lincoln only long enough to help settle me into my apartment before flying back to Tucson where her work was waiting.

This wrenching separation almost paralyzed me. The excitement of returning to mid-America paled. I wept, dreading the prospect of making this adjustment alone. We didn't know when or how we could arrange our lives so that we could be together again.

Driving back from the airport after dropping her off, I calmed my anguish by remembering the many times I'd moved and adjusted to a whole new life. I had to stop pining, to get busy and familiarize myself with Lincoln. I didn't want to be a burden to Patty and Terry. It was essential that I make my own connections, put down new roots—and do it right away. From experience, I knew that feeling at home is not a matter of chance. It's a matter of choice.

I began by looking up my few contacts in the community, among them Don Holloway, a friend from Kentucky. I knew he and Ellie had gotten a divorce when he revealed he was gay. His presence in Lincoln gave me not only a sympathetic friend, but an introduction to the city's gay and lesbian community.

Don was surprised to hear from me. It had been seven years since we'd seen each other. We had a lot of catching up to do and both realized that our friendship could continue to enrich us. He taught me to use a computer and was willing to play the dating game when I needed an escort to university affairs. The fact that he was handsome and charming led my faculty friends to comment on how quickly I'd "caught a man."

I enjoyed the deception game but recognized that it was only temporary. The gay and lesbian community had important work to do and I was eager to help. An amendment had been proposed by the city council to add sexual orientation to the list of specific considerations such as race, gender, and age that could not be used as a basis for discrimination. I jumped at the chance to promote this change, passing out flyers on campus even before I'd gotten oriented in my jobs. Many of my colleagues were surprised that I came out, spoke up, and rocked the boat so early in my tenure. The amendment was soundly defeated, but I knew I'd done all I could on its behalf.

I was pleased to find the challenges in both the International Programs and Home Economics Extension exciting. The extension service meant that, along with other specialists, I was on call as a resource to extension agents in every county of the state. By phone, I answered their nutrition questions; by car, I traveled all over Nebraska consulting and conducting training classes.

Extension specialists worked cooperatively in responding to these requests. For example, when Leon Rottman, a home and family specialist, received requests for classes on weight control, he asked me to help him design and carry out a program he named SOS, or Save Our Shapes. We made many trips out into the counties over the next few years, scheduling classes in contiguous counties if we were going clear across the state. Working with him gave me an easy introduction to many of the extension agents. I found that quite a few had overseas experience, either through church programs or the Peace Corps, and this created a strong bond between us.

I made countless trips across Nebraska driving Extension Service vehicles. For someone who'd once been reluctant to drive a car, I did amazingly well through snow, sleet, and high winds.

Each year I planned and held a training event for extension agents called Keeping Current in Nutrition, making it as practical and relevant as possible. The agents often asked for follow-up training on one or more topics for those in the counties they represented. One year, I held an evening course in North Platte for men and women who ran health food stores. They wanted accurate information about their products, but I knew that some of what I had to tell them would contradict the advertising information they were supposed to use. We were able to create an atmosphere of trust in which they admitted to wondering whether the sales pitches they'd been giving were accurate.

The three extension nutrition specialists in our department answered questions from people statewide—some by mail, others by phone. If we didn't know the answer, we researched until we found it. People asked about different foods and food values and about canning and other methods of food preservation. Certain questions arose repeatedly, so we prepared pamphlets with detailed information on these topics. These were then distributed by county agents or ordered through the mail.

Before leaving Tucson, I'd attended a conference on women in global development. Experts there were recognizing that women worldwide were excluded from the decision-making process that affected every aspect of their lives and they were also barred from the development strategy planning of their countries. The idea that women *should* participate was novel—many assumed that improvements in agriculture or business would be dreamed up and carried out by men and that women had little insight or opinion on such matters.

However, the important role of women in the advancement of community and country was being recognized. For example, the U.S. Agency for International Development (USAID) now required that every project it funded be evaluated for its potential impact on women's efforts to provide for their families. The agency even stipulated that a certain percentage of each grant proposal budget be devoted to ensuring that any such impact not be adverse. This requirement led project managers to rethink their proposals and was probably the reason I was hired to work with International Programs at the University of Nebraska. It was my job to get acquainted with the agronomists on campus who were writing proposals and help them think about the impact their projects might have on women.

I'd witnessed the consequences of excluding women from important decision-making processes while visiting Africa. In one country, a U.S.-funded project to improve crops and build a road connecting farms to the airport nearly destroyed an important sector of the area's economy. In developing the road, no one had thought to inquire about its impact on women entrepreneurs. The road actually ran in the opposite direction from the routes the women had established to sell their produce and it nearly wiped out their source of income. The American male planners had been oblivious to the fact that women brought in a significant percentage of household income.

My first public opportunity to highlight this concern over women in development came on World Food Day, held on October 16, 1982. That year's topic was "Women in World Food." Pat Young, my friend from White House conference days who now worked for the U.N. Food and Agriculture Organization (FAO), was in charge of promoting the annual event, which included a televised program from Washington, D.C. that would be downlinked to a University of Nebraska auditorium.

I invited four international women students from the departments of agriculture and home economics to talk about food

Kittu and her step-mother, Dorothy Parker, celebrate Kittu's 65th birthday in Lincoln, NE, 1984.

production in their countries. Though shy, each did an excellent job of addressing the main points of the teleconference and providing examples of what women did in their home countries. After the panel presentation, the women responded well to questions. And then someone asked, "What do the men do?"

The women looked at each other, obviously uncomfortable and hesitant to respond. Then one of them said softly, looking down at her feet, "Not much." Her simple, reluctant reply echoed through the room bringing new awareness of the importance of women's role in agriculture. I thought back to the Presbyterian conference on world hunger I'd attended where women weren't recognized as authorities on the matter. I hadn't known then what I do now—that in many countries, women perform 80 percent of the agricultural labor.

In the spring of 1983, Kate Cloud, leader of the women-in-development conference I'd attended in Tucson, alerted me to a small gathering being held at the Johnson Foundation's Wingspread Center in Racine, Wisconsin. About twenty faculty women from agricultural campuses were meeting to discuss mutual concerns. I decided to join them.

After a week of sharing ideas and reviewing possibilities, we formed the Association for Women in Development (AWID). Although headquartered in the U.S., AWID's membership is open to men and women worldwide. It has been and still is a vital force in encouraging women to become informed promoters of global development. Each year, AWID holds a conference involving women from all over the world. U.S. members pursue grant funding to underwrite the conference-related expenses of women from less wealthy countries, especially those who want to present papers or lead discussions. At AWID's first conference, in 1984, I was proud that the daughters of two dear friends were reporting their research and glad that I'd played a part in founding this valuable forum for exchanging information and ideas.

Through AWID, I found not only a supportive network of women with whom I could talk about possible approaches to my job, but also sources of funding outside the university for projects I wanted to pursue. Congress, for instance, had Biden-Pell funds available for carrying out development education in the U.S. These funds were allocated to projects that educated the American public about its role in world development. When I got back to Lincoln, I did two things. First, through International Programs, I completed and published a small brochure and created a slide-tape on Women and the Development of the World. These resources became useful in various facets of my work. Second, I contacted Lincoln women with international involvements and asked for their help in designing a proposal to access Biden-Pell funds for educating Nebraskans, especially women, about the role of women in development.

We located a nonprofit organization, the Foundation for Agricultural and Educational Development (FAED), to sponsor the proposal. Representatives of eight women's organizations with branches in rural Nebraska were interested in working with us, among them the YWCA, Women in Farm Economics, United Methodist Women, and the American Association of University Women. These representatives, along with international women students and wives of international students, became the advisory group that would administer the project as it developed.

In September 1982, at the same time that the proposal was being drafted and agreed upon, an incredibly welcome event was taking place. Margot was moving to Lincoln. While working for Neighborhood Housing Services in Tucson, she had been hired by its chartering organization, Neighborhood Reinvestment Corporation, to carry on similar work in the Lincoln area. We'd taken a summer road trip that took us through Jackson Hole, Wyoming, Yellowstone National Park, and rural Nebraska, and then headed back to Lincoln to look for an apartment in case the move worked out. We finally settled on a second-floor unit in a new complex near the Governor's Mansion. When the job came through, Margot put our Tucson house on the market, moved her belongings to Lincoln, and started a district office for Neighborhood Reinvestment Corporation. She worked with communities to provide improved, affordable housing and to nurture neighborhood identity and spirit.

Through AWID, I received word that in the spring of 1984, a special women-in-development workshop would be held in East Lansing, Michigan where Chuck and Jean lived. We'd kept in touch by letter but hadn't seen each other since Bill's wedding. I wrote, telling them I planned to attend the workshop, and they graciously invited me to stay with them. Knowing how happy they were together, I didn't hesitate to accept.

My daughter Dorothy suggested that while I was in East Lansing, I contact Dr. Ruth Useem of the sociology department of Michigan State University, who knew of my father. I learned that she had one of the few copies of my father's master's thesis on the adjustment problems of missionary children. She considered it the seminal work in a new field she was developing, the sociology of "third-culture" kids—in short, children brought up in one culture then forced to live in another that doesn't really honor the one they were raised in. They often lose their sense of belonging. To compensate, they create a "third culture" that combines elements of both. As she described these children, I realized she was describing me—I, too, often felt I didn't belong. Dr. Useem explained that this happens frequently to people who emigrate from the land of their birth or change belief systems or religions.

During the workshop, I mulled over her ideas. I was indignant to discover that men were allowed to participate in this gathering. But, as they shared their stories with the group, I came to understand that their presence was appropriate. One of the men, an Iranian, told us that he'd changed his chauvinistic thinking about women's roles in the world and now his male friends shun him. Like me—like many women—he was caught between cultures, searching for a place to belong, and I realized just how prevalent the "third culture" phenomenon is.

Each afternoon when I got back to Chuck's house, he had tea ready and we had delightful visits. We talked about our children, our India friends, my work, and his writing. In some ways, our relationship was easier than it had been when we were married because we were no longer dependent on or responsible for each other. Jean joined us when she came home from work. It was good to reestablish our three-way friendship, to affirm the fact that we still cared about each other. I was glad to see how well they nurtured each other.

When I returned to Lincoln and reported on this workshop at the university, I realized that I was becoming marked as someone who always brought up the women-in-development issue. Lest this alienate some of my colleagues, I started an informal but deliberate campaign to chat with men and women in different departments, encouraging them to become advocates of women's participation in international development. They were surprised to be asked to take initiative. But when they thought about how deeply entrenched the assumption was that women were unimportant to the decision-making process, they too realized it would take a wide-ranging approach to bring about change.

The first summer Margot and I were together in Lincoln some of my Woodstock classmates organized a reunion at Lake George in upstate New York. Margot and I flew to New York City and drove north to attend. The idea of a reunion frightened me a bit. It had been nearly fifty years since I'd seen many of my classmates. Would I recognize all of them? Any of them?

Of course I did. We sang the old songs, reveled in the taste of Indian goodies, and told our stories. Each of us had to adjust to life in the U.S., Canada, or England and we knew that everyone in the group understood how difficult that process had been. It was truly a reunion of "third-culture" kids. We had so much fun that we decided to do it again two years later. Since that first reunion, we've gotten together eleven times.

I'd been thinking about returning to China ever since President and Mrs. Nixon had visited the country and opened up diplomatic relations in 1972. When I saw an announcement for a nutrition and health tour in the spring of 1984, I signed up to go and Patty, a health educator, came, too.

The Beijing airport seemed no larger than when Chuck and I had first flown in from Shanghai in early 1947. We were taken by taxi to an enormous new Great Wall Hotel, one of a series that had recently been built to support tourism. To our surprise, two Chinese gentlemen were waiting for us. Dr. Paul Sun, an ophthalmologist from Tientsin and my English students at Truth Hall, and his son, Paul, had found out through Chuck that we were coming. We invited them to the hotel restaurant for dinner, not realizing that this was frowned upon. The Chinese government wanted to maintain a barrier between foreign tourists and the Chinese people. Our meal was an eye-opener for the Suns. They were shocked and dismayed to see the large gap between the hotel's lavish provisions and the meager supplies available to the ordinary citizen.

With their help, we found the compound where our family had lived. Tao Hospital, where Patty was born, had burned to the ground. But the new Sixth Teaching Hospital had been built on the tennis courts in front of our old house, now a residence for single doctors. We didn't go inside the dwelling, but I pointed out the rooms to Patty. We crossed the alley and entered the courtyard of Truth Hall, which was now coeducational. Patty wandered over to watch a volleyball game in progress. Word flew to the office that foreigners had arrived and an elderly teacher came out to convey the greetings of the principal. I gave my Chinese name and explained that I had taught there. We were not invited inside, but I was content to sit in the shade of young trees and look at the buildings. I pointed out to Paul the classroom where I'd taught him.

Our travel group attended daily seminars on the population's health care and nutritional status, yet there was also time for independent pursuits. One day I rose very early and went out into the streets to talk with the women sweeping the sidewalks. I'd practiced what I would say and told them in Chinese about the years I'd lived in Peiping. They were very curious and asked a lot of questions. Then one of them caught sight of a supervisor. With regret, and fearful that they might be doing something wrong, they dispersed. For me, hearing them speak the pure Mandarin tones was like listening to music. And making contact once again with Chinese women was a joyful experience, a connection of past to present.

But the highlight of our trip was a visit with Pastor and Mrs. Yin. The latter had been a member of the women's group that had helped me learn Chinese so long ago. Affirming the solidarity of our friendship was one of the most precious experiences I've ever had. When she told me she was willing to take me to see Mrs. Shao, another of the group members, tears sprang to my eyes because this was impossible—we were leaving Beijing the following day. Our time together had been too short. My heart cried out in protest, reliving the same wrenching emotions I'd felt at the railway station when we'd been forced out of China so many years ago.

The remainder of the trip was anticlimactic except for meeting a Chinese dietician who had trained under Dr. Adolph during the years we were in Peiping. Though we visited places I'd never been, they seemed as unreal as the paintings of Guilin's mountains, which I'd always thought were fanciful until I saw them myself by riverboat. We took the train from Canton to Hong Kong and flew back to the States. Crossing the wide Pacific, I made peace with my misgivings. I could see that although the Communist regime did not necessarily heed the people's will in its decision-making, it had brought about a degree of equality never before seen in China and was undertaking improvements that would truly benefit its people.

Patty and I were in Seattle just long enough to change planes, but to our great surprise, Bill met us at the gate and told us that his son, Charles William Riddle, had been born just two days earlier, on June 3, 1984. We toyed with the idea of dashing to the hospital to see the baby but decided that the chances of getting back to the airport before our flight departed were slim. However, I did go back a few weeks later to get acquainted with my exceptional grandson.

In that same summer, I learned that FAED, sponsors of the proposal I'd helped put together for a women-in-development project now entitled Nebraska in the World (NIW), had been granted Biden-Pell funds. With the money we could send teams of women from other countries out into the rural communities of Nebraska to tell their stories. Team members were recruited from the international student community and included women graduate students and the wives of students. In composing each team, we selected one woman each from an African, Asian, and Latin American country. Though we couldn't pay them, we did reimburse them for expenses incurred for their participation—for example, the cost of babysitters. Once we had set up an event, we'd rent a car for the team. We'd previously negotiated for them to stay overnight in local homes so there would be opportunities for conversation with the rural Nebraskan women.

The events were so successful that word spread across the state and requests began pouring in. Our program was very simple. After introductions, we showed the eleven-minute slide-tape I'd prepared to illustrate what was meant by "women in development." Then the three team members took turns speaking about their home countries. Each could say whatever she wanted about her life experience.

After the presentations, there was usually awed silence followed by remarks such as, "I didn't know there were such articulate and educated women in those countries," "You've told me more in an hour than I've learned from any other source about women in the world," or "I'd never thought about the fact that women aren't considered resources in solving their country's problems." These remarks were usually followed by the recognition that women in the U.S. weren't thought of as resources either. Then came the questions and I was impressed with their thoughtfulness. These women realized that we were talking about world-changing possibilities.

Our presentations gave the international women a chance to see rural America, to spend time in different homes, to ask questions, and to make new friends. Each of the speakers told the advisory group that she felt she was growing and gaining from this chance to tell her life story. Kunzang Roder from Bhutan told us that before this project started, she'd felt claustrophobic, cooped up with her children as she waited for her Swiss husband to complete his agronomy degree. Due to green card restrictions, she couldn't seek employment. But now, uplifted by the support of our group, she was considering graduate study herself.

The NIW project extended into Kansas where Pat Hill Martin was raising the awareness of farm women in rural areas. She had moved there from New Mexico to marry a childhood sweetheart, Pete Martin, and we saw each other often. She spearheaded events like the ones we carried out in Nebraska and was influential in getting Kansas women to think in terms of commitment to change—what they would do differently as a result of hearing these women from other countries.

Toward the end of the three-year project, men began to attend, too. In one instance, we were invited so speak to a men's group, the Future Farmers of America. The event was almost canceled when the sponsor got cold feet, concerned we'd try to cram "women's lib" down the male farmers' throats. Thinking quickly, I said that Dr. Rick Foster, an authority on international agriculture, would be part of our team. Fortunately, when I called Rick, he was happy to oblige.

I had no idea what he'd say to the twenty men huddled in the back of the meeting room. I was delighted when he told them that in the years he'd been teaching international agriculture, he'd learned that most of the agricultural work in other parts of the world is done by women, and that the women with him here tonight knew more about agriculture in their home countries than he did. The farmers, their interest piqued, moved up a few rows to listen to the women's presentations.

By the questions that followed, the men indicated that they were truly fascinated by this new, or new-to-them, angle on agriculture. After the meeting, they admitted they'd never thought about women's roles in agriculture. They kept us talking informally for nearly an hour saying that they wished more men had come. They also wished their wives had joined them.

As we drove back to Lincoln, we reflected on the evening. The women had talked about agriculture as naturally as they would have talked about any other facet of their lives, enabling their male audience to see them as they really are—as female agricultural experts. In continuing this conversation with the advisory group, we realized just how far we'd come during the project's three years. Our teams of women had bridged a gap in the nation's thinking. I wondered when the world as a whole would see women in more varied roles and further appreciate and make use of its most undervalued resource. Though funding for Nebraska in the World ended in 1987, the new ideas it fostered continue to be appreciated.

In 1983, Patty and Terry had left Lincoln and moved to San Diego. I was sad to see them go. Still, I was glad that Patty had not only found challenging work in the San Diego Health Department, but a delightful apartment overlooking the Pacific Ocean as well. In fact, it was such a wonderful location, with an inexpensive motel nearby, that I suggested a family Christmas there in 1985. To our great sorrow, Chuck's wife Jean had died of cancer earlier that year and it seemed appropriate that our family gather around him.

Margot and I traveled a fair amount. We visited Alaska and the British Isles, and in 1987, we drove out to the YMCA Center in Estes Park, Colorado for a Woodstock School reunion. Being there brought back many memories—after all, it was where Chuck and I had met nearly fifty years earlier. It also put me on the mailing list which would lead to a gratifying future relationship.

At about this time, the AIDS epidemic began raging, storming to the forefront of people's awareness. I was shocked when Don Holloway told me he was HIV positive and saddened when he moved to Colorado with his lover. He became politically active, joining groups that kept themselves informed about AIDS research, prevention and treatment, and helped those debilitated by the disease. With the help of local doctors and Dr. Bernie Siegel, author of *Love, Medicine, and Miracles*, he started an annual conference called "AIDS, Medicine, and Miracles" that became an empowering gathering, drawing people from across the States.

In the spring of 1989, I attended the conference. Don looked so well that I felt sure he'd be leading many more such gatherings in the

Patty, Kittu's daughter, Bill, her son, and Harriet and Don, her half-sister and brother, with Kittu on the YMCA Grounds, Estes Park, CO, 1987. They are attending a Woodstock School reunion.

future. However, in the fall, he became ill and his health deteriorated rapidly. I talked to him by phone several times before he died in February 1990. Though I didn't go to Colorado for his memorial service, I heard that it was a transforming experience for all who participated. Those who'd cared for him during his last weeks, including his daughters, knew that he harbored no bitterness and, even in weakness, was a conduit for love and gratitude. Later, when I was in Estes Park, I had the privilege of scattering some of his ashes in the mountains. I feel he accompanies me on my walks there.

In 1984 Margot and I bought a two-story bungalow several blocks south of where I worked on East Campus. It had been partially renovated, so our carpenter friend David completed the necessary changes before the lease on our apartment ended. We held a big open house when we were settled. It seemed only fair to let the neighbors see how this house, which had been undergoing remodeling for years, had turned out. One of the neighbors we met had cocker spaniel puppies for sale. We fell in love with two of the dogs and brought them home to join our family. Though they chewed on the furniture at first, Emily and Anna soon became a precious and integral part of our lives.

Dr. Hazel Fox, head of the University of Nebraska's nutrition department, supervised my work both in Extension Services and in International Programs. I was careful to report to her all that I was doing in both areas. She took part in the development of the Nebraska in the World proposal and was interested in knowing how it was working out. She herself had pioneered studies on the importance of protein in infant feeding in developing countries and was well known for her work in the Philippines.

I knew that many international women students on campus were conducting nutrition research. Being participants in a study, they lived in the Human Nutrition Lab on the same floor as my office in Ruth Leverton Hall and ate a specified diet prepared in the research kitchen. Dr. Constance Kies, in close cooperation with Dr. Fox, was in charge of the project.

Dr. Kies was very protective of the research and reported it only in interdepartmental nutrition seminars. She made it clear that she didn't want me fraternizing with "her" students or involving them in "my" international development work. The women were here to work, she said, and didn't need to be distracted. I didn't understand her opposition but accepted her directive.

Her stance made for many difficult situations. For example, when the governor of Taiwan visited campus, I was asked to introduce his wife to Taiwanese women students. Many of them were in the human nutrition program. When I asked Dr. Kies's permission, she reluctantly made an exception. This was an invaluable opportunity for her students to explain their research to an influential woman, a valuable contact in their home country.

When Dr. Fox originally interviewed me in 1981, she'd known I was sixty-two but stopped herself from commenting on my age, realizing the subject was out of bounds legally. She said nothing when I turned sixty-five. So as far as I was concerned, I could continue working until I was seventy, when I planned to retire. She, herself, was only a few years younger than I.

Then, out of the blue, in December 1985, as she and I were reviewing my plans for the coming year, she interrupted to tell me she wasn't going to recommend a continuation of my contract the following June. She gave no reason for her decision, and to this day I don't know what prompted it. I could see by the way she held herself that she was bracing for a fight—she knew I could bring up the subject of age discrimination.

For a moment, I sat speechless, wondering how to respond. Then it hit me that although she thought she was dealing me a blow, she was actually giving me a gift. I was tired of working, tired of the sparring that went on in the department. To my own surprise, I countered honestly, "You've just made my day. I'll be glad to retire. I have only one request: I want to be named Professor Emerita." Now it was she who was speechless.

"That's in the hands of the Chancellor," she protested.

"But it's for you to recommend." I replied. "I've worked with the Chancellor and know he'll agree."

Leaving it up to her that way meant that she would have to give me an honorable farewell. As soon as she announced the June date for my retirement party, I invited Bill, Barbara, and my grandson Charles to be present for the event. The room was packed with friends—men and women from our campus as well as the main campus. The Chancellor sent a representative who conferred on me a citation and the emerita status I had requested. I was surprised at the turn-out and I think Dr. Fox was, too.

My retirement came not long before funding for Nebraska in the World dried up, creating a big hole in my life that I wasn't yet sure how to fill. Requests still came in from across the state for talks by NIW team members, and when we could raise the money for transportation, we continued sending women out to present programs. But eventually even those funds dwindled.

I saw no reason why the women who'd worked on the project couldn't continue meeting for enriching discussions on topics of mutual concern. Why not get together for tea and talk as often as possible? I discussed it with some of the women and they agreed that we should announce a Friday open house. We typed up flyers inviting women interested in international conversation to come to our 37th Street house for "Tea and Talk" and tacked them up on campus. A new program was born, one that still continues today. Women from Nebraska in the World came along with women I'd never met. Each time we got together, the conversation took its own course. It seemed to fill a need not met by any other campus programs—the need to share what it was like to be a foreigner on the University of Nebraska campus.

My stepmother, Dorothy Parker, had been living in a cottage in Westminster Gardens in Duarte, California, a retirement colony for Presbyterian missionaries, for about six years. On one of my trips to see her, she announced that we would have tea with Nelle Morton, a classmate of hers from Biblical Seminary in New York. I was thrilled. Nelle, a theologian I wanted to meet, had corresponded with me at Nourishing Space but hadn't been able to visit.

Our meeting was serendipitous in every way. Nelle knew of Dorothy, my daughter, and when I mentioned Nourishing Space, it all came together. She knew who I was, too, though she hadn't connected me with her classmate, Dorothy, my stepmother. As we drank tea, she told us about her experiences of what she called goddess energy, the subject of her next book. I visited her several times after that, hungry to hear more.

When her book, *The Journey Is Home* was published, it seemed a likely candidate for group study and I sent invitations to about thirty friends in Lincoln who might be interested. More than a third of them showed up at the designated time. For six months or so, we—a good mix of Protestant, Catholic, Buddhist, Hindu and the unchurched—met every other week to wrestle with Nelle's ideas on the goddess energy within each of us. We also enjoyed corresponding with her, and together, mourned when word of her death came.

Ruth Thone, the former governor's wife, was a member of the group. I'd met her when she taught a class at the YWCA on women and aging. One day, in class, she asked the question, "What is the one thing you've always wanted to do and haven't done?" I said I wanted to take an independent trip. I'd always admired my stepmother's ability to get in the car and drive long distances alone. I'd been driving across Nebraska, but now that I'd retired, I felt the need to go a step further—to start out and travel without a schedule. Combining this with my desire to be alone on Christmas Day, I decided to drive my Chevrolet hatchback west in December, visit some friends and family, and find a solitary place to spend Christmas.

Of course I ran the risk of ice and snow, but I made it to Seattle to see Bill, Barbara, and Charles before heading south along the coast. Several days later, I reached San Francisco and visited Esther who had just had heart surgery. I drove east to the edge of Yosemite National Park and took a motel room planning to visit the park the following morning, but there was a huge snowstorm and the park rangers discouraged cars without tire chains from entering. So I switched plans and headed for Fresno, where my college roommate Jeanne and her sister Carol lived.

They asked me to stay for a few days, but one of the main purposes of my trip was to be alone in the desert on Christmas. From Fresno, the nearest desert was Death Valley, which I reached at twilight on Christmas Eve. I found space in a campground and slept in my hatchback, waking early to watch dawn break over the mountains. The biggest surprise of the trip was that about 10,000 other people shared my desire to get away from it all. Every motel room and camping space was full. Death Valley was crowded. By afternoon, I'd called my stepmother and found that, if I left right away, I could join her in time for a late Hindustani dinner with Donald, Harriet, and Harriet's family in Duarte, California.

Meanwhile, Margot, who'd driven out to Arizona to spend Christmas with her folks, was headed to Tempe to meet me at my daughter Dorothy's house. After several days there, we rented a car trailer for Margot's Blazer, loaded my hatchback onto it, and headed home to Nebraska. I'd had enough of my solo fling, but I was glad I'd done it.

Margot and I were living in the house of our dreams and had many friends. But hanging uneasily on the clothesline of our awareness was the knowledge that change loomed ahead. Margot's company, Neighborhood Reinvestment Corporation, was downsizing and streamlining its operations. In all probability, the Lincoln office would be closed and she'd be transferred to the district office in San Antonio, Texas.

I was more sanguine than she about another move. In fact, I recognized the phone call when it came. Before she'd even picked up the phone, I knew we were on our way.

In the spring of 1988, members of the Nelle Morton book group threw a party at the YWCA in our honor. All of our friends came and enjoyed themselves, swimming in the pool and taking time to visit with us and each other. The previous fall, the YWCA had presented me with a significant Tribute to Women award, letting me know that the work I'd done in conjunction with women and women's groups had been understood and appreciated. It was a gratifying acknowledgment and a fitting ending to my years in Lincoln.

We put our house on the market, forwarded our belongings, bade our friends farewell, and drove south to San Antonio, where I was confident I'd find new opportunities to work for the empowerment of women.

Chapter Twelve
Full Circle

Margot and I drove south through Kansas and Oklahoma, pleased that this time we'd be starting out together. This was the first move I'd ever made without contacts in the new location, but I was confident that connections would reveal themselves. The first was a beckoning invitation to meet Dr. Robert Conley, president of Union Graduate School, who was visiting San Antonio. At the reception I met Carol Barrett, a UGS faculty member living there. She, in turn, introduced me to a journal writing group held at the Resource Center of the Doté Foundation—an activity that became a steady and integral part of my creative life.

We live in north-central San Antonio, only fifteen minutes from the airport, an important factor considering Margot's frequent travels. Our neighborhood is friendly and diverse, our home comfortable. The dogs like the enclosed yard and I love lounging on the deck, where I can gaze up at tall live oak trees harboring squirrel nests. Lizards climb the fence walls as they do in India. The shrubbery around the deck and the hanging plants and flowers add even more beauty. I've now lived in this house longer than any other—it brings a sense of constancy, a welcome anchor to my nomadic life.

Moving in July 1988 meant getting used to the heat, but when summer broke and fall turned to winter, we enjoyed the fact that the cold wasn't nearly as bitter as Lincoln's. In spring, the glory of south Texas burst upon us. Fields and woods overflowed with bluebonnets.

Friends and family came to visit us and see the city. I chauffeured them to points of interest, quickly learning what to see and where to park so we could visit the River Walk with its restaurants and shops, shaded walks, and boat tours. Nearby, on the grounds where the 1968 HemisFair had been held, I loved showing off the extensive, artistic water displays. At noon, we could dine in the Tower of the Americas and see the expanse of the city as the room rotated. I found it amusing that the Tower had been built 200 feet taller than Seattle's Space Needle—in Texas, everything is bigger. I also chuckled when I saw a license plate that read "I'm the parent of a Trinity University alum" and realized it applied to me, too—Patty graduated from there.

While exploring San Antonio, I found an Indian store where I could buy basmati rice from Dehra Dun and spices. Also, to my surprise, there were tins of mustard greens from Jullundur. Best of all, the store manager was a dignified elderly gentleman from Lahore with whom I could reminisce in Urdu about the days when Lahore was in India and there was no Pakistan.

Margot and I soon discovered a lesbian bar and became participants in a Tuesday night discussion group that met there. The bar scene can be a good way to get to know other women and form lasting friendships. Through our new acquaintances, we learned that Texas was then the only state that held an annual lesbian conference.

In 1989, I, with Esther, attended a San Francisco gathering of old lesbians at which the topic of ageism was introduced. It hadn't dawned on me that every old person faces condescension—if not outright discrimination. Old lesbians face ageism after having dealt all their lives with a host of other "isms"—heterosexism, which requires that they hide their sexual preference, the sexism that all women face, and, for those lesbians of color, racism.

Wanting to bring up this topic at the 1990 Texas Lesbian Conference, I offered to lead an ageism workshop. Among the participants were Arden and Charlotte, Houston women who'd founded a local organization called Lesbians Over Age Fifty (LOAF). We contacted the recently formed Old Lesbians Organizing for Change (OLOC) and invited their steering committee to meet in Texas in December 1990.

After that meeting, Arden, Charlotte, and I joined the steering committee which was preparing a handbook on ageism to alert women to the issue and empower them to rebut the negative stereotypes surrounding old age. Arden and Charlotte volunteered to make Houston OLOC's headquarters, and ever since, old Texas lesbians have played a prominent role in the organization's activities.

When a National Lesbian Conference was held in Atlanta in April 1994, Esther and I traveled to Georgia to attend. The city of Atlanta not only welcomed the 2,000 women who came, but posted their welcome in lights on the Conference Center's electronic billboard outside. The presence of nearly two hundred old lesbians added an important dimension. One of the events that OLOC had scheduled was the Fishbowl on Ageism. As facilitator, I introduced eight members of OLOC who sat in the center of a circle of interested women. Each old lesbian spoke in turn about how she had experienced ageism. After one had finished, I asked a listener in the outer circle to repeat what had been said, giving everyone a chance to clear up misconceptions—and there were many. Those in the outer circle discovered the ways that old lesbians experience ageism from young lesbians. Many of the five hundred or so in the audience rated the experience as one of the most valuable events of the conference.

Through OLOC, I've met many wonderful women and heard their stories. Some have been lesbians all their lives. Others, like me, had married and borne children. Everywhere I go, OLOC provides a wonderful connection to women my age. Though I've since resigned from the steering committee, I still firmly support OLOC's goals and continue to write for its newsletter.

During the first fall Margot and I were in San Antonio, my Woodstock class held a reunion at Ghost Ranch in Abiquiu, New Mexico. She and I carefully packed our china cups and teapots for the tea we planned to serve there. On the green lawn of the conference center with the late afternoon light filtering through autumn-leaved trees illuminating the red cliffs in the background, we poured tea for members of the class as they arrived. Ghost Ranch staff members, knowing only that we were a group of senior citizens in our early seventies, were hardly prepared for the fact that the first thing the class wanted to do was to climb to the top of the cliffs. It was a delightful reunion.

While there I visited Chuck and his new wife, Jeanne Rhodes, in the Presbyterian retirement cottages in Santa Fe. When they told me they were going to visit India and Nepal, we compared itineraries, as I was planning to lead a small group of women to some of the same places. Two Lincoln friends had asked me to show them the India I'd known, and I'd agreed to the venture if they could line up others to join us. Our party eventually grew to eight women, including my daughter Patty, and Ada Munson, who'd been part of Nebraska in the World's advisory group. We decided to spend three weeks in India and Nepal, after which Ada and I would go on to Bhutan to visit Kunzang Roder and her family.

Patty and her friend Elaine went ahead to Mussoorie while the rest of us visited Delhi's colorful and variegated cloth shops. Later, we had difficulty reaching the station for the night train to Dehra Dun due to the Dussehra holiday throngs. When our taxis could go no farther, we paid the drivers off, piled our luggage on two bicycle rickshaws, and walked behind them the last mile, pushing our way through the crowds. I felt both excited and scared, hoping we'd make it.

Our train reservations were for a sleeping compartment, so we were granted sheets and pillows and could stretch out. I placed an order for breakfast and the next morning the group was surprised when the trays of tea, eggs, and *parathas* (Indian fried bread) were delivered through the window. All were entranced to see the mountains approach as the train chugged into the doon valley.

When we arrived in Dehra Dun, we were able to take taxis clear to the top of Landour Hill—quite a change from the travel arrangements of fifty years ago. We had only a short walk to the estate of Oakville where we'd stay as guests. Watchmen, servants, and others nearby recognized and greeted me and word went out across the hillside that Parker Sahib's daughter had again returned.

Before going into the house, we stood at the edge of the garden looking down at the doon from which we had come. The view and the accompanying cool breeze were refreshing. I felt myself relaxing in the ambiance of this hillside, familiar to me since birth. The trip was going well and I felt reassured that I could take care of this group of tourists and their individual needs. I was, after all, back in the land that had nourished me, where I felt comfortable and knew what to do. It was important to soak it all in, for though I'd returned many times, I was now nearly seventy and doubted I'd be back again in this lifetime.

After a delicious Indian lunch of lentils, rice, *chappatis*, and salad, I urged the group to take naps. We were now at an elevation of 8,000 feet and I was concerned about altitude sickness. Meanwhile, I planned to walk the mile or so down to Woodstock school to find Patty and Elaine and confirm arrangements for our group visit to the school. Marilyn and Rena from Colorado wanted to accompany me. They assured me that they were used to high altitudes and didn't need extra rest. We hiked at a fast pace and I took all the shortcuts I knew. They later admitted that initially they wondered whether I'd make it and eventually realized their mistake.

When my companions awoke, they were delighted to find that *wallahs* had spread out on the verandah wares from Kashmir, Saharanpur, and other Indian regions. The women were in shopping heaven—drinking refreshing tea while looking and selecting. Later, we walked out along the Tehri Road and watched the snows on the northern horizon turn pink with the sunset. We spent some lovely days visiting the school and shopping in the bazaar.

All too soon it was time to go downhill. The taxis dropped Patty and me off at Mrs. Vijaya Lakshmi Pandit's home in Rajpur for lunch while the others went to a restaurant to eat. I would have liked the whole to group meet this great lady, but at age eighty-eight, she was too frail for such an incursion. Chand, her first-born child, was there too, so we were two mothers and two daughters.

Madame Pandit was, as always, vivacious with abundant good humor. She'd finally recovered from the illness that kept her housebound the previous winter and prevented her from attending the fortieth anniversary celebration of the United Nations. In 1947, she had led the Indian delegation to its first meetings. Not only was she a founding member of the U.N., she'd also been its first woman secretary general. We had a wonderful visit, especially poignant in hindsight because it was our last. Two years later, she died.

Our tour group returned to Delhi and moved on to Agra and the Taj Mahal. There, we watched the sun set, and under an October full moon, ate a picnic supper in the gardens. Once again, I was able to enjoy its bejeweled walls sparkling in the moonlight.

I'd been disappointed we couldn't go on to the Punjab, the part of the Indian plains I knew best, but there was danger of communal rioting there—the Sikhs were protesting for a homeland. We went instead to Rajasthan, a large arid region south of the Punjab. There, the headman of a small village took us into his home. The group had a chance to walk through the village, watch women cook, observe the comings and goings of commerce, see artisans at work, order tooled leather shoes, and admire the dowry wardrobe of the headman's daughter who was soon to be married. At night, we watched and participated in festive dances. By day, we rode camels. But best of all, my group got a feel for the lifestyle led by about 85 percent of India's population.

From Rajasthan we flew east to Shillong, Meghalaya, in what used to be Assam. Stanley Nichols-Roy, who had been in Woodstock with me, arranged our tour. I'd never been there and had always pictured Cherrapunji, known as the wettest spot in India with over 350 inches of rain a year, as being a lush tropical forest. Instead, I found that its bare cliffs stand high above Bangladesh, and are lashed by all of the monsoon rain that sweeps north from the Bay of Bengal.

Then to Katmandu, Nepal, where we had glorious expansive views of the snow-covered Himalayas. The country was celebrating its Queen's birthday with parades and ceremonies. Members of our group split up. Some took a car to view Mt. Everest and some visited temples, fascinated with how Hinduism and Buddhism lived hand-in-hand there. Prayer flags were at every elevation. Others followed a funeral procession carrying a sheet-covered corpse to a burning ghat by the river. From a distance, they watched the cremation, impressed with the reverence of those in attendance and by the ritual's simplicity.

Our tour group had been together three weeks—it was now time for us to go our separate ways. Most of the group would fly back to

Delhi and on to the States. Ada and I would go to Calcutta and then to Bhutan. On our last evening, we shared what this trip had meant to each of us and I was satisfied that my companions had truly seen India.

Before leaving Katmandu, Ada and I visited a young Nepali woman who'd been a geography student at the University of Nebraska and now held a position in the Nepalese government. Ada told her about our Nebraska in the World project. When we mentioned Women in Development, she showed us an invitation to a workshop in Katmandu on women's roles called together by ICIMOD, International Centre for Integrated Mountain Development, an organization whose members came from various Himalayan nations.

The workshop meetings would include women from Nepal, India, Pakistan, and Bhutan. Attendees would address the fact that women had been excluded from the planning that had gone into preserving Himalayan forests and water resources. Certain resolutions had been adopted by ICIMOD, but women had been neither consulted in their creation nor informed of their passage. Now, women, the primary users of these resources, were being blamed for their noncompliance. We talked about the fact that this situation repeated itself over and over throughout the world. At one point, our hostess's face lit up—she now understood what the issues were and realized that she, too, could participate by drawing up protests for ICIMOD to present to the respective governments.

Ada and I flew to Calcutta and from there flew northeast, past the towering snow peaks of Everest and Kanchenjunga, up into the high mountain valleys of Bhutan. We landed in Paro, eager to see Kunzang. Walter Roder, her husband, was there to meet us and guide us to the capital city of Thimpu, where they lived.

Kunzang, who worked at the United Nations Development Fund there, didn't get home until evening. She wore her Bhutanese clothes—a long, layered silk and wool outfit wrapped in front. A few days later, she donned an even more formal outfit worn only by relatives of the royal family and took us to see the *dhzong*, a combination fort and enclosed monastery. Ordinary citizens were not allowed entry, but Kunzang's attire identified her as someone permitted access.

Walter, working on a Swiss project to introduce potatoes into Bhutanese farming, took a day off and drove us east. We stopped for lunch at a very high overlook, gazing at the snows to the north. As we drove, we saw farmers at work on their terraced fields and in some places rice was being threshed. The women worked as hard as the men. We traveled many miles through this sparsely populated mountain kingdom of about a million residents to visit a famous *dhzong* built at the confluence of two rivers and there learned some of its important history.

One evening, Kunzang invited women friends over to meet us. Not all were Bhutanese, but each was devoted to the country. Among them were a Thai journalist, an Indian educator, and an Englishwoman formerly married to a Bhutanese prince. The Englishwoman still had her own palace and she also read the evening news in English on Bhutanese radio every day. Seldom have I participated in such fascinating conversation as I did there.

When I returned to San Antonio, I had much to share with Margot about the trip and much to write about for my journal group. It took a conscious effort to adjust to life at home after such a protracted journey and the months of planning that had preceded it. At loose ends, I knew I had to start another project right away. But before I was able to, my life took an unexpected turn.

Margot and I had long wanted to see the fall colors in the northeastern U.S. In October 1989, we flew to Boston, then drove up to Portland, Maine and took a boat to Halifax, Nova Scotia, where Dorothy taught at Dalhousie University. After a good visit there, we drove south through Maine, planning to see friends in New Hampshire and Vermont. But on Friday, October 13, while enjoying the vibrant autumn colors along our two-lane road, something went wrong with the car's steering and Margot found herself fighting to bring the vehicle to a safe standstill.

There wasn't much room to maneuver. She steered us toward some bushes hoping they'd provide a soft cushion to stop against. But their looks were deceiving—they hid large rocks. Though our seatbelts prevented us from flying through the windshield, we were stunned nonetheless. We sat there wondering what had happened to us as we tried to collect our wits. Traffic came to a halt and people ran toward us, relieved when they opened Margot's door and could see that we were alive. A truck driver called for an ambulance.

I noticed that my right thigh had a strange, hard bump and I could see that my foot was near the gear shift, even though it felt like it was by the door. Then I realized that my leg had been broken quite badly.

Margot was able to get out of the car to answer the sheriff's questions, but I sat in place, waiting for the ambulance, holding on to my strength. The words that ran through my mind were *Kittu, your life has just changed completely. Don't wonder why this happened. Margot can move and talk and you can still think. Just be thankful it's no worse.* That encouragement, wherever it came from, was an amazing gift that calmed my uneasiness and nipped any resentment I might have felt toward Margot for losing control of the car.

When the medics came, they laid a board across the driver's seat and turned me so I could lie down on it. Then they gently pulled me out the driver's door, steadying my leg as they worked. Once inside the ambulance, the medics tied me down so I wouldn't slide around.

I awoke in a hospital emergency room to the sound of a drill and I was shocked to find it was being used on my leg. The doctor explained that my femur was broken. He was putting a pin through my shin to hold a stirrup. This would be attached to a series of pulleys and a heavy bag of water whose weight would gradually pull the two halves of my femur apart.

Margot and I were put in the same room. She had a cracked breast bone and was under observation to make sure there was no damage to her lungs or heart. When Dorothy arrived the next morning, the two of them moved into a nearby motel.

Kittu and Dorothy, her daughter, in Halifax, Nova Scotia, Canada, just before Kittu broke her leg in 1989.

Dorothy told me later that when she arrived, I'd had very gray skin and little awareness. Alarmed, she'd yelled for a nurse who told her that everything was under control and that I was "just old." Dorothy persisted, and finally, they determined that I was barely getting enough oxygen. Once this was taken care of, I revived and was transformed into my usual self.

For more than a week, I lay suspended in time and traction, my leg inert, resting in lamb's wool. I had to grab a trapeze overhead to hoist my body up when I wanted to change position or use the bedpan. My horizon shrank. I concentrated on healing.

Margot came every day and updated me on how all the insurance claims, police reports, and other details of the accident were being handled. She was feeling better and encouraged me to eat the delicious food on my tray—fresh blueberry muffins and pancakes with real maple syrup. Any fear that I'd gain weight, being so inactive, was dispelled when the doctor reminded me that I had a negative nitrogen balance—any extra calories were being used to build new tissue and heal the wound.

Doctors talked about fatty emboli in my bloodstream and expressed concern about the low level of oxygen showing up in my arterial blood. They couldn't perform surgery or use anesthesia until the oxygen level was higher. It was eleven days before conditions would be right for the operation. In the meantime, my job was to stay happy and heal, to consciously absorb the care being given and the good wishes being sent just as the body absorbs nutrients from the food it is fed. Though I would never have asked for this accident to happen, the sudden halt to my usual schedule proved to be an invaluable opportunity to experience, in full color, the everyday details of life. I realized I'd been living in black and white. Now I had time to appreciate this colorful richness.

When my blood oxygen rose high enough and the operation could be performed, the surgeon made an incision in my thigh and inserted a 42-cm steel rod through the two parts of my broken femur, pulling them together so they could heal. Later that day, I walked a few painful steps.

Then came physical therapy and the "knee-bender" machine. Slowly, relentlessly, it lifted my leg, bent it, unbent it, and lowered it again. This went on for hours. And though the exercise regime was tiresome, I could feel improvement in the muscles of my leg. In between these sessions, I got out of bed and moved around using a walker.

It was wonderful to lie in bed and simply receive the healing energy that poured into me from friends, family, and hospital staff. I marveled at all that happened each day within my small space. When the time came for me to go home, I wasn't sure I wanted to leave my little room, with its cards and flowers and views. There was a lump in my throat as I said goodbye to all those who had cared for me so beautifully. But they'd done their job well and it was time to move on. I found out later that the fatality rate from broken femurs among people my age was very high and breathed in yet another thanks for the careful care I'd received.

My cousin Verlene helped bring us home, and when she returned to San Diego, Patty came to help. Friends took turns staying with me during the day. A woman from my journal group introduced us to a law firm that dealt with personal injury cases and they took care of the insurance issues relating to the accident. We never did discover the cause of the crash, but the fact that we received a generous settlement led us to believe a defect had been found in the car.

Margot surprised me with a special marvel—an electrically controlled lounge chair that would rise up so I could ease off the seat, or tilt back, and raise my feet to the same level as my heart. It has proved extremely useful—not only for me but for all the children who visit us and enjoy riding up and down on it! We didn't know then that I'd have further trouble with my legs. Many is the time I've breathed words of gratitude for that chair's ability to make me comfortable.

That Thanksgiving was truly joyous. Margot's daughters came from Tucson and Lincoln and joined us and her brother's family from Houston for a wonderful reunion dinner. Debbie and her fiancé Eric prepared the meal with the help of Laurie and her friend Doug, whom she later married. My first public outing was to an Indian restaurant with Ada Munson and her husband. There, she introduced us to her nephew Ted Saad and his pregnant wife Linda. Soon after, Linda gave birth to twin girls, Bethany and Laura. A sister, Alexandra, followed seventeen months later. The Saads have been like family to Margot and me and we consider the girls our "granddaughters."

In early 1990, I was able to return to my journal group. Among the members, I felt the strongest resonance with Louita Wilson because she, too, had lived in many countries and held a similar broad view of the world. She was only a few years older than I and we had much in common. A geologist and anthropologist who'd worked toward a doctorate in genetics, she traveled frequently around south Texas. Sometimes I went along and learned much from her about the state's geography and history. Already listed in *Who's Who of American Women*, she successfully nominated me, so now I, too, am listed.

Her conclusions about how women had saved the human race from extinction time and time again were fascinating. I wish she'd had time to write them down before she died in 1992. She believed that when we die, we return to the stars from whence we came. The night of her death the moon was full and in partial eclipse—what a show the heavens put on for her!

She and her friend, Kay Price, had bought the house where our journal class met, making it available to many women's groups for meetings. The mortgage payments were cleverly financed. Louita rented part of the building as her own apartment and the rest of the space was leased to other women for offices. With my connections to Don and the "Love, Medicine, and Miracles" conference in Boulder, it was significant to me that this house was the first place in San Antonio where women with AIDS could gather and where the organizations that served them could coordinate their efforts.

Along with others, Louita and Kay had founded a nonprofit organization, the Doté Foundation. *Doté*, Spanish for "gift" or "legacy," symbolizes the heritage that women pass down to each other through their lives and works. The Foundation endeavors to make a difference in the kind of world women inherit by supporting a variety of women's educational ventures. I served for many years on its Board of Directors, glad for the opportunity to continue my work on behalf of women's empowerment.

Through the Doté Foundation, I published *Storyletters* two or three times a year. Each issue of this newsletter contained stories that women around the world sent in about their lives and experiences. This was my way of continuing the work of Nebraska in the World and helping women learn more about other women different from themselves. Dorothy, who had moved to Canada and become president and CEO of Service Growth Consultants, made a sizable contribution to the Doté Foundation. That money, along with other donations, covered our operating costs. So, thankfully, I didn't need to worry about subscriptions.

I wanted to make the publication available to the women overseas who'd left Nebraska to return to their home countries as well as their friends. Melanie Stafford, a new journal group member, offered to help and keyed in and laid out the first several issues. Though she moved away from San Antonio, she continued to provide support and excellent suggestions. Maggie Reasor, leader of my journal group, designed the *Storyletters* masthead. I obtained mailing labels from AWID and other international organizations and sent out an introductory letter in 1993. From replies, we developed a mailing list of about six hundred women, nearly a hundred of whom lived overseas. We encouraged recipients to share their copies and make duplicates, as long as they weren't used in profit-making ventures.

Margot now does the layout after I've keyed in the text and together we work on illustrations. We've enjoyed hearing from many *Storyletters* readers. A woman from Botswana wrote, "It's wonderful that you are responding to a need to establish a link amongst women in a unique way—the sharing of experiences in story form. I'm sure women all over the world will realize the similarities relating to their shared experience."

Sometimes reading women's stories from abroad made me pine for hills like those where I was raised. Thankfully, ever since we attended the 1987 Woodstock reunion at Estes Park, we'd been on the YMCA Center mailing list. One of their brochures announced an Adopt-a-Cabin program, explaining that if a donor made a significant contribution to the YMCA, the Center would upgrade a cabin of the donor's choice, maintain it, and rent it out when the donor didn't plan to use it. This caught my full attention, as I'd been looking for a way to stay on the grounds for an extended period of time. Ever since I'd worked there as a college student, I had longed to return. I envied those who were able to spend a few weeks there each year.

Margot and I discussed this as a way for me and our dogs to escape San Antonio's summer heat. She encouraged me to pick out a cabin as soon as possible. We were able to swing the "adoption" financially by using the final insurance settlement from our car accident—the exact amount adopting a cabin would cost! We chose Sweetbriar cabin, and since 1991, I've lived there with our dogs for several months each summer.

Being there has been a dream come true, reminding me of childhood summers in the mountains of India. The YMCA Center's rugged paths switchbacking up steep hillsides were like those I'd learned to walk on so many years ago. The heavy growth of pines on northern slopes, the meadows full of wildflowers, and, of course, the overshadowing mountain ranges all seem familiar. I could explore, hike, breathe the pine-scented air, hear the wind whooshing through the Ponderosa pines, listen to the creek murmur its way down the valley, marvel at every dawn, reach for the full moon as she rose over the ridge across the valley, and gaze with wonder at the thick clusters of stars overhead.

I also enjoyed hikes led by staff members. If I mentioned that I first came here in 1939, I was looked at as a relic from another time. The fact that I'd climbed Longs Peak—14,255 feet in elevation— brought looks of awe. But when I huffed and puffed up the hills with everyone else, they realized that I was human after all.

Emily and Anna, our cocker spaniels, walked with me on the grounds several times a day, always eager to escape the confines of the porch. They ventured with me along the mesa, down the slopes below the cabin, along Wind River, or out on the more deserted meadows.

My connections with the YMCA Center became even more profound when I discovered the Pifer family had occupied Sweetbriar in 1920 when it was new. Isabel Pifer, whom I'd known in Chicago at the House of Happiness, and her sister Ann were featured in the book *Magnificent Mountain Women of Colorado*, which told how these two young women led hikes, including many up Long's Peak, a twenty-six-mile round-trip from the YMCA grounds. Also, in the YMCA museum, I found pictures of the employees of 1939 and 1940—pictures in which both Chuck and I appear.

For me, and for Margot, when she could get away from work, Sweetbriar became a second home, adding a settled dimension to our lives. We knew exactly where we'd be spending each summer. It tempered the sense of rootlessness I carried with me from having lived in so many different places. Even without television, I stayed abreast of the important political and economic changes taking place on the planet. In Sweetbriar, I acted as a world watcher, brooding on the workings of the universe and radiating the hope that we can all learn to live together and honor each other.

Many friends have come up to visit and enjoy the mountains. Each of my three children manage to visit each summer. My most avid visitor has been my grandson Charles who started coming when he was seven and staying a week or two, fishing, attending day camp, and wandering around the grounds. We've had a great time together.

In the midst of such bliss, in February 1991, came the shocking news that a mole on my left thigh was malignant melanoma. It had been twenty years since I'd beaten breast cancer and the word 'cancer' no longer frightened me, but melanoma was different. A friend who'd experienced it in her family told me that it could be devious and deadly. The growth was skillfully removed and I came under the care of Dr. Steve Kalter in the San Antonio Cancer Center.

Some months later, I felt a lump about an inch away from where the mole had been. The melanoma had reappeared. Though I knew a reoccurrence was serious, I felt sure I could overcome it. This time, the surgery required a graft from my right leg and the removal of nodes in my groin. The latter wound took a long time to heal.

Before going to Estes Park in the summer of 1992, Dr. Kalter started me on interferon treatment. I gave myself the shots which wasn't hard, but the drug sapped my energy. For the first time, it was difficult to hike. By the end of the summer, I was having great trouble with diarrhea and assumed it was a side effect of the therapy.

Left: Charles William Riddle, Kittu's grandson in 1998, age 14.

Below: Kittu Riddle and Margot Kostenbader, Estes Park, CO.

However, I was wrong. Somehow I'd contracted giardia, a disease caused by a protozoan prevalent in Colorado streams and lakes. The dogs, who loved the water, had also contracted it, so they needed treatment as well. For several years after that, I boiled all the water we drank. After the interferon treatment ended, my vitality and energy returned.

Some years later, I was alarmed when a cancerous lump showed up in Patty's breast. But thankfully, she got by with a simple lumpectomy. This shared experience created a special bond between us.

In May of 1994, I turned seventy-five. I knew my three children were coming to San Antonio to celebrate, but I didn't know they'd planned a whole weekend of fun and a large dinner for nearly a hundred friends and family. Those who couldn't come sent cards and letters that filled up a huge notebook I frequently leaf through. Guests shared remembrances, then Patty introduced a slide show of pictures reproduced from old family albums. I became the narrator, telling stories I thought I'd long forgotten. Chuck and my sister Barbara filled in when memory failed me.

In August 1994, I fell not far from the cabin. My head in the clouds, I'd been taking a last look at the beauty of the mountains before Margot and I headed back to Texas when I tripped and fell flat on my face. I managed to sit, prop myself up with my left hand, and call out for help. People came running, called 911, summoned Margot, wrapped me in a blanket, and offered me a towel to catch the blood dripping from my mouth. I could hardly speak. My lips were badly cut and bleeding. My teeth were in all the wrong places in my mouth. I wondered whether I'd ever feel or look as I had just two minutes ago.

I was chagrined about my teeth. My dentist had recently told me that, barring some unforeseen circumstance, I'd be able to live out my life without any more major dental work. Now here I was, right in the middle of that unforeseen circumstance.

We spent the day in the emergency room where a dentist put a temporary restraint on my displaced teeth. We didn't leave Estes Park for several days. In San Antonio, my doctor, Dr. Hasi Venkatachalam referred me back to Dr. Westfield who had done the skin graft during the melanoma surgery. He reconstructed my lip and took care of my damaged facial bone structure. My dentist referred me to an orthodontist and for six months I had to wear braces. Grandson Charles and I had even more in common.

Restoration took place much more quickly than I'd anticipated, and soon, I looked and felt almost like my former self. Again, I was awed by the healing process. I could almost feel my cells revving up immediately after the first shock, working valiantly to set things right. They had to rid my body of the broken, dead, and now useless bits of tissue and start rebuilding according to my genetic pattern. Despite the health challenges I've faced since moving to Texas, I'm grateful for the good care I've received and my alert, well-nourished body, which soon bounced back into shape, ready to participate in more of the joys of life.

Staying connected with friends, especially women who have been significant in my life, has become increasingly important. I've kept our mail carrier and e-mail busy. Before we leave this life, we can help each other prepare to do so intentionally and lovingly. A brief visit with Mary Chaffee, my Bible study leader from Berkeley and a fellow missionary wife, helped me to acknowledge that how we lived and what we accomplished formed the record of our lives. Over the years, we'd each done our best to serve the One who chose us. The joy that welled up as we embraced and said farewell filled me with thankfulness.

After she retired, Esther Pashek gave me the gift of a five-day visit. She was frail and I was not surprised when she died a month later. I didn't need to grieve. Though I miss her, I rejoice in the times we had together. The last time I saw my kindergarten teacher, she was ninety-four. Our talk of my parents and the years we'd spent in India brought life full circle for me.

To my disappointment, I couldn't attend the Beijing Conference for Women in 1995. I'd closely followed the previous U.N. conferences for women and had urged others to attend. These conferences are the only forum where an international women's agenda could be agreed upon and goals to end sexual discrimination set. Plus, simply meeting and getting acquainted with other women brings greater mutual comprehension of how women's energies and talents can better the world as a whole.

Though I wasn't there in person, I did give some orientation to four women from San Antonio. Mariá Berriozábal, former city council member and mayoral candidate, was the only Hispanic in the official U.S. delegation, led by Hillary Rodham Clinton. Dr. Ruth Burgos Sasscer, then president of San Antonio College, Ginger Purdy, founder of the San Antonio Women's Chamber of Commerce and an activist in women's networking, and Patricia Castillo, who worked with the Benedictine Resource Center to prevent domestic violence were the other three. When we met in preparation for their trip, I shared what I knew from personal experience about the city and the people of Beijing.

When they returned, I was glad to hear their reports on this historic gathering of more than 30,000 women from every country of the world. The platform that came out of the conference spelled out areas where work needs to be done, among them poverty, education, health care, and economics. It also addressed the need to include women in decision-making, prevent violence against women, and increase opportunities for young girls who are overlooked in many societies. The platform's importance was downplayed by governments because what women do is not seen as essential to the life and health of the planet. But now that women from all over the world have met and are beginning to realize that they have much in common with each other, these issues will never again be looked upon as only local. Mariá Berriozábal thought that the most significant aspect of the gathering was that women from completely different cultures and walks of life met face to face and communicated, deepening their mutual understanding. Our challenge now is to figure out how we can make this happen in our own neighborhoods.

The 1994 visit of ten Tibetan lamas from the Drepung Monastery in south India to San Antonio was a spiritual revival. Known as The Awesome Voice, they were traveling to various U.S. cities to promote a deeper awareness of the divine and to remind people of the sacredness of the earth. Wearing yellow hats, they danced, chanted, and played drums, cymbals, and Tibetan horns. Their aura was one of peace and harmony. The program notes stated that their aim was to shatter the ego. I couldn't tell whether that happened to me, but I felt lighter in recognizing that my ego often gets in the way. I was reminded I live under a purpose much larger than any personal ambition.

As I listened, I thought about the universality of music and how it touches me on a core level deeper than any religious belief. A great sense of peace washed over me and I felt a oneness with all the earth. I was content simply because I was. Life is like music—you can't hurry it, you can only enjoy it by letting it unfold.

Though I no longer follow any formal spiritual discipline, I follow the Light revealed to me by my own higher self. I'm learning not to be upset by disappointments and irritations and choosing instead to radiate love to every person and situation I meet. I'm always willing to believe the best about the world around me.

Margot's work has involved weekly travel to cities where there are local Neighborhood Housing Service organizations. The services she provides shift with local need and the ability of National Reinvestment Corporation to respond. Recently, she devoted much of

Clara Jo, Kittu, and Barbara at Dorothy Parker's 90th birthday celebration, Westminster Gardens, Duarte, CA, 1998.

her attention to a technical manual on community based lending and authoring a workbook on loan servicing. We—the dogs and I—have tolerated her absences reasonably well.

Margot and I have been together for twenty years and she is now the age I was when we met. We identify with the lesbian community, its many activities and its ways of helping the surrounding community. We also enjoy simply being together and taking care of each other. Our abilities are complementary. She, the doer, helps me actualize my dreams. With her support, I find ways to expand my dedication to women and my devotion to bringing them together—regardless of lifestyle, nationality, or religious preference—to involve them in their own nourishment and that of the world.

I feel a deep contentment with life. There are times when I hear the humming engines of the universe and glimpse the interconnectedness of everything in it. Clues about how the world works come in unexpected ways. One day, while driving past an oak-shaded yard, I saw three motor boats standing side by side along the back fence. I wondered idly whether, if all the boats in the world were launched, the oceans would flood the world. This triggered a series of images, including ones of human peril. The next image was of a huge armada ready to sail to the aid of those in need. The overwhelming message I was left with was, "Never fear, the armada is always at hand!"

Our morning paper carried an article that reinforced this vision. Cathy Arends, founder of Let There Be Light, set a goal of having one person for every 10,000 San Antonio residents pray daily to make the city a microcosm of world peace. Since she started this crusade, crime rates have plunged. Even though there are no meetings, I feel that I'm part of this group that visualizes San Antonio surrounded by light. With goodwill in our hearts and the power of divine intention in our minds, we contribute to birthing the world we long to see.

I feel fortunate to be part of a family whose members live their lives with goodwill in their minds and hearts. My stepmother, Dorothy Dragon Parker, who turned ninety in 1997, called us all together for a family reunion in Duarte, California. She reserved Packard Hall in Westminster Gardens so that we could meet. Despite her recent stroke and subsequent hip fracture, she was a lively, involved participant.

As I looked at her, I remembered the phone call she'd made when her sister had died, telling me that she was now the last living member of the Dragon family. I'd asked her a question, and she responded with stoic acknowledgment. "How do you feel about it?" I'd asked.

"Strange," came her reply.

We'd been silent for a while, thinking about the implications. The Parker name, too, would soon be gone. My brother Donald will probably be the last to carry it.

Thinking about the transitory nature of life made it even more important to attend the reunion and be together while we could. More than forty members of her family came together as she'd planned and spent a whole day together. Dorothy was wheeled in from the health center and remained in her wheelchair throughout the day. We took the time to visit and catch up with each other, play games, sing, celebrate with a birthday cake, and remember our past. We took a lot of pictures.

The next morning, we began to disperse. In the middle of fond farewells, Patty remembered I'd wanted "my five children," as I called Dorothy, Bill, Patty, Harriet, and Donald, to have their picture taken with me as a remembrance of their school days in Landour. My sisters Barbara and Clara Jo objected to not being included, saying, "We went to Woodstock, too!" and the photo lineup grew. One of us began singing the school song and the rest of us found ourselves straightening up, standing at attention, and clasping hands as we joined in. I felt the vibrant connections between us as individuals as well as the bonds across the generations. As our voices soared together, I was present in the moment yet simultaneously carried back to childhood. In my mind's eye I was with my schoolmates singing the anthem in Parker Hall. It was deeply moving—and another instance of my life coming full circle.

Not long after the reunion, much to my surprise, I received an invitation from the People to People Citizen Ambassador Program to join a delegation of women's studies specialists on a visit to South Africa. Margot accompanied me. When we arrived in the spring of 1998, I was struck by how committed the country's political leaders were to eradicating the last vestiges of apartheid in an effort to make South Africa a truly nonracist, nonsexist democracy. Reconciliation between once diametrically opposed racial factions is becoming possible through the remarkable resolution process of the Truth and Reconciliation Commission. As members of the delegation, Margot and I felt we were glimpsing what is possible for the world. We felt privileged to hear women leaders speak about the steps they were taking for the transformation of their country.

There at the tip of Africa, where the Indian Ocean meets the Atlantic, I felt the different facets of my life come together—my youth in the East and old age in the West, and all the back-and-forth in between, my personal transformations and professional successes. The significance of one of my contributions was affirmed when a woman doctor told me about the mother-and-child clinic at Stellenbosch University describing how the mothers kept the charts documenting their children's growth, using them as entry into the clinic. "Having the charts is a very empowering tool," she said. I smiled, thinking back thirty years to a planning session in Nairobi and remembering how strongly I'd stressed that the charts belonged with the mothers.

On our flight back to the States, there were many long hours to reflect on my life and how it has come full circle in so many ways. The Parker family reunion and our joyous rendition of the Woodstock school song sprang to mind and I remembered the school pledge we'd taken so many years ago promising "to transmit this school better, stronger, and more beautiful than it was transmitted to us." I believe I have kept my promise, not only to Woodstock and my family, but to women and the global community. I have nourished the world I live in, transmitting it better, stronger, and more beautiful than it was transmitted to me. I have radiated and engendered love.

References

Adolph, William A. "Pre-War Nutrition in Rural China" *Journal of the American Dietetic Association*, 1946, Vol. 28, p. 869.

Cheney, Joyce, editor of *Lesbian Land*, 1985, Word Weavers, Minneapolis, MN.

Gifft, Helen H., Washbon, Marjorie B., and Harrison, Gail. *Nutrition, Behavior, and Change.* 1972, Princeton Hall, Inc. Englewood Cliffs, NJ.

Morton, Nelle, *The Journey is Home*, 1986, Beacon Press, Boston, MA.

Nehru, Jawaharlal, *Glimpses of World History*, 1939, Lindsay Drummond Limited, London.

Pandit, Vijaya Laksmi, *The Scope of Happiness: a Personal Memoir*, 1979, Crown Publishers, NY.

Robertson, Janet, *Magnificent Mountain Women of Colorado*, 1990, University of Nebraska Press, Lincoln, NE.

Seigel, Bernie, *Love, Medicine and Miracles*, 1988, Caedmon.

Taylor, Dr. Clara Mae, and Riddle, Mrs. Katharine P., *A Bibliography of International Nutrition Education Materials*, 1972, Colombia University Press, NY.

DATE DUE

OC 22 '08		
DE 10 08		